JEAN FISCHER

EVERYDAY BIBLE ENCOURAGEMENT

DAILY DEVOTIONS AND PRAYERS

BARBOUR kidz
A Division of Barbour Publishing

Everyday Bible Encouragement for Boys/ Print ISBN 978-1-63609-980-4
Everyday Bible Encouragement for Girls/ Print ISBN 978-1-63609-981-1

Published by Barbour Publishing, Inc., 1810 Barbour Drive, Uhrichsville, Ohio 44683, www.barbourbooks.com.

Our mission is to inspire the world with the life-changing message of the Bible.

Member of the Evangelical Christian Publishers Association

Printed in the United States of America.

002309 1124 BP

DAY 1

In the beginning God made from nothing the heavens and the earth.
GENESIS 1:1

The very first verse of the Bible explains that God created our universe. But where did God come from? Sometimes the simplest questions are hardest to answer.

Read a little further in the Bible and you'll find God explaining His own being. . .kind of. When speaking to Moses (Exodus 3:13–14), God calls Himself "I AM." There never was a time when God wasn't, and there never will be a time when He won't be. God simply *is*—He always has existed, and He will forever. It's a difficult thing for our human minds to understand because everything in our world has a beginning and an end.

For about as long as humans have existed, they have tried to figure out how the universe and its people began. But the Bible holds the answer: everything came from God, the Great I AM. It's one of those things that you just have to accept as real—you have to have faith that God *is* and that everything came from Him.

Father, many things about You are bigger than I can understand. When I don't understand, please help me to trust You, have faith in You, and believe. Amen.

DAY 2

God has shown His love to us by sending His only Son into the world. God did this so we might have life through Christ.

1 JOHN 4:9

Not only has God always existed, but He has always cared for us. He helps us in ways that we may never realize. Why does God spend so much time guiding us? Because He loves us! God loves us so much that He sent to us His only Son, Jesus Christ, to make a way for us to live with Him in heaven after we die.

Many things about God are a mystery. We can't understand the ways He works and thinks. But there is one thing we *can* understand: we can know that God loves us. There is nothing we could ever do to make God *stop* loving us, because we did nothing to make Him start. God has always loved us because we are His. He is concerned about everything we do. He celebrates our victories and cries with us during our difficult times. First John 4:9 reminds us that God proved His love for us long before we were born!

You have always loved me, God, and You will love me forever. I am so grateful! Compared to Yours my love is small, but I love You with all of my heart. Amen.

DAY 3

God is able to do much more than we ask or think through His power working in us.
EPHESIANS 3:20

One of Jesus' greatest followers was a man named Paul. Our Bible verse today comes from a letter Paul wrote to his friends. He wanted them to remember that our human strength comes from God's power working in us.

God is able to do what no human can. His power is greater than any superpower you could ever imagine. God's power and greatness can't be measured. We see it all around us in His creations and the things He does.

You might think something in your life is impossible—and then it happens. You say, "Wow! How did God do that?" Nothing is impossible for Him. God is able to do wonderful things that our human minds can't begin to understand.

But God doesn't keep all that power to Himself. He shares it with us! His power works in us to help us do things that we think might be impossible. When we pray and ask for God's help, He will do more for us than we can imagine.

O Lord, You do things that I think are impossible. You know my hopes and dreams, and I believe that You are able to help me accomplish them. Amen.

DAY 4

Do you not know that you are a house of God and that the Holy Spirit lives in you?
1 CORINTHIANS 3:16

The Bible tells about a woman who asked Jesus in which of two churches she should worship. Jesus surprised her by saying that people would not worship God at *either* place but "the true worshipers will worship the Father in spirit and in truth" (John 4:19–24). What did Jesus mean? The Bible gives us a clue: "The Most High [God] does not live in buildings made by hands" (Acts 7:48).

So, if God doesn't live in buildings built by humans, where does He live?

The answer is God's Spirit lives inside us! He is with us wherever we go.

Today's Bible verse is another written by Paul. He says we should think of our bodies as churches where God lives. We need to remember to keep our bodies and minds clean and good like the inside of a church where people go to worship and pray (1 Corinthians 6:19; 2 Corinthians 6:16–17).

Think about it. God's Spirit lives inside your heart right now, and He is always with you. Isn't that awesome?

Heavenly Father, how wonderful it is that You have chosen to live inside me and with me forever. Help me always to remember that Your Holy Spirit lives inside my heart. Amen.

DAY 5

"Yet they did not obey or listen, but walked in the way they wanted to and in the strong-will of their sinful heart. They only stepped back and did not go on."

JEREMIAH 7:24

Our scripture verse today tells of a time long ago when people thought they pleased God just by making sacrifices to Him. Back then, a sacrifice meant giving to God one of their best animals. But God told the people He wanted more. Along with giving Him their best, God wanted them to obey everything He told them to do.

Did the people obey God? No. They did whatever they wanted, and God saw that their "stuff" meant more to them than He did. The people were turning away from God instead of toward Him.

Humans have never been perfect. Sadly, we often go about our business forgetting God's commands, His rules that help us lead good and happy lives.

God wants from us what He wanted from those people long ago: to follow His rules. The Bible tells us "loving God means to obey His Word" (1 John 5:3). We show God our love by doing our best to live according to His rules in the Bible.

Sometimes, Lord, I am guilty of focusing on the world instead of on You. Help me to obey Your rules. Amen.

DAY 6

May you have loving-favor and peace from God our Father and from the Lord Jesus Christ.
1 CORINTHIANS 1:3

Paul lived long ago in a time before computers, tablets, and smartphones. He didn't send text messages or emails. He wrote letters—lots of them. Paul wrote to his friends telling them about Jesus and God.

Think about this. When you text someone, how do you begin your message? Do you begin by identifying yourself? THIS IS KEVIN WRITING TO YOU. Of course not! But in Paul's time, a person began a letter with their name followed by the name of whoever they were writing to. After that, the person added a special greeting.

Paul's letters often began like this: *Paul, to (whomever he was writing). May you have loving-favor and peace from God our Father and from the Lord Jesus Christ.* Along with *loving-favor* and *peace*, Paul sometimes added *loving-kindness* to his greeting. These were favors, or blessings, that he wished for God to give his friends.

Favor, peace, and kindness are God's gifts that help us through life. Like Paul, you should want God to bless your friends with these things and more. Ask Him to do so when you pray.

Father God, thank You for blessing me daily, and please also bless my family and friends. Amen.

DAY 7

When my worry is great within me,
Your comfort brings joy to my soul.
PSALM 94:19

You can think of the book of Psalms in the Bible as an ancient book of song lyrics. Psalms were written for people to sing praises to God. King David wrote most of the psalms. Others were written anonymously—we don't know who wrote them. Psalm 94 is one of them.

If you read the whole psalm, you would see that the writer was frustrated and upset with evil people who were causing plenty of trouble. He lists some of what they were doing, and he begs God to punish them. He warns those people to shape up and start following God.

Psalm 94:19, today's scripture verse, is a turning point in the song. This is where the writer is so totally upset that he has no more words to describe his feelings. Instead, he praises God because even when he is all filled up with worry, God is the one who brings him comfort and peace.

How do you handle it when you are filled with worry? Remember this: God knows. He understands. Trust Him to comfort you and work things out.

Dear God, on those days when frustration and anxiety overwhelm me, please come to me, comfort my soul, and remind me to praise You. Amen.

DAY 8

They chose Stephen who was a man full of faith and full of the Holy Spirit.
Acts 6:5

In ancient times, some people risked their own lives to help others, just as some people do today.

Stephen was one of those guys. He went among his enemies where he wasn't welcome. Wherever he went, Stephen wasn't afraid to talk about Jesus. He was a chosen leader, a great man of faith who trusted God to guide him.

Some people hated the whole idea of Jesus as God's Son. They hated Stephen for talking about Him. But Stephen never lost faith in Jesus. He refused to stop telling people to turn their lives around and follow God. He didn't lose his faith even when men dragged him outside and threw rocks at him until he died.

Watching Stephen die that day was a man named Saul, another Jesus hater. What Saul didn't know then was that someday he would turn his life toward God. He would write many of the Bible's New Testament books. This man named Saul would someday be one of the greatest Jesus followers ever. Who was he? The man we know in the Bible as Paul!

Lord, bless me with strong faith like Stephen had. Teach me to be a blessing to others and never to be afraid to tell them about You. Amen.

DAY 9

"The city and all that is in it must be destroyed because everything in it belongs to the Lord."

JOSHUA 6:17

The Bible tells about the city of Jericho, a city protected by tall, strong walls. Jericho was a safe place for God's enemies, or so they thought. In their minds, nothing could bring down those walls. But God knew better. He planned for His followers to knock down the walls and take over the city.

His plan worked. God's people took Jericho. Then God commanded them to destroy everything inside except gold, silver, bronze, and iron. Grain was valuable too because it could be traded for all kinds of useful things. But God wanted all the grain destroyed too.

Why, the people wondered, did God want to destroy that precious grain? Still, they did what God said.

In recent years, archaeologists have found the ruins of Jericho including clay jars filled with burned grain—a reminder to us that the Bible story is true.

Sometimes God's ways are a mystery to us humans. Nevertheless, He always wants us to follow His commands. One thing we can believe by faith is that God has His reasons for doing what He does. And everything He does is right.

God, sometimes Your ways are mysterious to me. Still, I believe that Your reasons are right, and I will keep trusting in You. Amen.

DAY 10

If you do not have wisdom, ask God for it. He is always ready to give it to you and will never say you are wrong for asking. You must have faith as you ask Him. You must not doubt. Anyone who doubts. . .will get nothing from the Lord.

James 1:5–7

James, the author of today's scripture, was Jesus' half brother. It must have been hard for James to live with a brother who was perfect. James was not sure that his brother was God's Son. But years later, after Jesus died, was buried, and came alive again, James believed. He became a leader in the church, and he wrote a book in the Bible to help us know how God wants us to live.

James said that if we need wisdom, we should never be afraid to ask God because God wants us to make wise choices. When life gets hard, God wants us not to get discouraged. If we have faith in Him during the hard times, God will help us. Faith is the most important message in this scripture passage from James. A strong faith in God is what helps us grow in wisdom and strength.

Father, when life gets hard, help me to hold on tightly to You. Open my eyes, Lord. Teach me. Make me wise. Amen.

DAY 11

"This book of the Law must not leave your mouth. Think about it day and night, so you may be careful to do all that is written in it. Then all will go well with you. You will receive many good things."

JOSHUA 1:8

It's easy for sin—bad thoughts and actions—to creep into our lives. On our computers, tablets, and smartphones, we can instantly view whatever we want. This is good when we need information, but it has a dark side too.

There is garbage lurking in cyberspace! Stinky sin—bad stuff that you know you shouldn't be reading or looking at. Sin wants you to take this trashy stuff in instead of hauling it to the curb. The problem is, sin is sneaky. It can find its way inside your heart and mind if you're not careful.

Joshua 1:8 tells what you should do to keep sin away. Read the Bible! Study it. Fill your mind with God's Word day and night so you know how God wants you to live. Then follow God's commands. If you do that, there won't be room in your heart and mind for sin to creep in.

Dear Lord, plant Your words inside my mind and heart, and let the Bible always be my guide. Amen.

DAY 12

"For God so loved the world that He gave His only Son. Whoever puts his trust in God's Son will not be lost but will have life that lasts forever."

JOHN 3:16

John 3:16 tells us about God's great love.

After He created the world, God put humans here to care for it. If they had obeyed God, the world would be a perfect place. But, right away humans let sin creep in. Before long, people everywhere did sinful things.

Still, God loved His humans. He knew He couldn't let them into heaven after they died because sin has no place in heaven. So, God made a way to clean our hearts of sin *before* we die. He sent His Son, Jesus, to earth to take our sin away.

Jesus was nailed to a cross and left to die. When He died, our sin died with Him. Then, Jesus rose from the dead—just like we will someday if we believe in Him. If we believe that Jesus died to take our sin away, then when we die we will wake up in heaven alive and sin free.

That's how much God loves you. He wants you to live with Him in heaven forever.

God, how can I ever thank You for giving us Jesus? I will do my best to show my love for You with everything I do. Amen.

DAY 13

Trust in the Lord with all your heart, and do not trust in your own understanding. Agree with Him in all your ways, and He will make your paths straight.

PROVERBS 3:5–6

Have you ever had to make a decision but didn't know what to do? King Solomon, the author of today's scripture, has the answer.

Solomon was a wise king. He knew that our human problem-solving skills don't always measure up. So, Solomon said—kind of—"If you don't know what to do, quit trying to figure it out on your own." Solomon knew that God is the only one who has the answers to all of our problems. He said, "Agree with [God] in all your ways, and He will make your paths straight." In other words, if we pray and ask God to help us make the right decision, God will show us the way.

The next time you don't know what to do, ask God. Go someplace quiet and tell Him what's going on and what you need. Then trust God to work it out. Listen to your heart, and believe that God will give you the answer.

Often, Lord, I run on ahead of You and make decisions on my own. Help me to remember that even with small decisions I need to seek Your help. Amen.

DAY 14

That is why we must listen all the more to the truths we have been told. If we do not, we may slip away from them.
HEBREWS 2:1

In Bible times, fishing was an important job. Fishermen provided food for the people. The Sea of Galilee was the best fishing spot, but it was a dangerous place. The nearby hills reached as high as 1,500 feet. To the east, mountains with peaks of more than 3,300 feet surrounded the sea. This put the sea in a kind of circle that often had sudden and violent storms.

Fishing boats held four men, and the boat's small size made it dangerous in bad weather. If fishermen were careless about what was happening around them—like a storm brewing—they could find themselves in trouble quickly. Their boat would be carried off by the wind and waves.

Hebrews 2:1 warns us that we can be like careless fishermen. If we don't keep our eyes open for sin, then sneaky sin can easily carry us away from God.

So, keep your eyes open. Watch out for sin, and don't let it carry you away.

Heavenly Father, I know that sin can find many ways to send me off course. Help me to keep my eyes open and my mind set on You. Amen.

DAY 15

Then King David went in and sat before the Lord, and said, "Who am I, O Lord God, and what is my family, that You have brought me this far?"

2 SAMUEL 7:18

David had been just a simple shepherd boy. But because he trusted God, his heavenly Father blessed him in amazing ways. You might remember that David, as a young boy, used his slingshot and a stone to bring down the giant, evil soldier Goliath. No one could believe how brave young David was. God had blessed him with bravery, and God kept on blessing him. David became the greatest of God's kings! God promised David even more. David could not understand why God had given him so much, but he was grateful. He always remembered to praise and thank God.

David wasn't the only one who received God's blessings. Abram (Genesis 15:1–17), Moses (Exodus 3:1–22), and Joshua (Joshua 1:1–9) are just a few people in the Bible who were given great promises and blessings from God.

God gives you blessings too. Think about all the wonderful things He does for you. Then be like King David. Pray and thank God every day.

Father, I praise You! Your blessings are endless and so beyond what I deserve. I accept them with gratefulness and joy. Amen.

DAY 16

Love means that we should live by obeying His Word. From the beginning He has said in His Word that our hearts should be full of love.

2 John 1:6

Obey God's Word and have a heart full of love. It sounds easy, doesn't it? But the truth is, it's hard! Humans have never been good at following God's commands.

In the beginning, God put Adam and Eve in a beautiful garden with everything they needed. He put them in charge and gave them just one command—He told them not to eat fruit from one of the trees. Eve wondered what would happen if she ate the fruit. So, she disobeyed God. She ate it! And what happened? Sin entered the world. It changed everything. Adam and Eve had to leave that beautiful place and work for their living.

We humans are often curious to see what will happen if we disobey. It never leads to anything good.

Don't be like Eve. Trust that when God gives you a command, He knows what He's doing. Do your best every day to obey Him. If you allow God to lead you, then your heart will be filled with His love.

God, I don't want to disobey You. Please help me to trust You, especially when I'm curious to see what will happen if I disobey. Amen.

DAY 17

Pilate said to Jesus, "What is truth?" After Pilate said this, he went out again to the Jews. He said, "I do not find Him guilty."

John 18:38

Soldiers took Jesus away to be crucified—to die nailed to a cross. Why? Because an angry crowd did not believe that Jesus was God's Son—God's great King—the one who came to save us from sin. When Jesus called Himself King of the Jews, they thought He was a liar.

The Roman governor, back then, was a man named Pontius Pilate. He questioned Jesus and tried to get at the truth.

"Are you the King of the Jews?" he asked Jesus.

Jesus said, "You are right when you say that I am a King. . . . I came to speak about the truth" (John 18:37).

"What is truth?" Pilate asked. But he didn't wait for Jesus' answer. Although in his heart he found Jesus not guilty, Pilate made a sinful decision and allowed the angry crowd to take Jesus to the cross.

Always remember: Jesus is all about truth. He is God's Son, the world's Savior. Believe that, and listen to His words.

Jesus, You always tell the truth. You are God's Son and my Savior. Trusting You is the only way to heaven. Help me always to believe in You and to listen to Your words. Amen.

DAY 18

It was Hezekiah who stopped the upper opening of the waters of Gihon, and made them flow to the west side of the city of David. And Hezekiah did well in all that he did.

2 Chronicles 32:30

The city of Jerusalem has an ancient history. It is the center of many events in the Bible and remains an important place today.

Jerusalem, protected by heavy walls, sits atop a mountain. It gets its water from the Gihon spring, which lies outside its walls.

Early in Jerusalem's history, a twenty-foot-deep trench covered with rock slabs made a canal carrying water from the spring into a pool inside the walls. This wasn't very good, though, because enemy soldiers could get into the city by going through the trench.

A king named Hezekiah finally solved the problem by covering the outside route to the Gihon spring and cutting a tunnel back to the pool. This way, water could be safely gathered and the enemy soldiers kept out.

Although Hezekiah's plan was good, it was not as good as God's plan. No one can keep His people from the holy city of Jerusalem.

**Wherever the way is blocked, You know a detour.
Whenever there is a problem, You know its solution.
So, lead me, Lord. I want to follow You. Amen.**

DAY 19

He who lives in the safe place of the Most High
will be in the shadow of the All-powerful.
PSALM 91:1

The names given to God in today's verse remind us of His loving protection and care. *Most High* means that God is greater than any problem we face. *All-powerful* tells of His super power and majesty.

The word *shadow* makes us think of a shelter, covering, or protection from heat and storms. Just as a tree's big, leafy branches shield us from the hot sun, God provides us protection wherever we are and whatever problems we face. When we put our trust in the Most High, we live in the shadow of His protection—a place where nothing can harm us.

In another psalm, 46:1, there are these words: "God is our safe place and our strength. He is always our help when we are in trouble." God promises to be with us all the time to help and protect us. We can run to Him, and He will keep us safe.

Whenever you feel afraid, remember that you are not alone. God is with you wherever you go. Call to Him in prayer and then trust that He will help you.

Most High and _All-powerful_ God, there is nothing that can harm me because You are always with me. You are my safe place. Amen.

DAY 20

Let the teaching of Christ and His words keep on living in you. These make your lives rich and full of wisdom. Keep on teaching and helping each other. Sing the Songs of David and the church songs and the songs of heaven with hearts full of thanks to God.

COLOSSIANS 3:16

Colossians 3:16 tells us that we become wise when our lives are filled with God's Word. That means we need to study and learn what's in the Bible and keep it in our hearts. As we learn, we should praise God for everything He gives us. We also need to live what we learn. No matter how smart we think we are, there is nothing compared to God's wisdom. He shares His wisdom with us through the Bible and instructs us to share it with others. When we do that—live following God's commands—we set a good example.

The Bible helps us find peace, wisdom, and happiness. Isn't that wonderful? Take time today to praise God for giving us His special book, the Bible. Then spread some of God's wisdom around. Share the Word of God with your friends.

Dear Jesus, my Lord, may my words and my actions be a reflection of Your Word, the Bible, and pleasing to Your sight. Amen.

DAY 21

While Jesus was in one of the towns, a man came to Him with a bad skin disease over all his body. When he saw Jesus, he got down on his face before Him. He begged Him, saying, "Lord, if You are willing, You can heal me." Jesus put His hand on him and said, "I will, be healed."

LUKE 5:12–13

A sick man asked Jesus if He was willing to heal him. Of course Jesus was willing! Jesus came to the world willing to help. Everything He did, He did willingly. He didn't have to help anyone. He *wanted* to.

Jesus wants us to be willing too. He wants us to be willing to do His work here on earth. He wants us to try to be more like Him—kind, caring, and willing to help.

Ask Jesus to show you what He wants you to do. Then keep your eyes open for ways that you can help others. Don't worry that you aren't old enough, smart enough, or strong enough to do great things. Jesus will give you the power to do His work, as long as you are willing.

Jesus, I am willing. Use me. Work through me to accomplish whatever You want. Whether it is something great or something small, I am ready. Amen.

DAY 22

"The LORD bless you and keep you."

NUMBERS 6:24 NKJV

"God bless you." Has someone said that to you? Maybe you've heard it said in Sunday school or church or by your parents. But what do the words *God bless you* mean?

To be blessed by God means that He covers you with His goodness and protection; He does good things for you.

In a talk Jesus gave to a huge crowd, He blessed certain groups of people. Jesus blessed

Those who believe goodness comes from God,
Sad people,
Those who believe they are no better than anyone else,
Those who want to be right with God,
Kind people,
People with pure hearts,
Peacemakers,
And those who are made fun of or given a hard time for doing right (Matthew 5:1–11).

Jesus told these people to be happy and celebrate because God loves and protects them. This tells us that the result of God's blessings is happiness!

God loves and protects you too. So, be happy and celebrate His blessings. Give praise and thanks to God for all the wonderful ways He blesses you.

I praise You, Lord, for the abundance of blessings You give me each day. I am so grateful! Amen.

DAY 23

Jesus took the sour wine and said, "It is finished." He put His head down and gave up His spirit and died.

JOHN 19:30

God always has a plan, and His plan is always perfect. If you read the Bible from beginning to end, you will see that the greatest part of God's plan included Jesus. In the Old Testament, prophets (people to whom God revealed part of His plan) predicted that God would send a Messiah (a leader or savior) to earth. It happened! Jesus, the Messiah, was born as a baby in Bethlehem.

God had a purpose for Jesus—salvation. Jesus' purpose was to save people from sin. God would allow His own Son to die in our place so someday we could live in heaven.

Just before Jesus died on the cross, He said the words "It is finished." He meant that God's plan to save us was done. Mission accomplished! From that day forward, anyone who believed in Jesus and asked for forgiveness for their sins would be welcomed into heaven.

God's plan for Jesus is not done yet. Although His Spirit is always with us, the Bible says that one day Jesus will return to earth in a body that we can see.

Thank You, Jesus, for completing God's plan of salvation. Thank You for saving me from sin. Amen.

DAY 24

"There is not one person who is right with God. No, not even one!"
ROMANS 3:10

Do you worry that maybe you're not good enough to get into heaven? Many people feel that way. They know how great God is, and they feel that they could never be good enough to please Him.

Today's Bible verse comes from Paul. He wrote it in one of his letters. Paul reminds us that nobody is good enough to always please God. *Nobody!* Not even one.

Why? Because God is the only one who is, always has been, and always will be perfect. No human can ever be as perfect as He is. We all have times when we sin by disobeying God's rules. Because we can't help sinning sometimes, we can't be perfect like God. That's why we need Jesus—to clean away our sin when we die so we can live with God forever in heaven.

Don't worry about being perfect. You can't be. Ask Jesus to be your Savior and then do your best to live a good life for Him. That is what God wants from you. Because of Jesus, He loves you and accepts you just the way you are!

Father, on days when I feel not good enough for You, myself, or others, I come to You believing that You will accept me just as I am. Amen.

DAY 25

"But God raised Him up. He allowed Him to be set free from the pain of death. Death could not hold its power over Him."

ACTS 2:24

When people die, they leave their bodies here on earth. If they believe in Jesus, then their spirits go to heaven to live with God forever.

Jesus told His followers that three days after He died on the cross He—body and all—would come back from the dead. And that is exactly what happened. Jesus' dead body had been put in a tomb sealed with a rock. Three days later, His body was gone. Jesus showed Himself to His friends and talked with them. He had risen from the dead!

Jesus' resurrection—His body coming to life again—was God's way of showing the world that Jesus really was who He said He was, God's Son, the Messiah who came to save us from sin.

Death had no power over Jesus, and it has no power over us either. If we believe in Him, then we will wake up someday to a new and forever life in heaven.

Lord, I praise You because You are the only one who brings forever life to all believers. Thanks to You, I look forward to a new life in heaven someday. Amen.

DAY 26

But when Peter came to Antioch, I had to stand up against him because he was guilty.

GALATIANS 2:11

Think about this: What would you do if you saw someone make a wrong choice, one that could hurt that person or others?

Paul was faced with that problem. He saw his friend Peter make a decision that went against God's will. Worse, other people were following Peter's choice. Paul knew this had to stop, so he talked with Peter about it. He helped Peter see why his decision was wrong.

Sometimes people make wrong choices because they don't know any better. Sometimes they choose wrong because they want to fit in with their friends.

God wants us to be strong and do what we know is right. That's why it's so important to know and follow God's rules. You will learn His rules by reading the Bible. If you know God's rules, then, like Paul did, you might even help someone else if you see them making a wrong choice.

Pray and ask God to teach you and guide you so when you are faced with a decision, you will make the right choice.

God, guide me in Your ways. Help me to learn Your rules so that I will make good choices in my life. Amen.

DAY 27

Next to them Uzziel the son of Harhaiah, who worked with gold, did the needed work. Next to him Hananiah, one of the men who made perfume, did the needed work. They made Jerusalem like new as far as the Wide Wall.

NEHEMIAH 3:8

The Bible's Old Testament tells about Nehemiah, a cupbearer to the king of Persia. When Nehemiah heard that most of Jerusalem had been destroyed by enemy soldiers, he asked the king for permission to leave his job to do God's work. His goal was to rebuild the broken city.

After receiving the king's permission, Nehemiah called on all who believed in God to help. Uzziel, the goldsmith, helped. So did Hananiah, one of the men who made perfume. All sorts of people set to work rebuilding stone upon stone: men from different tribes, merchants, rulers of districts, priests, servants. Together, they worked side by side, and *in just fifty-two days* they rebuilt Jerusalem and its walls!

That's how God expects us to work today, side by side with other believers. When Christians band together to do God's work, they can accomplish great things. Best of all, they build a strong "wall" of faith that keeps Satan's evil plans from getting in the way.

Heavenly Father, lead me to work together with others who believe in You. Please guide us toward You and Your work. Amen.

DAY 28

But Mary hid all these words in her heart.
She thought about them much.
LUKE 2:19

Jesus' mother, Mary, had much to think about. God had chosen her to care for His Son, Jesus, here on earth. Mary didn't know why God chose her for such an important thing—but He had! It was her responsibility to raise Jesus knowing that He was not like any other human.

The Bible says that when Jesus was born, angels appeared to shepherds watching over their sheep. The angels told the shepherds that the baby born nearby, in Bethlehem, was God's Son, the one who would save the world from sin. The shepherds went to see the baby, and they told Mary what the angels had said. Mary was not surprised. She already knew that her baby, Jesus, was God's Son.

The Bible does not tell us exactly what Mary thought. It just says that she thought much about the responsibility of raising Jesus. Certainly, she prayed and asked God to guide her.

Whenever you face an important responsibility, remember Mary. Take time to think and pray. Let God be your guide.

Sometimes, Lord, I jump right into something without taking time to think about what You want me to do. Remind me to slow down, even stop, and turn my thoughts toward You. Amen.

DAY 29

The Lord said to him, "What is that in your hand?"
EXODUS 4:2

Have you ever experienced a miracle? The Bible tells us that Moses did.

God surprised Moses by setting a bush on fire and appearing in its flames. He told Moses that He had chosen him to lead the Israelites out of Egypt to God's Promised Land. But Moses lacked the confidence he needed to be a leader.

"Why me?" Moses asked. "I'm a nobody."

God assured Moses, "I will certainly be with you."

Moses still wasn't sure. So, God did another miraculous thing.

"What is that in your hand?" God asked.

Moses was holding a stick.

"Throw it down," God said.

And when Moses threw it down, the stick turned into a snake! Moses grabbed it by the tail, and the snake morphed back to a stick!

"I will *certainly* be with you," God said.

It took several miracles for Moses to believe that God would help him and certainly be with him.

Maybe you are like Moses and you aren't sure that God is with you all the time. If you ask God to help you believe, He certainly will!

Heavenly Father, I do my best to believe You are always with me, but sometimes I need reassurance. Help me, please, to believe. Amen.

DAY 30

Your heart should be holy and set apart for the Lord God. Always be ready to tell everyone who asks you why you believe as you do. Be gentle as you speak and show respect.
1 PETER 3:15

Like Paul, Peter, another of Jesus' followers, was a letter writer. Today's Bible verse is part of a letter he wrote to Christians living among nonbelievers. Peter wrote to give them advice about how to set a Christlike example and what to say if anyone asked them about Jesus.

First, Peter told them to make God more important in their hearts than anything else. He said they should remember to be amazed by His absolute greatness. Second, Peter told his friends to be ready to tell nonbelievers about Jesus—that He came to save them from sin so they might live forever in heaven. Finally, Peter wrote that they should explain Jesus to nonbelievers with gentleness and respect.

Remember Peter's words, because someday one of your friends might ask you about Jesus. Will you be ready? Think about what you will say and how you will say it.

Dear God, please prepare me to explain Jesus to anyone who asks. Teach me to explain in a way that honors You with gentleness and respect. Amen.

DAY 31

A man's wisdom makes his face shine.
The hard look on his face is changed.
ECCLESIASTES 8:1

Whether or not you have a smile on your face depends on one thing. Can you guess what it is? A positive attitude! Even on bad days, your face can wear a smile.

Solomon, the author of today's Bible verse, says wisdom is what makes a person's face shine. A wise person knows that a smile and a positive attitude can make a bad day turn around. When you find something to feel good about, it makes you feel better.

A wise way to boost your attitude is to think about God's blessings. In one of his letters, Paul wrote, "Keep your minds thinking about whatever is true, whatever is respected, whatever is right, whatever is pure, whatever can be loved, and whatever is well thought of. If there is anything good and worth giving thanks for, think about these things" (Philippians 4:8).

If your attitude stinks, remember this little poem:

You can smile when you can't say a word.
You can smile when you cannot be heard.
You can smile when it's cloudy or fair.
You can smile any time, anywhere.
(A. H. Ackley)

Father, put a smile on my face today. Bless me with a positive attitude that I can share with others. Amen.

DAY 32

Jesus said to them, "You are wrong because you do not know the Holy Writings or the power of God."
MATTHEW 22:29

The Sadducees, a rich and powerful religious group in Jesus' time, tried to trap Him into saying that He was not the Son of God. They asked Him question after question trying to make Him contradict Himself. They wanted to show the crowd the importance of their religious ways and their superiority over Jesus. It irritated them that Jesus drew a big crowd everywhere He went. They wanted to be recognized as wiser than He, but instead the crowds preferred to listen to every word that came from Jesus.

Jesus knew what they were up to. His answer to them is found in Matthew 22:29. He basically told them that they didn't know what they were talking about because they didn't know God or what's in the Bible. If they did, they would *know* that He was the Son of God.

Imagine being alive during the time Jesus was teaching and being able to hear the voice of the Son of God as He spoke!

God, as I read Your Word, open my eyes to Your truth. Teach me Your ways so that I may apply them to my life and walk in the footsteps of Jesus. Amen.

DAY 33

Jesus said to him, " 'You must love the Lord your God with all your heart and with all your soul and with all your mind.' "

MATTHEW 22:37

The Sadducees couldn't trap Jesus, so another religious group, the Pharisees, tried to do it. They asked Him which of God's commandments was the most important.

Jesus answered them with Deuteronomy 6:5, which says that we should be completely full of love for God. He also told them that the second most important commandment was to love others as we love ourselves.

Everything Jesus ever taught and lived revolved around love. Everything Jesus did, He did with love. Even when He was angry with people, it was because He knew their actions were going opposite to God's will. There was never a time when Jesus spoke to another person, went anywhere, or did anything without being filled with love for people.

This is how we should live. Our Lord is the God of love, and there is nothing more important. We should be like Jesus and focus on what is right with the world and with other people and not be so concerned about what is wrong with them.

I sometimes find it hard to focus on the goodness in people. Change that, Lord. Lead me to love others just as You love them. Amen.

DAY 34

I say to myself, "The LORD is my portion;
therefore I will wait for him."
LAMENTATIONS 3:24 NIV

The word *portion* means a part of something that is yours. If your mother promised that you could have just one piece of pie, that one piece would be your portion. Your mom promised it to you, and it is yours to enjoy.

The writer of today's verse says that the Lord is his portion. He meant that everything God is and does belongs to him. That applies to all of us. We are God's children, and He wants us to share in His goodness.

God promises us a portion of something else—heaven! He promises that if we believe in Jesus, we already have a home waiting for us there when we die.

The author of Lamentations 3:24 was sure that his place in heaven was already there. He knew that God always keeps His promises, although sometimes we have to wait to receive them.

You will likely have to wait a long time before you get to meet God in heaven face-to-face. But you can be sure that when you get there, a beautiful home awaits you.

What an amazing promise You have made to me, Father, that one day I will be with You in heaven. My hope is in You as I wait for that day. Amen.

DAY 35

Let me hear Your loving-kindness in the morning, for I trust in You.

PSALM 143:8

How did your day begin today? Did you get up early and enjoy the peaceful quiet of the morning after a good night's sleep? Or maybe you spent a restless night worrying about something at school or whether you will play well in your soccer match this weekend.

King David, the man who wrote Psalm 143, had learned the secret to getting each morning off to a good start. He chose to begin every day thinking about God's love. It didn't matter to David if the sun was shining or if he'd had a good night's sleep. It didn't matter if David was worried about a problem. He made a choice to trust God first thing every morning, no matter what. Thinking about God's love throughout the day reminded David that the Lord was with him, not only in the morning but all day long and through the night.

Tomorrow morning, give it a try. Be like King David. Choose to begin the day talking with God and trusting in His love.

I awake in the morning, and You are there. You are with me all day long and throughout the night. Thank You, heavenly Father, for Your ever-present love. Amen.

DAY 36

"Everyone who has power and wins will wear white clothes. I will not take his name from the book of life. I will speak of his name before My Father and His angels."

REVELATION 3:5

God created each of us. He knew us before we were born, and He knows everything about us, even how many hairs are on our heads (Matthew 10:30)! Before we were born, our great and powerful God had already planned all our days (Psalm 139:16).

The Bible mentions the Book of Life, a book in heaven where God writes all our names. God also writes in the book about the things each of us does here on earth (Revelation 20:12). He even jots down the places we go and how many tears we cry (Psalm 56:8)!

Today's Bible verse is about people who have believed in and accepted Jesus as their Savior. When a believer dies and goes to heaven, that person will wear spotless white clothes. Jesus will speak the person's name to God and His angels. Can you imagine what a great introduction that would be? A believer's name will never be erased from God's book. It will stay there forever.

Thank You, dear God, for caring so much about me that You've written my name in Your heavenly book. Amen.

DAY 37

"But is it true that God will live on the earth? See, heaven and the highest heaven are not big enough to hold You. How much less this house which I have built!"

1 KINGS 8:27

King Solomon built a magnificent temple, a special place to honor God. His temple was made from the finest wood and stone and carvings overlaid with gold. It took more than thirty thousand men, working seven years, to complete the work.

When his temple was finished, Solomon felt God's presence there, but he also recognized something else: God is not in just one place. He is everywhere all at the same time! Maybe Solomon remembered the words his father, King David, had written: "I can never get away from your presence! If I go up to heaven, you are there. . . . If I dwell by the farthest oceans, even there your hand will guide me, and your strength will support me" (Psalm 139:7–10 NLT).

God Himself says, "Am I not everywhere in all the heavens and earth?" (Jeremiah 23:24 NLT). He sees and cares for each of us. God knows our whereabouts at all times and guides us through good and bad times.

Isn't that wonderful?

You know exactly where I am. I call and You lead me. I am grateful, Lord! I love You, Lord! Amen.

DAY 38

"Come to Me, all of you who work and have heavy loads. I will give you rest. Follow My teachings and learn from Me. I am gentle and do not have pride. You will have rest for your souls. For My way of carrying a load is easy and My load is not heavy."

MATTHEW 11:28–30

"It looks like you have the weight of the world on your shoulders." Maybe someone has said that to you when you've looked stressed out. Stress wears us down. It makes us feel sort of heavy inside—heavy with worry.

In today's scripture, Jesus is speaking to everyone who feels stressed out. "Come to Me," He says. "I will give you rest." Jesus meant that we should trust Him with everything in life. When we have a problem that weighs us down, we can bring it to Jesus in our prayers. We can give to Him whatever stresses us out and have faith that He will handle it for us. It is His promise to us. And Jesus always keeps His promises.

Is something bothering you today? Give it to Jesus, and then relax. You can trust Him to work it out.

Jesus, I'm glad that You want to take on my troubles. I give them to You right now, and I trust You to give me rest. Amen.

DAY 39

If we tell Him our sins, He is faithful and we can depend on Him to forgive us of our sins. He will make our lives clean from all sin.

1 JOHN 1:9

Maybe you feel guilty after you've done something wrong. You hear a little voice in your heart that keeps reminding you. Would you like that voice to go away? Here's how:

First John 1:9 teaches us that if we pray to God and tell Him we are sorry for our sins, He will forgive us. God cleans away our sin. In Isaiah 1:18, God says, "Come now, let us think about this together. . . . Even though [your sins] are dark red, they will be like wool."

And there is this promise in Romans 10:13: "For everyone who calls on the name of the Lord will be saved from the punishment of sin." Jesus came to take our sins away. Believing in Him is what guarantees us that our sins are forgiven.

We all sin, every one of us! God knows that, and He wants to fix it. You can trust Him to forgive you and heal your guilty feelings.

Sometimes I feel so ashamed of my sins that I avoid confessing them to You. Help me to remember—You will forgive me, if I just come to You and ask. Amen.

DAY 40

But we are citizens of heaven. Christ, the One Who saves from the punishment of sin, will be coming down from heaven again. We are waiting for Him to return.

PHILIPPIANS 3:20

If you have accepted Jesus as your Savior, you already have a home waiting for you in heaven. You don't have to do anything else to become a citizen there. Paul tells us in Philippians 3:20 that we already are citizens of heaven, even while we live here on earth.

For every Christian, heaven is home. From the moment we accept Christ, we are adopted into God's family with the promise of spending forever with Him and all the Christians who have gone before us. Although we are alive here on earth, God thinks of us as citizens in heaven, and our names are written in His book.

As heaven's citizens, we will enjoy all the rights and privileges of our heavenly Father. Meanwhile, God wants us to act like heavenly citizens while we live here on earth. That means putting Him first in our thoughts and acting in ways that please Him.

Heavenly Father, thank You for Your gift of salvation. As a Christian, I know that my forever home is there with You in heaven. I cannot imagine how wonderful it is! Amen.

DAY 41

"For the eyes of the Lord move over all the earth so that He may give strength to those whose whole heart is given to Him."
2 CHRONICLES 16:9

God is exploring the world, searching in every corner. He is busy looking for something. What is He looking for? He is searching for people with a particular type of heart—a heart ready for Him.

God wants a relationship with those who have open and receiving hearts. He is not looking to turn people away or judge them, but His mission is to find hearts committed to knowing Him and learning His ways. God is looking for people who want to talk and listen to Him and who are willing to serve and please Him.

God gives loyal hearts a gift—His strength. He pours His Spirit into these open hearts in order to draw near and build a close relationship with them.

God looks all over the earth for those who will love Him. He searches our hearts and knows if we welcome Him there. When we open our hearts to receive Him, He will find us.

Find me, Lord; draw me near to You. Open up my heart so that I may fully receive all that You want to pour into it. Amen.

DAY 42

When Jesus heard that John had been killed, He went from there by boat to a desert. He wanted to be alone. When the people knew it, they followed after Him by land from the cities.

MATTHEW 14:13

Jesus understands what it feels like to be sad. When His cousin John died, Jesus wanted to be left alone. He went out onto the sea in a boat in search of peace.

Jesus must have felt sad and alone in a way He never had before. Still, He knew that He couldn't stay in that boat feeling sorry for Himself. People needed Him. A crowd was waiting for Him on the shore nearby.

The Bible says that Jesus came back to the shore. Seeing the people and their needs, "He had loving-pity for them and healed those who were sick" (Matthew 14:14). Then, in one of His best-remembered miracles, Jesus fed five thousand people with five loaves of bread and two fish.

Jesus taught us an important lesson when He came back to shore. Feeling sorry for ourselves shouldn't last forever. Life isn't about us; it's about the wonderful things we can do for God when we put our own sadness behind us and turn our thoughts toward others.

Dear God, when I feel sorry for myself, remind me to think about what others need. Amen.

DAY 43

The Holy Spirit proved by a powerful act that Jesus our Lord is the Son of God because He was raised from the dead.

ROMANS 1:4

Do you believe that Jesus is the Son of God? Some people don't. This is nothing new. The fact that some people did not believe is why Jesus was crucified on the cross.

Jesus told the Jewish people, "I am the Son of God." He also told them that if they didn't believe what He *said*, they should believe because of the miracles He did (John 10:36-38). Still, some people did not believe. They thought He was a liar and His miracles were tricks.

The final proof came when God's Holy Spirit raised Jesus back to life after He was in the grave for three days. The Bible tells us in Romans 1:4, "The Holy Spirit proved by a powerful act that Jesus our Lord is the Son of God because He was raised from the dead."

That same powerful Spirit who raised Jesus from the dead lives inside our hearts. He reminds us that Jesus is God's Son, and if we believe, we will live with Him forever in heaven.

Jesus, I believe You are the Son of God. I know that God's powerful Holy Spirit raised You from death, and someday He will do the same for me. Amen.

DAY 44

You do well when you obey the Holy Writings which say, "You must love your neighbor as you love yourself."
JAMES 2:8

Sometimes you might wonder if you are doing enough for God. You think about His commandments and what Jesus taught, and you wonder if you are living well enough for God to want you in heaven someday.

A rich, young ruler came to Jesus and asked Him what he must do to get to heaven. Jesus answered that there is nothing we can do to earn our way into heaven. God is not as impressed by our work as He is impressed by our relationship with Jesus. God is most concerned about us loving Him and loving others as much as we love ourselves.

James 2:8 shows us that we are living as we should if we obey God's law to love one another. This isn't always easy. Some people are, well—just difficult to love! Sometimes it's really hard to see others as Jesus does. But, if we try to see people through the eyes of Jesus, that's good enough for God. When we do our best, then in God's eyes we are doing well.

Give me Your eyes, Lord. Allow me to see others as You see them. Then, with Your help, I can love those who seem unlovable. Amen.

DAY 45

The Lord God planted a garden to the east in Eden.
He put the man there whom He had made.
GENESIS 2:8

After God created Adam, the first man, He led him to a perfect garden. He put Adam in charge of the garden and gave him a companion named Eve.

All they had to do was obey God, but they disobeyed and let sin into their lives. God made them leave His garden. He could have left them and all the humans who came after them miserable forever in their sinful lives, but God didn't. He sacrificed His Son, Jesus, to give humans a way out of sin. That's how much He wants us in heaven with Him someday.

We humans have given in to sin from the start, and we often don't think we deserve God's forgiveness and love. We might think that heaven is for perfect people, not weak, scared people who mess up, like us. And when we think like that, we break God's heart. He isn't waiting for us to prove ourselves worthy of His love. He made us, He loves us, and He wants us to be with Him forever.

Remember this: God loves you just as you are, sin and all. He made you. You are His child.

Thank You for loving me, God, just the way I am. Amen.

DAY 46

Then the demons brought the kings together in the place called Armageddon in the Hebrew language.
REVELATION 16:16

Maybe you have heard people speak of Armageddon. This is a place, also called Mount Megiddo, about eighty miles north of Jerusalem. The Bible says that the last war on earth will be fought in this place. No one knows when this will happen—no one but God. *Armageddon* is also a word some people use to describe an event that will end the world.

The idea of the world ending is scary. But Christians don't have to be afraid, because God is in charge. The Bible tells us that God wins this last earthly battle. Afterward, He will create a new and absolutely perfect earth. It will be as perfect as the garden of Eden was before Adam and Eve sinned. Then everyone whose name is written in God's heavenly book will live on His perfect earth forever.

When you hear about Armageddon and people talking about the end of the world, don't worry. God wants you to follow Jesus and lead a happy life. You belong to God. He will take care of you today and every day.

Father, I will live happily and not be afraid when I hear talk about the end times. I know that You are in charge and that You will take care of me. Amen.

DAY 47

I am asking you for my son, Onesimus. He has become my son in the Christian life while I have been here in prison.
PHILEMON 1:10

Paul spent time in a Roman prison because he spoke of Jesus and some people hated him for that.

While in prison, Paul met a runaway slave named Onesimus who had been in service to someone Paul knew, a man called Philemon.

Onesimus had stolen from his master before running away. Such actions usually meant a death sentence for a slave.

While in Rome, though, and thanks to Paul, Onesimus became a follower of Jesus. He realized he needed to do the right thing, return to Philemon and give back the stolen goods. However, doing so could mean his death. Determined to do the right thing whatever the cost, Onesimus made plans to return.

The slave had been like a son to Paul. To help save Onesimus' life, Paul wrote a letter to Philemon telling him that Onesimus had become a Christian, and he asked his friend to forgive him.

Onesimus displayed great courage and trust in Jesus by returning to Philemon. How courageous are you in your trust? Are you willing to trust Jesus to help you do what is right?

God, please strengthen my trust in Jesus. Take away anything that prevents me from doing what's right. Amen.

DAY 48

When Joshua was by Jericho, he looked up and saw a man standing near him with his sword in his hand. Joshua went to him and said, "Are you for us or for those who hate us?"

JOSHUA 5:13

People sometimes view each other as "the good guys" and "the bad guys." In sports, for example, you might think of the opposing team as the enemy. Of course, this is all in fun—or it should be. If people really see each other as the enemy, that's when trouble starts.

God's friends are those who worship and honor Him. Those who don't are God's enemies. The things they do go against God's will.

God wants us to be watchful about who we associate with. Are they for God or against Him? Those who are for God lead us closer to Him. They always do their best to live in ways that please Him. Those who are against God don't know Him. They live carefree, sinful lives and try to pull others into doing things that they know are wrong.

Be careful when choosing your friends. Be close with those who love God. Pray that the others change their lives and learn to honor Him.

Father, help me to choose my friends wisely and to remember to pray for those who don't know You. Amen.

DAY 49

Jesus said, "Come!" Peter got out of the boat and walked on the water to Jesus.

MATTHEW 14:29

The Bible describes times when Jesus, the perfect Son of God, broke the rules of physics by walking on the waves. But there was someone far from perfect who also walked on water, Jesus' disciple Peter.

Earlier, Jesus had told His disciples to get into a boat and go on without Him to the other side of the lake. Jesus stayed behind to send His crowd of followers home and then to pray. Later that evening, the disciples, who were wrestling their boat against a strong wind, saw a ghostly figure approaching them.

"It is a spirit," they cried out with fear.

Jesus spoke to them and said, "Take hope. It is I. Do not be afraid!"

Then Peter decided to test the Lord. "If it is You, Lord, tell me to come to You on the water."

Jesus did—and Peter, briefly, walked on the waves.

Humans today don't walk on water, but ordinary people who follow God's commands have successfully accomplished difficult, even impossible, tasks.

So, don't give up when things seem hard. That's the perfect time to rely on God's strength.

You are my strength, Lord. Whenever I feel like giving up, I will turn to You for help. Amen.

DAY 50

Be holy in every part of your life. Be like the Holy One Who chose you. The Holy Writings say, "You must be holy, for I am holy."
1 PETER 1:15–16

What does it mean for humans to be holy? It means working toward perfection in all that you do. That's different from *being* perfect. God is the only perfect one, perfect in every way. No human has ever been or ever will be as perfect as Him. That's what sets us apart from God.

Our heavenly Father wants us to work to be like Jesus. He had a human body like ours, one that could hurt, bleed, and die, but in every other way Jesus was perfectly perfect. He is our example of how to live. The more we become like Him, the more pleasing our lives are to God.

You should keep doing your best to be holy in all that you do. Be kind, caring, and giving. Keep your mind focused on God. You won't be perfect on earth, no matter how hard you try. But when you get to heaven someday, you will be perfectly holy with God.

I give myself to You, Father, a work in progress. Come into my heart. Shape me and direct me toward holiness so that I might please You. Amen.

DAY 51

Peter said, "I have no money, but what I have I will give you! In the name of Jesus Christ of Nazareth, get up and walk!"
ACTS 3:6

Two of Jesus' disciples, Peter and John, were on their way to the temple to pray. Every day, friends carried a man to the temple. He was disabled, so he could not walk, and this man had no money. He sat outside the temple and begged.

He asked Peter and John for money, but they had none to give him. Still, Peter knew that he could provide the man with something even better.

"Peter said, 'I have no money, but what I have I will give you! In the name of Jesus Christ of Nazareth, get up and walk!' Peter took the man by the right hand and lifted him up. At once his feet and the bones in his legs became strong. He jumped up on his feet and walked!" (Acts 3:6–8). God had done a miraculous thing through Peter.

God will work through you too. Maybe you won't heal someone, like Peter did, but you can be generous with others through your kindness and caring and by sharing your talents.

God, please work through me. Guide me to use what You have given me to help others. Amen.

DAY 52

Now Lappidoth's wife Deborah, a woman who spoke for God, was judging Israel at that time.

JUDGES 4:4

Women today work alongside men in every imaginable job. But in Bible times, women were rarely seen working with men, especially not as leaders. So, who is this Deborah in today's verse? How did she end up ruling Israel?

Deborah was a prophet, a judge, and a military leader. A prophet is one called by God to speak on His behalf. Deborah inspired people to turn their hearts toward God. She must have been a remarkable woman to be accepted by men and given power at a time in history when men ruled everything.

Deborah is a role model for *everyone* today. We may not see ourselves as leaders, but we all can draw others closer to God.

Think about ways you can lead others to Him. You can be kind and caring, like Jesus. You can have a positive attitude, especially when things aren't going well. You can tell your friends about Jesus and even say little things like "God bless you" when someone is kind toward you.

Keep your eyes open for opportunities. Every day, your simple acts of kindness can draw others closer to God.

Heavenly Father, open my eyes and my heart! Lead me to share You with others. Amen.

DAY 53

"This Good News about the holy nation of God must be preached over all the earth. It must be told to all nations and then the end will come."

MATTHEW 24:14

Jesus is coming back someday. When He arrives, it will signal the end of earth as we know it. That will be a good day—a great day—for all who love God.

We don't know when Jesus will come back, but He said that the good news first has to be told to all nations. What is the good news? It is the news that Jesus was sent by His Father, God, to save us from sin. Jesus is the only ticket to heaven.

You might think that in this modern age the good news has already been preached in all nations through missionaries, radios, television, the Internet. . .but there are groups of people in far-off parts of the world who have not heard of Jesus—yet.

That's why it's important for you to pray and do your part to see that these people hear about Him. There is still work to be done before Jesus returns. Everyone needs to know about Him, in every country to the ends of the earth.

Lord, there are still some who haven't heard about You. Remind me to pray for those who need to hear. Amen.

DAY 54

Your ears will hear a word behind you, saying, "This is the way, walk in it," whenever you turn to the right or to the left.
ISAIAH 30:21

Most smartphones and many cars have a GPS to lead users when they don't know which way to go. But did you know that each of us has a GPS inside our heart? It's the God Positioning System! Whenever you face a decision and don't know which direction to take, you can ask God to lead you. Through the God Positioning System, you can be sure that your heavenly Father will show you the way.

Everyone faces big decisions, and today's Bible verse offers encouragement and hope to those who call on God. When we turn to Him in trust and use His navigational system, we can be sure that His map for our lives is perfect. Unlike an earthly GPS, God will never lead us down dead-end roads or send us onto nonexistent streets. Instead, He promises to hear us when we cry for help (Isaiah 30:19). And from that moment on, He gives us directions that we can 100 percent trust.

I'm grateful, Father, for Your God Positioning System. Each morning, remind me to turn it on so that Your voice can direct me in the way I should go. Amen.

DAY 55

If a person says, "I love God," but hates his brother, he is a liar. If a person does not love his brother whom he has seen, how can he love God Whom he has not seen?

1 JOHN 4:20

Who does not know someone they'd cross the street to avoid? That person might be a bully or might have caused hurt feelings—but God still loves that person! He wants us to love that person too through our kindness and good example.

If even one of these difficult people sees God through the way you behave, it makes God happy. So, do your best to be kind to those who are unkind to you. It's difficult, and God does not want you to get hurt or into trouble, but do your best to love them like Jesus would.

Maybe there are those who hurt you, people you trusted once and find hard to forgive. God wants you to forgive them and replace the hurt with love. It's a big assignment and one that might not always work, but you will be nearer to God for having tried!

God, sometimes it's hard acting in a Christlike way, especially toward those who are not my friends. Help me, please, to love everyone and not just those who love me back. Amen.

DAY 56

If the one who hates you is hungry, feed him. If he is thirsty, give him water. If you do that, you will be making him more ashamed of himself, and the Lord will reward you.

PROVERBS 25:21–22

Read today's scripture passage again and think about it.

Maybe the last thing you want to do is be kind to someone who is unkind to you. But, these verses from Proverbs 25 say that is exactly what God wants from you.

God says to find ways to be kind to your enemy. Maybe that difficult person needs some gentle words or help with a project at school. Maybe that person just needs a friend. You should ask God to show you what to do.

It may be hard to gather up the courage to show kindness to someone who is not your friend, but God will give you His strength. And God also hints in today's verse that your kindness might make that person feel ashamed of the way they have treated you. It might help them turn to God.

Whatever happens as a result of your goodness, God promises to reward you for trying.

Dear Lord, help me to be forgiving toward my enemies. Even if they hate me, teach me to bless them by showing them love. Amen.

DAY 57

In those days King Ahasuerus sat on the. . .throne in the city of Susa. In the third year of his rule, he gave a special supper for all his princes and leaders. . . . There was much wine, because the king was very able and willing to give it. . . . The king had told all the workmen of his house that they should give each person what he wanted.

ESTHER 1:2–3, 7–8

Kids your age and older are taught that bad things can happen if they drink alcohol or use drugs. Not following that advice has caused people trouble almost since the beginning of time.

Persia's king, Ahasuerus, held a banquet for important leaders in his kingdom. The purpose of the banquet was to plan an attack on Greece. There was much wine, and the king told his servants to give each person as much as he wanted.

The attack on Greece was a disaster. A much smaller army from Greece crushed the king's huge army. Likely, the king and his men had partied instead of worked on a plan to win the battle. Their poor planning left many in their army dead.

The Bible warns about drinking too much. Please keep that in mind as you get older. Always behave to honor God.

Lord, as I get older, please keep me away from alcohol and drugs. I want to live to please You. Amen.

DAY 58

Jesus looked at them and said, "This cannot be done by men. But with God all things can be done."
MATTHEW 19:26

A rich, young ruler asked Jesus what he needed to do to get to heaven. Jesus told him to sell all his possessions and give to the poor. Sadly, the man went home.

Jesus' disciples were troubled by what Jesus had said. *What would it take to get to heaven?* they wondered. *If everyone gave up everything they had, what would be left? And how would that please God?* Frustrated with the impossible idea of giving up everything, the disciples finally asked Jesus, "Who can be saved?" (Matthew 19:25).

Jesus told them exactly what it would take. He said no one can be saved by their own efforts! The rich young ruler had tried everything humanly possible, and still he failed. His greatest efforts could never measure up to God's requirements.

Only accepting God's grace—His forgiveness and favor, even when we don't deserve it—will admit us to heaven. Realizing we can do nothing is the key to gaining everything—God's gift of living in heaven someday.

Dear Father, I appreciate Your grace—Your loving-kindness that I don't deserve. There is nothing I have done to earn it. Grace is Your gift to me, and I thank You. Amen.

DAY 59

Go to the ant, O lazy person. Watch and think about her ways, and be wise.
PROVERBS 6:6

Each species of ants—over ten thousand—forms colonies that consist of one or more queens, a few males, and numerous female worker ants.

The queen ants do not lead or rule. They simply spend life laying eggs to populate the colony. The workers perform most of the labor necessary for the colony to survive and carry out their tasks without any leadership.

In some species, worker ants keep aphids the way people keep cows. The ants care for the aphids over winter and in spring place them outside on plants. When rubbed, these aphids secrete a sweet liquid used as a beverage by the ant colony.

Other ants cut leaves to grow fungus underground while their companions tend these underground gardens. Larger workers patrol the colony on the lookout for enemy insects.

Proverbs 6:6 contrasts these hardworking ants with lazy people. But sometimes people aren't lazy at all. Some just feel overwhelmed by the size of a task. If that describes you, then break a chore into small parts and celebrate completing each one. Become wise by planning ahead. Study the ants and learn from them.

When a task seems so big and overwhelming, remind me, Lord, that You will help me to accomplish it, one small step at a time. Amen.

DAY 60

There are many other things which Jesus did also. If they were all written down, I do not think the world itself could hold the books that would be written.

JOHN 21:25

The Bible contains four Gospels—books that tell about Jesus—but it doesn't have a single biography of Jesus.

Aren't the Gospels biographies?

Not exactly. Two of the Gospels ignore Jesus' birth completely, and only Luke mentions His childhood years.

Jesus' disciple John said that to write a complete biography of Jesus' life would require more books than the world has room for! So, when John chose which details of Jesus' life to include in his Gospel—he did it with great care.

All of the Gospel writers did. They each had a particular purpose in writing their accounts of Jesus' life. John explains his clearly: "These are written so you may believe that Jesus is the Christ, the Son of God. When you put your trust in Him, you will have life that lasts forever through His name" (20:31).

Jesus' story continues to be written—in us. The way we live our lives can lead others to faith in Him.

Jesus, the Gospels make me want to know more about You. Teach me to become more like You and to grow nearer to You as I learn. Amen.

DAY 61

Never stop praying.

1 THESSALONIANS 5:17

The Bible tells us that God listens to us when we pray. He hears every word, and He cares deeply about what we want.

Sometimes the answer to our request is "not yet." Sometimes the answer is "no." That's because God knows that what we want isn't always what we need.

When we pray and tell God what is in our hearts, He always finds a way to bless us and make everything work out for the best. God is so much smarter than we could ever hope to be. He knows what is best for us and provides it each time. All we have to do is share our concerns with Him and wait faithfully for what He will provide.

God never promised an easy life to Christians. If we will allow Him, though, God will be there with us every step of the way, every day of our lives. We need to get in the routine of praying all the time. Remember the three simple words from 1 Thessalonians 5:17. Then pray and trust God to provide exactly what you need.

Father, when I pray, remind me that prayer is not only about talking to You but about listening to You. Open my heart to Your words. Amen.

DAY 62

"Keep these words of mine in your heart and in your soul. Tie them as something special to see upon your hand and on your forehead between your eyes. Teach them to your children. Talk about them when you sit in your house and when you walk on the road and when you lie down and when you get up. Write them beside the door of your house and on your gates."

DEUTERONOMY 11:18–20

Have you ever seen a person of the Jewish faith wearing a small box attached to his forehead? "Frontlets" are tiny leather boxes tied to the forehead and left arm and worn at prayer times. Each box holds scrolls of parchment containing key Old Testament verses. For these Jews, the frontlets provide a way of carrying God's Word with them all the time. When they cross their arms, they draw the scriptures closer to their hearts. They believe this practice helps them fulfill the commandment in Deuteronomy.

So, how do we Christians carry God's Word with us all the time? By keeping important Bible verses in our hearts and minds. Memorizing Bible verses reminds us that God is always with us.

Give it a try!

What an awesome gift You have given me, God—the Bible! I will remember Your words and carry them with me wherever I go. Amen.

DAY 63

He said to them, "Where is your faith?" The followers were surprised and afraid. They said to each other, "What kind of a man is He? He speaks to the wind and the waves and they obey Him."

LUKE 8:25

It was calm on the lake that day when the disciples and Jesus set out in their boat to sail to the other side. During the gentle boat ride, Jesus fell asleep. Then it happened—a storm.

The boat took on so much water that it was going under. The disciples woke Jesus and begged Him to do something because they were going to drown. Jesus got up and spoke to the wind and the waves. The storm stopped.

Sailing again on calm water, Jesus questioned His followers about where their faith was. The disciples sat there amazed that Jesus had the power even to control nature.

Jesus used the terrifying boat ride not only to display His power over all creation but to provide an opportunity for the disciples to look at the depth of their faith.

What shape is your faith in today? Do you believe that Jesus can do anything?

Jesus, increase my faith. Teach me to trust even more in Your power and Your ability to calm the storms that come into my life. I love You, Lord Jesus. Amen.

DAY 64

Do not answer a fool by his foolish ways, or you will be like him. Answer a fool in the way he has earned by his foolish acts, so he will not be wise in his own eyes.

PROVERBS 26:4–5

If you find today's scripture passage confusing, you are not alone. It seems to give two opposite pieces of advice. The author, King Solomon, did this on purpose to make it clear that we are to respond differently in different circumstances. Solomon later pointed out, "There is a special time for everything," and "A wise heart knows the right time and way" (Ecclesiastes 3:1; 8:5).

Maybe you know someone who always thinks he is right. Maybe you know what that person says is foolish and wrong. What you should say to that person depends on the situation. God may lead you to give him a serious answer or a humorous, foolish answer (to show him how foolishly he's talking).

Sometimes God might lead you to say nothing at all (Proverbs 23:9). No matter what you say to some people, it won't keep them from saying foolish things and giving foolish advice.

Dear God, when I don't know how to respond to a foolish opinion, show me. Give me the proper answer, or lead me to keep still. Amen.

DAY 65

Then Jesus cried.

John 11:35

This one little verse in the Bible reminds us just how much Jesus understands our feelings. As God's Son on earth, Jesus felt things as we humans do. He laughed and He cried.

Jesus cried over the death of His friend Lazarus.

Lazarus' sisters had sent a message to Jesus asking Him to come when Lazarus was sick. They knew Jesus could heal their brother. But Jesus waited. Why? Because He had a big miracle planned.

By the time Jesus arrived, Lazarus was already dead and buried in his tomb. When Jesus saw how sad Lazarus' sisters were, that made Him cry. Jesus loved Lazarus and his family, and He hated seeing them hurting.

John 11 goes on to say that Jesus' great miracle was raising Lazarus back from the dead, returning him to his grieving sisters, Mary and Martha. That proved His power as God's Son—but before that, just like us humans, Jesus cried over the loss of a friend.

Jesus still feels our pain when we cry. And we can count on Him to comfort us. The next time you feel sad, remember that Jesus is right there with you, and He understands.

Jesus, when things in life make me cry, remind me that You care and understand. Hug me, Lord. Hold me in Your arms and comfort me. Amen.

DAY 66

"Then you will know which way to go, since you have never been this way before. But keep a distance of about two thousand cubits between you and the ark; do not go near it."
JOSHUA 3:4 NIV

These days, GPS systems and smartphones give us confidence that we won't get lost. The Israelites didn't have such tools; instead, they had something better for guidance, the *ark of the covenant*—a chest that contained the stones onto which God wrote the Ten Commandments.

Joshua led the Israelites across the Jordan River into a new land. The people hadn't journeyed in this direction, so the plan was for them to follow the ark, which the priests would carry. When they saw the direction the ark was going, they would know which way to go.

The Israelites could safely travel into the unknown only by believing that God was leading them.

Many times in your life, you are going to find yourself heading in a direction you are not familiar with. When God brings you to that unknown territory, you can be sure He'll guide you through it.

Sometimes You lead me into unfamiliar places, Father, but You always bring me through them. You know the way. You stay with me, guide me, and love me. Thank You, God! Amen.

DAY 67

"But I tell you, do not fight with the man who wants to fight. Whoever hits you on the right side of the face, turn so he can hit the other side also."

MATTHEW 5:39

Read today's verse again. Jesus is speaking.

Of course Jesus does not want you to stand still and allow someone to beat you up. But He also doesn't want you to get angry and beat someone up because they beat you. Instead, Jesus wants you to love your enemy and do your best to walk away from conflicts.

Jesus is all about love. He said we should love God (Matthew 22:36–37), love our neighbors (Matthew 22:39), and love our enemies (Matthew 5:44)!

It sounds great, but loving our enemies can be difficult. God knows we live in a world where walking away is often judged as cowardly. That's why He sent Jesus to be our example of love. Think about it: when Jesus was nailed to the cross by an angry mob, He prayed, "Father, forgive them" (Luke 23:34).

Do your very best to avoid any kind of fight. Battle against anger with love, and ask God to help you love your enemies.

Heavenly Father, when someone does wrong to me, please quiet my anger and soothe my hurt. Help me to love my enemies with Your kind of love. Amen.

DAY 68

Be glad you can do the things you should be doing.
Do all things without arguing and talking about
how you wish you did not have to do them.
PHILIPPIANS 2:14

If anyone had a right to complain, it was Jesus' friend Paul. He had a tough life. Paul had suffered through shipwrecks; he had been made fun of, beaten, and put into prison for doing nothing wrong. Still, he wrote the words of Philippians 2:14: "Be glad."

Are you someone who does tasks willingly, or do you grumble? Most kids complain sometimes about doing homework and chores around the house. Grown-ups grumble too. Complaining is something all humans do. But God wants us to be like Paul, turn that around, and have a positive attitude.

Try this: Put a rubber band or bracelet on your wrist. Every time you notice you are complaining or arguing, switch it from one wrist to the other. Keep track of how many times you made the change. If it was often, then promise to turn your attitude around.

Think every day about how God has blessed you. Do willingly what you don't want to do. Be happy, and replace your grumbles with sunshine.

Lord, I argue and complain, and often I am not even aware. Remind me to look on the bright side and to share a little sunshine with others. Amen.

DAY 69

While Paul was waiting for Silas and Timothy in Athens, his spirit was troubled as he saw the whole city worshiping false gods.

ACTS 17:16

When God gave the Ten Commandments to Moses, the very first one was "Have no gods other than Me" (Exodus 20:3). In His second commandment, God said, "Do not make for yourselves a god to look like anything that is in heaven above or on the earth below or in the waters under the earth" (Exodus 20:4). The people in Moses' time did not obey these commands, and humans don't obey them still.

In ancient times, people often created statues that they called gods. They bowed down and prayed to them. This happens, still, in some parts of the world.

But our false gods today are usually everyday things that we make more important than God. For some people, money is the most important thing. Others might worship a person or even an idea. Maybe you can think of other examples where people make something more important to them than God.

The best way to make God your only god is to keep your mind on Him all the time. Don't allow anything to become more important than Him.

Dear God, I want You to be my one and only God. Please help me to stay focused on You. Amen.

DAY 70

Turn my eyes away from things that have no worth,
and give me new life because of Your ways.

Psalm 119:37

How well do you see with your heart? Wait! Don't we see with our eyes? Yes, but we also see with our hearts. God works through our hearts to help us understand the world as He sees it.

Some things in life take our eyes off Jesus and pull us farther away from Him—things that distract us, like television shows and video games. You can compare this to being nearsighted and seeing only what the world plops in front of you. Other things, like worrying about what might happen tomorrow or next week, keep us from seeing what God is doing for us right now. You could compare that to farsightedness, focusing only on things far away. Perfect heart vision comes when we remember to keep God's Word in our hearts and focus our thoughts always on Him.

Are there things in your life that are keeping you from having perfect vision of the heart? Think about it. What changes can you make to focus your heart on Jesus?

Jesus, there are so many distractions in life, things that get in my way. Help me to make them less important and to center my focus on You. Amen.

DAY 71

Give me your heart, my son. Let your eyes find joy in my ways.
PROVERBS 23:26

It is almost impossible for us to be joyful about everything in life. Some things that happen make us feel discouraged, frustrated, and sad. The Bible tells us, though, in James 1:2 (NIV) that we should find joy in *all* things: "Consider it pure joy, my brothers and sisters, whenever you face trials of many kinds."

We find joy by knowing that God is in control of our lives, and He wants only what is best for us. Sometimes God allows us to experience difficult things because those things build up our faith in Him. At other times, God will bless us with something to be joyful about when we feel discouraged, frustrated, or sad.

Proverbs 23:26 reminds us that we have to keep our eyes open for God's blessings and not allow circumstances to keep us from noticing them. At times, some little thing that God does could turn your frown to a smile. Remember always that God is in your heart. That alone is a good reason to feel joy!

God, thank You for all of Your blessings, especially those little ones that I forget about. Open my eyes to find joy all around me all the time. Amen.

DAY 72

"For it is by your words that you will not be guilty and it is by your words that you will be guilty."
MATTHEW 12:37

The words we say come out of our mouths without us thinking much about them. Words can be kind like a gentle spring rain, or they can cut like a sharp knife. Words can stir things up or settle things down. Our words are so important that Jesus spoke about them.

Jesus said that people would someday have to stand before God and give an answer for every unkind or stir-things-up word they have ever spoken (Matthew 12:36). According to Jesus, our words are like a mirror that reflects what we've stored up in our hearts. If there are good things in our hearts, our words will be kind and good. If our hearts are filled up with bad stuff, then our words will reflect that too.

Other people, who can't see into our hearts, learn what's there by the way we speak. Think about the words you've said today. Were they good and kind? Or maybe you need to apologize for some of what you've said.

Dear God, please help me to choose my words wisely. I want each and every word that comes from my mouth to be pleasing to You and to others. Amen.

DAY 73

"Do not steal."

EXODUS 20:15

Each of God's Ten Commandments is equally important. When put all together, they tell us how God wants us to live.

God thinks these commands are so important that He carved them into flat stone tablets and gave them to Moses to read to the Israelites. Then God had them make a special chest, called the ark of the covenant, to hold His stone tablets. The Israelites carried the ark with them during their journey to the Promised Land.

"Do not steal," the eighth of God's Ten Commandments, is one of the simplest to remember. But, stealing can be more than just taking an item that belongs to someone else.

If you think about it, there are other ways to steal. You can steal someone's place in line by being selfish and cutting in front of that person. You can steal a person's self-esteem by bullying them. You can steal someone's good character by saying bad things about them. Can you think of other examples?

God wants us not just to follow His commandments but to meditate on what they mean. The words might be simple, but they give us much to think about.

Dear Father, help me to memorize and remember Your Ten Commandments and not just know them but think about them. Amen.

DAY 74

Paul looked straight at the court and said, "Brother Jews, I have lived for God with a heart that has said I am not guilty to this day."
ACTS 23:1

Poor Paul. Everywhere he went he got into trouble—and for nothing. Some of the people hated him for talking about Jesus. They said things about Paul that were not true and got crowds of people all upset. Before long, Paul was beat up and accused of starting a riot. This caused him to be arrested and have to go to court.

But, standing before the judges in court, Paul said that he was not guilty. He told them that he lived according to God's laws and that he lived every day to serve God. His conscience was clear.

What does it mean to have a clear conscience? It means that in your heart you know that what you did is right. When our hearts tell us we have done wrong, then we feel guilty. But knowing we have done right brings us peace.

In Acts 24:16, Paul reminds us: always try to live so your heart says you are not guilty before God or man.

What is your heart saying today?

Help me, Lord, to live a clean life so that I can stand before You and others with a clear conscience. Amen.

DAY 75

There is a way which looks right to a man,
but its end is the way of death.
PROVERBS 14:12

In school, you learn about writing stories. You discover that in every story there is a conflict—some problem that a character has to overcome. Every story has a climax—an event where the character has to make a decision. Sometimes that decision means life or death.

Often in a story, someone makes a wrong decision that gets them into trouble. This happens in real life too. We humans make decisions that can get us, and others, into a deep mess. But, just like in stories, we have a hero who comes to rescue us. It's Jesus!

Jesus is the one who gets us out of our messes. We can count on Him to save us, no matter what. All we have to do is call on Him in prayer and then trust Him to arrive, at just the right time, to pull us up out of the mud and carry us safely in His arms.

Lord, come rescue me from the mess I'm in. Lead me out of my frustration and fear. I put my trust in You. I stand waiting, knowing that You will save me. Amen.

DAY 76

My Christian brothers, you should be happy when you have all kinds of tests. You know these prove your faith. It helps you not to give up.

JAMES 1:2–3

Today's scripture comes from a letter written by James, Jesus' oldest brother, to a group of Jewish Christians. James told them not to give up. They had endlessly been made fun of and punished for holding tightly to their faith, and they were tired and worn out.

James added words similar to those of Peter's in the Bible: "You can be happy even if you need to have sorrow and all kinds of tests for awhile. These tests have come to prove your faith and to show that it is good" (1 Peter 1:6–7).

God encourages us today through the words of James and Peter. When we're tired and beaten down with our own problems and tests, we can be happy just knowing that God is right there with us. God promises that He will never leave or abandon us. All He asks is that we hold tightly to our faith and not give up.

Father God, when I face hard times, please strengthen my faith. Show me Your mercy, gentleness, and love. In You I find pure joy, and I praise You! Amen.

DAY 77

"Return to Me, and I will return to you," says the Lord of All.
MALACHI 3:7

Malachi's name means "my messenger." He is the last prophet to speak God's words in the Old Testament.

The people of Israel had wandered far from God and faced all kinds of trouble. Sadly, they continued to sin. God chose Malachi to deliver His final message to the people before Jesus came. Malachi warned the people of Israel about their sin. But he also reminded them of the love of their heavenly Father. "Return to Me, and I will return to you," God said.

After speaking through Malachi, God was silent for about four centuries. Then Jesus was born, and later Jesus' cousin, John the Baptist, came preparing us for Jesus' ministry and God's plan to save us from sin.

"Return to Me, and I will return to you." These words from God were a promise to the people of ancient Israel but also for us. It is a promise we can still count on today.

Whenever I stray from You, Lord, I feel empty and alone. So many times, I've returned and asked Your forgiveness, and always You've loved me. Thank You, God! Amen.

DAY 78

As you have put your trust in Christ Jesus the Lord to save you from the punishment of sin, now let Him lead you in every step. Have your roots planted deep in Christ. Grow in Him. Get your strength from Him. Let Him make you strong in the faith as you have been taught. Your life should be full of thanks to Him.

COLOSSIANS 2:6–7

How do we plant our roots deep in Jesus?

First, we remember that Jesus lives in our hearts. Living with someone means spending time together. Spend time learning about Jesus and His ways.

Second, remember that strong roots run deep. Mighty trees have deep roots to support them. Our "roots" are made strong with prayer and studying the Bible.

Next, we believe what we have learned about Jesus in the Bible and what we have been taught by others. Their words, or the examples of how they live, strengthen our faith.

Finally, we give thanks to God. Thankfulness comes easy during good times. But even in hard times, expressing appreciation to God renews our spirits.

That's how we plant our roots deep in Jesus. He guides us through prayer and study, the fellowship of others, and practicing daily gratitude.

Guide me, Lord. Nourish and strengthen the roots of my faith. Lead me to those who will teach me Your ways, and then, Lord, keep me mindful of what I have learned. Amen.

DAY 79

Happy is the man who does not walk in the way sinful men tell him to, or stand in the path of sinners, or sit with those who laugh at the truth.

PSALM 1:1

It should make you happy knowing that you have done the right thing, even if those around you have not.

God knows what is in our hearts and minds. He loves us and cares about us so much that He is interested in everything we do—even the little things. He sees when we make bad decisions or follow those who make bad choices!

Following Jesus means having wisdom. And wisdom is available from God to everyone just by asking for it; however, not everyone chooses to make wise decisions.

Sometimes it is easier to simply go along with the crowd. This might take pressure off us and make us feel better in the moment. Later, though, we realize what we have done and how we have pushed ourselves away from God.

The next time you are tempted to follow the crowd, be wise and remember the words of Psalm 1:1.

Be happy. Do the right thing!

I am happy, God, when my actions please You. But if I give in and follow the crowd, thank You for being a forgiving God, a God of second chances. Amen.

DAY 80

Then Jesus turned to Peter and said, "Get behind Me, Satan! You are standing in My way. You are not thinking how God thinks. You are thinking how man thinks."

MATTHEW 16:23

Jesus told His followers that He would be killed and three days later He would be raised from the dead. Peter couldn't stand the idea of Jesus being killed. So, he said, "Never, Lord! This must not happen to You!"

Then Jesus turned to Peter and said, "Get behind Me, Satan! You are standing in My way. You are not thinking how God thinks. You are thinking how man thinks."

Sharp words, but Jesus was right. God had a wonderful plan far beyond what Peter, or any human, could understand. Peter was about to do the wrong thing and get in Jesus' way of carrying out God's plan.

We can get in the way of His plans for us too when we carelessly go our own way and do our own thing. It's so important not to act without talking with God and seeking His will. He knows everything that's happening in our lives and what each new step should be.

Jesus, if I get in Your way, please stop me. Help me to remember that Your thinking and plans are so much greater than mine. Amen.

DAY 81

Then the Lord said to Satan, "See, all that he has is in your power. Only do not put your hand on him." So Satan went out from the Lord.

JOB 1:12

Some people picture God and Satan as powerful enemies locked in an ongoing battle. They believe that in good times God must be winning and in bad times Satan is winning.

Not true! God rules over Satan, always.

Today's verse comes from the Bible story about Job, a good man who followed God's rules. God had blessed Job with many wonderful things. Then, along came Satan. He said to God, "Just take away his stuff and watch what happens then." So, God allowed Satan to test Job's faith. He let him take away Job's stuff, and He allowed Job to feel sick and suffer. But God told Satan that he could not take Job's life.

Satan can't work without God's permission, and sometimes God allows us to be tested too. But no matter how bad things get, they are never out of God's control.

And what about Job? Through all his misery and suffering he held on to his faith, and when the test was over God blessed him even more.

When I ask, "Why do bad things happen to good people?" Father, remind me that You are always in control and You love me. Amen.

DAY 82

Who then can say we are guilty? It was Christ Jesus Who died. He was raised from the dead. He is on the right side of God praying to Him for us.

ROMANS 8:34

Have you ever thought, *I'm not good enough*? Or maybe someone hurt you and knocked down your self-esteem? Well, there's good news! You *are* good enough. Satan is the one making you feel that you're not, and you can fix that with Jesus' help.

When people hurt your self-esteem, Paul says in the Bible that you shouldn't pay attention to them (1 Corinthians 4:3). And when you feel in your heart that you aren't good enough, Jesus' follower John says, "Our heart may say that we have done wrong. But remember, God is greater than our heart. He knows everything" (1 John 3:20).

When Jesus died on the cross, He took your sins away. You are forgiven for whatever you have done, and you don't have to carry any guilt in your heart. Jesus is in heaven with God, praying for you and helping you.

So, cheer up! Let Jesus lift your spirits. He is always on your side.

If I don't feel good enough, Jesus, You lift me up. If others say I'm not good enough, You are on my side. Lord, You are my treasured friend, and I love You. Amen.

DAY 83

"If anyone asks you, 'Why are you doing that?' say, 'The Lord needs it. He will send it back again soon.'"

MARK 11:3

Today's verse is set just outside the city of Jerusalem. Jesus was about to enter the city to celebrate the Jewish festival of Passover. The people anxiously awaited Him—the Messiah, the one who would save them.

Jesus told His disciples to borrow a young donkey so He could sit on its back when He entered the city. How strange, it seemed, for Jesus to need a donkey. But this was all part of God's plan. In fact, many years before, God had given the prophet Zechariah a glimpse of what would happen in the future: "Be full of joy. . .O people of Jerusalem! See, your King is coming to you. He is fair and good. . . . He is not proud and sits on a donkey" (Zechariah 9:9).

Everything on earth belonged to God. Jesus could have taken His Father's donkey, but He borrowed and then returned it. Jesus was the great King of kings, but He never acted like a wealthy, greedy king. He was humble and gentle and always did the right thing.

Dear God, help me to remember that everything I have is Yours. Remind me to share what I have and to give back what I borrow. Amen.

DAY 84

Now in the city of Susa where the king lived there was a Jew whose name was Mordecai. . . . He had brought up. . .Esther, the daughter of his father's brother. For she did not have a father or mother. . . . When her father and mother died, Mordecai took her as his own daughter.

ESTHER 2:5, 7

The book of Esther in the Old Testament is the true story of a young queen, her cousin Mordecai, and how she saved his life.

Do you know that every story in the Bible is true?

Over and over again, the Bible is shown to be true and trustworthy. Esther's story takes place in 460 BC. Ancient tablets have been found by archaeologists to confirm that Mordecai was a scribe or minister at the royal court of Esther's husband, King Xerxes. Other archaeological finds prove that people in the Bible really existed and the events told about in the Bible really happened.

Second Timothy 3:16 says that everything in the Bible comes from God. And we know that God does not lie. We can always trust that His Word, the entire Bible, is 100 percent true.

Father, how exciting it is to know that all the stories I read in the Bible really happened! I want to read about Your people and share what I learn with my friends. Amen.

DAY 85

He said, "For sure, I tell you, unless you have a change of heart and become like a little child, you will not get into the holy nation of heaven."
MATTHEW 18:3

Jesus heard His disciples arguing about which of them was the greatest. They asked Jesus, "Who is the greatest in the holy nation of heaven?" (Matthew 18:1). In other words, "What do we have to do to become great when we get there?"

Jesus answered them using little children as an example. Young children, like babies and toddlers, haven't been in the world long enough to think they are better than anyone else. They see the world as a good place without a lot of bad stuff mixed in. They depend on their parents for everything.

Jesus said that everyone, young and old, needs to behave in a similar way. We should depend on God for everything and notice all the good things He puts around us in the world. Especially, we should never think that we will be greater than anyone else.

Jesus told His disciples that instead of worrying about being the greatest here or in heaven, they should change their attitudes and think with the pure heart of a little child.

Lord Jesus, if ever I feel like I'm better than anyone else, help me to remember Your words in Matthew 18:3. Amen.

DAY 86

Elijah said to Elisha, "Ask what I should do for you before I am taken from you." And Elisha said, "I ask you, let twice the share of your spirit be upon me."
2 KINGS 2:9

Elijah was a great prophet of God. When God spoke to him, Elijah passed His words on to the people. Elisha was a follower of Elijah. He listened to Elijah's words and saw the miracles that God did through him. Second Kings 2:9 is the beginning of the end of their story.

God was about to take Elijah up to heaven. But, just before that happened, Elijah asked Elisha what he could do for him. Elisha could have asked for anything. But he asked to become a prophet like Elijah and carry on God's work.

It seemed an impossible request, but God allowed it to happen! He made Elisha the prophet who took Elijah's place.

What might God give you if you asked for the impossible? God loves you. If your heart lines up with His will for you, He might surprise you. If God can take an ordinary man like Elisha and turn him into a great prophet, what great thing might He do for you?

Lord, when I ask for what seems impossible, I know You will provide what is best for me. Whatever Your answer, I know that You love me. Amen.

DAY 87

Do not be ashamed to tell others about what our Lord said, or of me here in prison. I am here because of Jesus Christ. Be ready to suffer for preaching the Good News and God will give you the strength you need.

2 TIMOTHY 1:8

Paul is probably the Bible's greatest letter writer. Today's verse comes from one of his last.

When Paul was an old man in prison for preaching about Jesus, he wrote to a younger friend, Timothy. Paul worried that Timothy and others might be afraid of ending up in prison too if they talked about the Lord.

"Do not be ashamed," Paul wrote. (In other words, *Don't worry.*) "God will give you the strength you need."

Paul had suffered a lot for talking about the Lord. People who hated Jesus also hated him. But Paul never gave up. He knew that all his suffering was worth it if it caused some to believe in Jesus so they could go to heaven.

If people make fun of you for talking about Jesus, don't you give up either! Remember Paul's words to Timothy. Keep spreading the good news about Jesus so others will believe and go to heaven someday. Trust God to give you the courage to share Jesus' story.

Lord, lead me to never be afraid to tell others about Jesus. Amen.

DAY 88

He has made everything beautiful in its time. He has put thoughts of the forever in man's mind, yet man cannot understand the work God has done from the beginning to the end.

ECCLESIASTES 3:11

Isn't our God awesome? Take a few minutes to look around and think about all the wonderful things He has made. Then praise Him for promising that you will live with Him in heaven one day.

God thinks about everything before He puts it on earth or allows it to happen. Everything God makes and does is perfect in His sight—even if it looks imperfect in ours. What we humans might see as ugly or broken or unfinished is just the way God wants it right now. Ecclesiastes 3:11 says that God makes everything beautiful at exactly the right time.

Sometimes it's hard to find beauty in everything. But we have to remember that God's mind is so much greater than our own. And His timing isn't like ours. What we think needs to be fixed right now, God might not fix for months or years or ever on this earth. But He always knows what He's doing, and He loves us.

God, I have so many unanswered questions about life and about You. There are things I don't understand. But I know this—You love me. Amen.

DAY 89

Christ was before all things. All things are held together by Him.
COLOSSIANS 1:17

Imagine Jesus, in heaven now, holding our world together. It's not that He wraps His arms around our universe to keep it from falling apart. Instead, Jesus makes sure that everything in the universe is working perfectly.

Earth's distance from the sun is perfect. If Earth were 5 percent closer, rivers and oceans would evaporate. Move 5 percent farther away, both water and carbon dioxide would freeze. Too cold or too hot means no life.

Even our moon makes life possible by stabilizing the tilt of Earth's axis. Without the moon's steady pull, Earth's tilt could randomly swing over a wide range resulting in temperatures too hot and too cold for life.

Astronomers are also discovering how other planets in our solar system actually help Earth. For example, the huge planet Jupiter stops many comets from entering the inner section of the solar system where they could easily hit Earth and wipe us out.

Jesus holds it all together. Isn't it amazing that with all He has to do, He holds on to you too and cares about everything you do?

Jesus, I love You! I can't imagine how You hold everything in the universe together and still have time to take care of me all night and all day. Amen.

DAY 90

"I looked at them with joy when they were not sure of themselves, and the light of my face gave them comfort."

Job 29:24

Job is speaking in today's verse. When he talks about "the light of my face," he means his smile. Job says his smile brought comfort and joy to his friends.

What if we lived in a land without words? What if we communicated only through our actions or just by being there without doing anything at all? What messages would our bodies send?

Our bodies and actions often show what is going on inside us. Job must have been happy inside. His smile lit up his friends' lives. It made them feel comfortable with Job, and it brought some sunshine into their troubled lives.

Look at yourself in the mirror. What do you see? Are you someone who smiles often, or do you keep your smiles to yourself?

A smile, a gentle hug, an act of kindness, or a silent prayer might be just what someone needs. How can you share some sunshine today?

Remind me, Jesus, to love others through my actions. A warm smile, a simple act of kindness, or a loving hug might be just what someone needs. Remind me, please. Amen.

DAY 91

"My sheep hear My voice and I know them. They follow Me."
JOHN 10:27

Sheep graze in large flocks. They often spread out to find the best spot for some tasty grass or cool water to drink. They wander down ditches and ruts unaware of dangers such as deep holes and wild animals. Sheep are not very smart animals. They need someone to watch over them and lead them to the best places. Sheep know one thing well: the sound of the shepherd's voice. They hear him call, even from great distances. His voice directs them back to safety. They know to call for his help when they get into trouble.

People are kind of like sheep. We wander away from God, looking for what we want and ignoring the dangers. And we also have a good shepherd—Jesus—to watch over us and call us to safety. If we listen, we can hear His voice even when we drift away. Jesus wants us to hear and follow Him.

So, open your ears to the good shepherd's voice. He will keep you out of trouble.

Lord, open my ears to hear You. Shout to me over the noise of the world. Whisper to me in the darkness. Lead me away from trouble, and keep me safe. Amen.

DAY 92

But Moses said to the Lord, "See, the people of Israel have not listened to me. How then will Pharaoh listen to me? I am not able to speak well."
EXODUS 6:12

God chose Moses to lead the Israelites out of Egypt where they were slaves. Egypt's pharaoh, their leader, was not a very nice guy. Still, God wanted Moses to go to Pharaoh and say, "Let My people go!"

You would think God would choose a confident, sure-of-himself person to lead. But Moses wasn't all that sure. Words didn't come easy for him. So, why should an important man like Pharaoh listen?

Still, God chose Moses to lead. And a great leader he was! Moses had a gift more important than the gift of speaking well. His gift was listening to and obeying God. Moses was faithful to God, and because of that he bravely led the Israelites out of slavery.

Maybe in some ways you are not sure of yourself. You might think there are things you can't do. Be like Moses! Listen to God. Obey Him, and He will help you do great things.

Heavenly Father, I'm not always sure of my ability to do the things You want me to do. Help me, please, to get strength from You. Keep me from getting in my own way. Amen.

DAY 93

Watch your talk! No bad words should be coming from your mouth. Say what is good. Your words should help others grow as Christians.

EPHESIANS 4:29

Have you checked your language lately? What kinds of words come from your mouth? Are you proud of the things you say?

God wants your speech to be pure and good, the way Jesus spoke. It makes God very unhappy to hear people saying swear words and using His name like a swear word. Bragging words aren't pleasing to Him either. Nor are loud and angry words and words that pull others away from following Him.

Words have power! They can build people up or tear them down. They can lead people toward doing something good or guide them to doing wrong. Words can help others trust God or make them think God does not exist.

Ephesians 4:29 reminds you to choose your words wisely. Be careful what you say. Try to always use words that are gentle and kind. Delete all the bad words from your vocabulary. Speak words that please God and show others what it means to be a Christian.

Dear God, I don't often think about my words. Thank You for reminding me. I want everything I say to please You. Amen.

DAY 94

How can a young man keep his way pure? By living by Your Word.

PSALM 119:9

Today's verse asks a question: How can a young man keep his way pure? Well, this also applies to girls! Let's think about what it means to keep your way pure.

Imagine an aquarium filled with beautiful fish. The water is always clean because it passes through a filter that takes out all the bad stuff, like uneaten fish food and fish waste. The fish happily go on their way swimming around in clean water. But if it weren't for that filter, their water would be filthy and the fish not so happy.

We are kind of like those fish, and we can think of God's Word, the Bible, as our filter. We depend on the Bible to help filter all the dirty thoughts and actions out of our lives. When we rely on the Bible, it's like swimming in fresh, clean water.

Learn all that you can from the Bible. As you think about and put into action God's Word, you build up your filter and keep all the bad stuff away. That's how you keep your way pure!

Lord, teach me every day from Your Word. Help me to learn from the Bible and to live a pure and clean life. Amen.

DAY 95

No person who has become a child of God keeps on sinning. This is because the Holy Spirit is in him. He cannot keep on sinning because God is his Father.

1 JOHN 3:9

We were all created by God, so in that way we are all His children. But it isn't until we accept Jesus into our hearts that we become adopted into God's family. That's when God's Holy Spirit comes and washes away our sins.

Accepting Jesus into our hearts doesn't mean that we stop sinning. Every human sins—we can't help ourselves. But the Holy Spirit is the one who reminds us to do our best not to sin. And the Holy Spirit also reminds us that Jesus died so we can be forgiven when we do sin.

The Holy Spirit is like our conscience. It is God's way of speaking to us about our sin and helping us to do what is right. Some people refer to the Holy Spirit as *that little voice inside me*.

Even when you do sin, you never have to worry about being kicked out of God's family. You are His child. He made you, and He loves you just the way you are—forever!

Dear Father, help me not to give in to sin. And when I do sin, thank You for forgiving me— Your gift to me through Jesus. Amen.

DAY 96

I look up and think about Your heavens, the work of Your fingers, the moon and the stars, which You have set in their place.

PSALM 8:3

Almost three thousand years ago, King David looked at the clear night sky. He gazed at the moon and stars and thought about God's greatness. He wondered how someone so wonderful and creative could care about him.

In the summer of 1969, another man wondered the same thing. American astronaut Edwin "Buzz" Aldrin saw the night sky from the surface of the moon. We can only imagine the thoughts that filled his mind.

For Aldrin, it was a deeply religious experience. As he stood on the moon's surface and gazed at the sky, he remembered the words of David as written in the King James Version of the Bible. He quoted those words in a television interview from space. Aldrin said, "When I consider thy heavens, the work of thy fingers, the moon and the stars, which thou hast ordained; what is man, that thou art mindful of him? and the son of man, that thou visitest him?" (Psalm 8:3–4 KJV).

Three thousand years apart, two different men looked up at the sky—and they saw the same God.

God, You are so great and yet You care for me! I love You. Amen.

DAY 97

You will know how to live in the family of God.

1 TIMOTHY 3:15 NCV

Moms, dads, sisters and brothers, grandparents, aunts, uncles, and cousins! Think about all the good things families bring into our lives. Things like help when we need it, company when we're lonely, forgiveness when we mess up, and laughter—lots of laughter! Families spend time together, have fun together, and learn from each other.

But family is more than relatives. There is another family that you belong to, the family of God. When you asked Jesus to come into your heart, you became part of His family. You have many Christian brothers and sisters here on earth. Can you name other people you know who believe in Jesus? You can find them at church, at school, in your neighborhood, everywhere!

Your Christian family members and friends are your family of God. As you share the Bible together and discuss God and Jesus, you learn things like joy, courage, forgiveness, unselfishness, and love!

Did you know that you can invite others into God's family? Pray and ask God to show you who needs to know Him.

Lord, lead me to those who need You. Open my heart to welcome them into my own family and Yours. Amen.

DAY 98

Have loving-kindness for those who doubt.

JUDE 1:22

Not everyone believes that God is real. All over the world you will find people who doubt. Some have scientific reasons for not believing. Some can't imagine a heaven where they can live forever. Others doubt that Jesus was the real Son of God. There are many reasons why people doubt.

In your own school and neighborhood there are probably unbelievers. You might know who they are. Maybe not. But how does God want you to treat those who don't believe? Jesus' disciple Jude has the answer: treat them with loving-kindness.

Jesus is the best example of loving-kindness. He was kind to everyone whether they believed or not. Even when unbelievers sent Him to die on the cross, Jesus prayed and said, "Father, forgive them. They do not know what they are doing" (Luke 23:34). What an awesome example of kindness that was! They wanted Jesus dead, and yet He prayed and asked God to forgive them.

God wants you to treat everyone with loving-kindness too. Never be afraid, if anyone asks why you are so kind. Maybe knowing you will turn their doubting into believing.

Heavenly Father, Jesus welcomed unbelievers, and He led them to You. I want to be like Jesus. Show me how to change doubt into faith and trust in You. Amen.

DAY 99

"Love your neighbor as yourself."
LEVITICUS 19:18

Which is the most important commandment? If you chose any of the Ten Commandments, you would be wrong—according to Jesus.

When someone asked Jesus, "Teacher, which one is the greatest of the Laws?" Jesus said to him, "You must love the Lord your God with all your heart and with all your soul and with all your mind" (Matthew 22:37). But Jesus wasn't done with His answer. He said that the second greatest commandment is "You must love your neighbor as you love yourself." Jesus was quoting today's Bible verse, Leviticus 19:18. Jesus said if we obey these two commandments, we are more likely to obey God's other commandments too.

God wants us to love Him more than anyone and anything. He wants to be our one and only God all the time. God wants us to love ourselves too because He made us. Then God wants us to share all that love with our neighbors.

Who are your neighbors? Everyone is your neighbor! Every man, woman, and kid in the world! Go spread some love around. Get in the habit of doing something nice for someone every day.

Dear Jesus, thank You for teaching me the two most important commandments. I love God, and I want to love Him even more. Please help me to do that and also to be a kind and loving neighbor. Amen.

DAY 100

This is love! It is not that we loved God but that He loved us. For God sent His Son to pay for our sins with His own blood.

1 John 4:10

"I love you with all my heart." Maybe someone has said that to you, or maybe you've said it yourself. Love is a powerful feeling. It fills up your heart.

That's how our love for God should be. It should be a *love-you-with-my-whole-heart* kind of love. But no matter how full of love our hearts are for God, we can never love Him as much as He loves us! True and perfect love can only come from Him. It's a kind of love not found anywhere on earth.

God loved us so much that He couldn't imagine living without us. He made a home for us in heaven so we could live with Him someday. But He knew we couldn't come to Him filled with sin—it isn't allowed in heaven. So, God sent Jesus, the Son He loved with all His heart, to suffer and die, so when we get to heaven we won't bring any sin with us.

Could you allow someone you love to suffer and die to save someone else? That's real love! God's kind of love.

Dear God, I'm grateful for how much You love me! I love You too. Amen.

DAY 101

"For as the heavens are higher than the earth, so are My ways higher than your ways, and My thoughts than your thoughts."

ISAIAH 55:9

In Isaiah 55, God tells us, "My thoughts are not your thoughts, and My ways are not your ways" (v. 8). Then He goes on to describe the huge difference between the way He thinks and the way we humans think and between the way He solves problems and the way people try to work things out. God works on such a high level that He compares it to the heavens, which are so much higher than the earth that they can't be measured.

God has given us intelligence and common sense, and He wants us to use our brains to think through everyday problems and come up with solutions. We are not as wise as He, however, and sometimes the solution to our problem may be different from anything we can imagine.

God knows best, and though we may feel certain that God's way won't work, we have to trust Him. God is so wonderful and great that we can't begin to understand His ways.

Father, sometimes You do things that I don't understand, and then I discover that it leads to something great. I praise You for always knowing what's best! Amen.

DAY 102

"I say to you, on the day men stand before God, they will have to give an answer for every word they have spoken that was not important."
MATTHEW 12:36

Our world is filled with careless speech. Swear words slip into television shows, movies, and music. People gossip and spread rumors. Some say nasty things to each other and later regret it.

How easy it is to speak without thinking! Yet Jesus reminds us that our words are powerful—and we will be held responsible for how we use them. He says that someday when we see God face-to-face, He will ask us about the way we spoke here on earth. He will want us to have an answer for our careless words.

When you read about Jesus in the Bible, you discover that every word He spoke was important. He spoke kind words, wise words, words that people have learned from and lived by for more than two thousand years.

What would our world be like if we all talked like Jesus? Remember always to think before you speak. Do your best to speak words that are pleasing to God's ears.

Jesus, every word You spoke had power and purpose. Help me to use my words so that they will always bring You glory and honor. Amen.

DAY 103

Keep your heart pure for out of it are the important things of life.

Proverbs 4:23

When you were younger, peer pressure was stuff like your brother or sister trying to get you to do something naughty. Maybe you got away with it, or maybe your mom and dad found out and punished you. Hopefully, you learned that giving in to peer pressure to do something wrong can get you into trouble.

Now that you are older and heading for your teen years, you will face peer pressure from friends at school. Maybe someone will try to get you to take drugs, drink, or steal. You know that these things are wrong. Still, there's a strong pull toward giving in to your friends just to stay on their good side.

When you feel that pull, stop! Remember that God requires you to have a pure heart. That means avoiding sin as best you can. Out of a pure heart comes everything good and important in life. Out of a sin-filled heart comes nothing but trouble.

So, keep your heart pure, live to please God, and don't give in to sin. Always stay true to God, and He will reward you.

Father, please help me to do only what is good and right and not give in to sin. Amen.

DAY 104

"When you pass through the waters, I will be with you. When you pass through the rivers, they will not flow over you. When you walk through the fire, you will not be burned. The fire will not destroy you."

ISAIAH 43:2

Today's verse is God's promise that when we face trouble in our lives, He will not abandon us.

In Isaiah 43:2, God provides some real examples. When Moses and the Israelites approached the Red Sea, with the Egyptian army chasing them, God split open the sea making a dry path for the Israelites to escape through to the other side (Exodus 14:10–31). When three of God's followers, Shadrach, Meshach, and Abednego, were thrown into a fiery furnace for refusing to bow down to a golden idol, God brought them out of the fire unhurt. He was there in the fire with the three young men, seen as a fourth person (Daniel 3).

Isaiah 43:2 does not mean that our bodies won't ever get hurt or sick and one day die, but Isaiah 43:2 isn't about our bodies. It reminds us that God is with us in whatever trouble we face. Nothing can change that. Whatever happens, God will be with you forever.

Father, when I face trouble, I will put my faith in You and believe that You are with me. Amen.

DAY 105

He was hated and men would have nothing to do with Him, a man of sorrows and suffering, knowing sadness well. We hid, as it were, our faces from Him. He was hated, and we did not think well of Him.

ISAIAH 53:3

Eight hundred years before Jesus was born, the prophet Isaiah predicted that Jesus would take on the sins of the world to save humans from sin. He described Jesus' last days, a time when many people would hate Him and hang Him on a cross to die.

Those people who hated Jesus weren't meant to be like that! Sin had twisted their lives.

You probably know some nasty and unpleasant people. They weren't meant to be like that either. Just like those who hung Jesus on the cross, the unpleasant people in our lives don't know who Jesus really is—God's Son, who came to earth to save us from sin.

When you face unpleasant people, don't think badly about them. Remember that inside them there is a soul God loves. Pray for them to know and love Jesus. Pray for them to allow Jesus into their hearts so they will live happy lives. Then believe that God hears your prayers.

God, in each unpleasant person, there is a soul You love. Show me how I can help them to love You. Amen.

DAY 106

"Is not this the son of the man who makes things from wood? Is not Mary His mother? Are not James and Joseph and Simon and Judas His brothers? And are not all His sisters here? Then where did He get all these things?"

MATTHEW 13:55-56

Imagine being a kid growing up with Jesus as your brother. His siblings didn't know Jesus was here to save the world from sin. And Jesus never sinned, not once! He did everything perfectly. How would you feel about living with a perfect brother?

As a young man, Jesus did great miracles. Imagine the questions His siblings were asked: "Hey, aren't you guys Jesus' brothers and sisters? What's wrong with your brother? How come He can do strange things?"

It must have been hard for Jesus' brothers and sisters to be His siblings, but Jesus understood. He knew what it was like to grow up in a human family, but He also knew what it was like to be God's perfect Son.

Remember this: Nothing happens in your family that Jesus doesn't understand. Pray for your family members. Ask Jesus to save them from their troubles. He cares about your family just as He did His own.

Jesus, You understand what it's like to be part of a human family. I'm glad that You know what it's like to be me! Amen.

DAY 107

I did not give up waiting for the Lord. And He turned to me and heard my cry. He brought me up out of the hole of danger.

PSALM 40:1–2

Bible heroes often went through hard times. You'd think that because they were close to God they would've been spared trouble. They weren't. You might think because they had great faith in God, He would rush right in and save them. Not so.

King David wrote today's Bible verses about a time he was trapped in trouble with no apparent way out. He cried to God to rescue him. Then he waited. It took time for God to answer, but He did. David probably learned patience while he waited and wondered if God cared about the trouble he was in.

Another Bible hero, Jeremiah, didn't get immediate answers to prayer either. He tells of a time when he was in a dangerous situation and didn't know how to get out. After Jeremiah prayed, God took ten days to answer (Jeremiah 42:7). But the answer came. . .in time.

We humans sometimes find ourselves in some sort of mess, and we pray hard for God to save us. He will. We just need to be patient.

Help me to be patient with You, God. I know that You will answer me when the time is just right. Amen.

DAY 108

God's Word is living and powerful. . . . It tells what the heart is thinking about and what it wants to do.

HEBREWS 4:12

The Bible is a book like no other book. It is God speaking to us through His own voice and the voices of His greatest followers.

Each time you read the Bible, you can learn things about your own life right now. But as you learn and grow older, those same things you read now might have a different meaning. It's like the Bible is alive. It grows with you. Can you think of any other book that does that?

People change, technology changes, thoughts and ideas change. . .but the Word of the Lord, the Bible, does not change. It will be as up-to-date two thousand years from now as it was two thousand years ago!

Think about it: Right now, you can learn what God says about your life in the present by reading the Bible and filling your mind with His words—exactly like the ancient Israelites and the people in Jesus' time did. The Bible is awesome! Reading it is sort of like traveling in a God-made time machine. You can be in the past and present, both at the same time!

Thank You for the Bible, Lord. Help me to fill my heart with Your Word. Amen.

DAY 109

*"Let the greatest among you be as the least.
Let the leader be as the one who cares for others."*
LUKE 22:26

Sometimes when you're wrong, you're really wrong.

What if you decide to surprise your mom by getting up early to get your baby sister ready to go to day care? You do it and then lead your sister to show your mom the great thing you did. But wait! You realize you've messed up big-time—it's Saturday. No day care on Saturday!

Don't worry. Even the world's great leaders mess up. God doesn't judge them for the honest mistakes they make. He wouldn't judge you for your mistake either. In fact, according to Jesus, you *are* a leader because you wanted to help your mom.

Jesus says in Luke 22:26: "Let the leader be as the one who cares for others." Being a leader doesn't mean you must rule great crowds or lead an army. It doesn't mean you have to be the best at everything. Jesus says that leaders are those who care for others.

If you help out at home, at school, in your church or community, then God thinks of you as a leader. So, wherever you go, lead! Show others that you care.

**Jesus, open my eyes to the needs of others,
and lead me to help wherever I can. Amen.**

DAY 110

"Whoever makes you walk a short way, go with him twice as far."
MATTHEW 5:41

The ancient Romans had a custom of forcing someone to carry their baggage for them while they traveled. Against their will, the people pushed, pulled, and carried these belongings the length of a mile.

Jesus talks about this in today's verse. He said don't just go the minimum distance—be willing to go twice as far. In other words, do more than is required of you.

Think of all God does for you. He gives you far more than you could ever require of Him. He gives you His blessings, forgiveness, and strength even in your toughest circumstances. He gives you much more than He has to, and He wants you to follow His example.

Choose to forgive when someone mistreats you. If someone leaves a mess in your house, clean it up. Help people without thinking about what you might get in return. Pray for the people others ignore. Love the unlovable. When you do these things, you will surely please God.

God, help me to willingly do more than is expected of me, for no other reason than to please You. Amen.

DAY 111

"If any man comes to Me and does not have much more love for Me than for his father and mother, wife and children, brothers and sisters, and even his own life, he cannot be My follower."

LUKE 14:26

Families are put together by God to love each other. Mothers, fathers, their kids, and extended family like grandparents, aunts, and uncles are all a part of your circle of love. And you love them too!

But in today's Bible verse, Jesus says something like, "Love Me so deeply that your love for your family will seem small by comparison." And that's not the only time Jesus said something like that. In Matthew 10:37, He says, "He who loves his father and mother more than Me is not good enough for Me. He who loves son or daughter more than Me is not good enough for Me."

Jesus meant that He wants to come first in our lives. We have to love Him with all our heart before we can truly love our family members or anyone else. Loving Him works like a circle. The more we love Jesus, the more we can love others. . .and the more we love others, the more we show our love for Him.

Jesus, please fill me up with love for You.
Then let Your love shine through me to others. Amen.

DAY 112

"The Lord your God is with you, a Powerful One Who wins the battle. He will have much joy over you. With His love He will give you new life. He will have joy over you with loud singing."

ZEPHANIAH 3:17

God shows His great love for us in many ways. Today's scripture verse reminds us that God's mighty power saves us. His love brings peace and quietness to our hearts. He gets so much happiness from us, His children, that He expresses His joy over us with singing!

People sing back to God to honor Him. They sing hymns and praise songs. The book of Psalms in the Bible is like a songbook filled with praises to Him. Heavenly beings sing to God too! Angels sang the night Jesus was born (Luke 2:13–14). And Revelation 5:11–12 helps us imagine a beautiful picture of heaven filled with songs of praise.

God has a song written just for you. Your name is its title. And the composer, God Himself, sings your song over you as you go about life here on earth. Close your eyes. Can you imagine Him singing to you?

Lift up your voice and sing to Him a song of praise!

O Lord, what an awesome thought—Your voice singing to me—my song. Open my ears to Your voice! Amen.

DAY 113

Jesus answered him, "You do not understand now what I am doing but you will later."
JOHN 13:7

Jesus' disciples, eating supper with Jesus, felt worried because Jesus had been telling them that soon He was going to be killed. How could that be when He had done nothing wrong? And then, Jesus did something else. Jesus got up from the supper table, wrapped a towel around His waist, and began washing the disciples' feet. Walking around in sandals all day, feet got very dirty. It was the custom for feet to be washed before dinner, but by servants—not Jesus! One of His disciples, Peter, said, "Jesus, why?"

Jesus told Peter that he wouldn't understand until later what He was doing. But Jesus knew His foot washing was a symbol of what was to come. Those who hated Him would treat Jesus like a slave, a servant, and Jesus would die to "wash away" our sins.

Sometimes we say, "Why, God?" when we face hard times. And God answers us, "You won't understand until later." We just have to trust that God knows what He's doing. He has a good reason for everything.

"Why, God?" I ask that question, and Your voice whispers, "Trust Me. I have it all under control." I trust You, Father. It is enough that You know why. Amen.

DAY 114

But Moses said to the people, "Do not be afraid! Be strong, and see how the Lord will save you today. For the Egyptians you have seen today, you will never see again."

EXODUS 14:13

The Bible is filled with exciting stories about brave women and men.

Under Moses' leadership, God helped the Israelite slaves to be freed from Pharaoh's Egypt. They had traveled only a short while when Pharaoh regretted freeing the Israelites and ordered his entire army after them. Pharaoh's army reached the Israelites as they approached the Red Sea.

The Israelites panicked, but not Moses. God had promised to deliver the Israelites from the Egyptians, and Moses believed Him.

God told Moses to hold his staff—his walking stick—over the water. Then, in an awesome display of power, God divided the sea. The Israelites walked to the other shore on dry land. But when Pharaoh's warriors followed, the walls of water collapsed, drowning the entire army!

Moses acted bravely because he trusted in God's promise.

As you read the Bible, you will find many promises God has made to us all. Just like Moses, you can trust God to keep every one.

Father, show me the promises in Your Word. Set them in my mind and heart. When I face trouble, remind me of Moses and the Red Sea, and I will be fearless. Amen.

DAY 115

Christian brothers, I want you to know that what has happened to me has helped spread the Good News.
PHILIPPIANS 1:12

Long ago, Christians were mistreated, even tortured and killed, because of their faith in Jesus. Paul, author of the book of Philippians, was one of them. He was hurt by stones hurled at him, imprisoned, and shipwrecked during his missionary journeys. But all his sufferings had a purpose—to advance the gospel he preached—to tell the world about Jesus.

Paul could have escaped his suffering by turning away from his faith in God, but he didn't. He put up with every mistreatment. As he boldly shared the gospel, Paul grew even stronger in his faith. It became more important to him than his own comfort and even his own life.

After Jesus rose from the dead, He said to His disciples, "Go to all the world and preach the Good News to every person" (Mark 16:15). When we choose to follow Jesus, it is our duty to share the gospel proudly and without worry, the way Paul did.

Whom will you share Jesus with today?

Jesus, You've told me to share the gospel with the world. Where should I share it today? Lead me to someone who needs to know You. Amen.

DAY 116

A dish of vegetables with love is better than eating the best meat with hate.
PROVERBS 15:17

Veggie lovers unite! This scripture verse is for you (and for veggie haters too). King Solomon says in Proverbs 15:17 that parsnips, broccoli, brussels sprouts, cabbage, spinach, turnips. . .they all taste better when served with love! And Solomon must be right because he was considered the wisest of all men.

But was Solomon really telling us in this verse to eat our veggies? No. He simply meant that everything is made better with love. Solomon understood the human need for love and friendship.

Imagine a world without love. It would be like eating your most favorite food but tasting nothing. Love is like a secret ingredient that makes everything—even your least favorite veggie—taste better.

The Bible says that those who don't love don't know God. That's because God *is* love (1 John 4:8). When something unpleasant happens in our lives, God is the one who makes it better. *He* is the secret ingredient! So, fill up on God's love. You can never have too much of it, and it always tastes good.

Heavenly Father, I love You with all my heart, all my soul, and all my mind. Help me to love You even more. In Jesus' name I pray, amen.

DAY 117

For they all saw Him and were afraid. At once Jesus talked to them. He said, "Take hope. It is I, do not be afraid." He came over to them and got into the boat. The wind stopped. They were very much surprised and wondered about it.

MARK 6:50-51

The storm came quick and strong. Angry waves and wind tried to capsize the boat. The fishermen in the boat held on, almost sure they were about to die. And then, the very Son of God appeared standing on the water! "It is I," He said. *Jesus!* He climbed into the boat, and everything became calm. The storm ended. The danger was gone. Imagine how those fishermen must have felt!

This story in the Bible really happened, and Jesus continues to work the same way in us today. When we have trouble and we see no way out of it, Jesus reminds us that He is still there. Then, just as He climbed aboard the boat, He stays with us and shows us that we don't have to be afraid, because He is with us.

Trust Jesus to help you. He will never leave you alone in a storm.

Jesus, nothing can keep You from me—not fire, flood, storms, not even the deepest ocean. I trust You to help stop anything that stands in my way. Amen.

DAY 118

The bread from heaven stopped on the day after they had eaten some of the food of the land. So the people of Israel no longer had bread from heaven. But they ate food of the land of Canaan during that year.

JOSHUA 5:12

For forty years while the Israelites wandered in the desert heading for the Promised Land, God miraculously provided "bread from heaven" for them to eat (Exodus 16:1–16). God's special bread continued to appear all around them while they went on their way. It even covered the ground when they camped!

Forty years! For 14,600 days, day after day, God provided them with bread (Deuteronomy 8:2–3). But the day after the Israelites ate the Passover meal in the Promised Land, the bread stopped coming. God had begun to provide for them in a different way—food that grew by natural means.

Think about it: God provides for us in different ways at different stages in our life. He knows exactly what we need and when we need it—every day, all the time! Isn't He wonderful?

Thank You, God, for providing for me. You know my every need, and You fulfill it at the perfect time and through Your perfect will. I love You, Father. Amen.

DAY 119

"Those who have sorrow are happy,
because they will be comforted."
MATTHEW 5:4

Jesus spoke the words of today's verse. What did He mean when He said, "Those who have sorrow [sadness] are happy"? Aren't sadness and happiness opposites? How can you be happy and sad at the same time?

When Jesus said these words, He was speaking to a large crowd. They didn't know yet that He would die and save them from sin. He was preparing them for what was about to happen. He would die on the cross. Those who loved Him would be sad. But then when He rose from the dead, all those who believed would have life forever in heaven. And *that* would make them happy!

The next thing Jesus said was "They will be comforted." Jesus understands when we are sad, and even today He comforts us with His presence. The Bible says that when we worry, God comforts us (Psalm 94:19). It says God takes away the tears from our eyes (Revelation 7:17).

In life, tears will come—but so will God's comfort. When we feel sad, we can be happy knowing that He is with us, loving us all the time.

Father God, when I feel sad and tears fall from my eyes, I am blessed because You calm me with Your forever, comforting love. Amen.

DAY 120

Have you not known? Have you not heard? The God Who lives forever is the Lord, the One Who made the ends of the earth. He will not become weak or tired. His understanding is too great for us to begin to know.

ISAIAH 40:28

Being a kid isn't always easy. Sure, there are plenty of good times with family and friends and at school, but once in a while there are days that you feel like no one understands you. It's a normal part of growing up.

But there is someone who always understands. That someone is God. He made you and He understands you, whatever stage of life you're in. God understands kids, teens, grown-ups, old people—everyone! How deeply He understands us is beyond anything we can begin to know.

On those days when it seems like no one understands you, talk with God in prayer. In Isaiah 1:18, He says, "Come now, let us think about this together." God understands what you are going through, and He will help you to sort out anything that troubles you.

Dear God, there are days when I feel like no one understands me. But You do, God! You always understand. Please remind me of that and help me to find my way. Amen.

DAY 121

And now we have these three: faith and hope and love, but the greatest of these is love.
1 CORINTHIANS 13:13

First Corinthians is another letter from Paul, and in it he reminds us about the importance of love in our lives. He says it is even more important than faith and hope.

This is what else Paul says: "If I understand all secrets, but do not have love, I am nothing. If I know all things and if I have the gift of faith so I can move mountains, but do not have love, I am nothing" (v. 2).

Paul explains about love: "Love does not give up. Love is kind. Love is not jealous. Love does not put itself up as being important. Love has no pride. Love does not do the wrong thing. Love never thinks of itself. Love does not get angry. Love does not remember the suffering that comes from being hurt by someone. Love is not happy with sin. Love is happy with the truth. Love takes everything that comes without giving up. Love believes all things. Love hopes for all things. Love keeps on in all things. Love never comes to an end" (vv. 4–8).

And what is love? God! There is no greater love than Him.

Dear God, please help my love for You to grow stronger every day. Amen.

DAY 122

Be quiet and know that I am God.
PSALM 46:10

Read about David in the Bible, and you will learn that he experienced a great deal of trouble. The only way he survived was by trusting in the Lord. He had to believe that God was indeed God, the Creator of the heavens and the earth, powerful enough to help him out of his problems. To gain such confidence, David had to turn away from his trouble, stop worrying, quiet his heart, and focus on God. Only when he was perfectly still and trusting could he know in a very real way that God is God.

David wrote in Psalm 4:4, "When you are on your bed, look into your hearts and be quiet." Remember that. When you lie down in bed tonight, instead of tossing and turning, think about God and how wonderful He is. When you learn to trust that God can protect you and work out your problems, then you can lie down peacefully and sleep.

"I will lie down and sleep in peace. O Lord," says David, "You alone keep me safe" (Psalm 4:8).

Dear God, quiet my mind. Remove from it all the worldly thoughts that come between You and me. Create stillness within me and turn my thoughts toward You. Amen.

DAY 123

"I will give them one heart, and put a new spirit within them. I will take the heart of stone out of their flesh and give them a heart of flesh."

EZEKIEL 11:19

Our heart is a part of our human body, but we can also think of our heart as that place deep inside us where God wants to live. That heart can be cold. It can be angry, jealous, and slow to forgive. It might be a selfish heart that runs after whatever it wants. The Bible calls that kind of heart "a heart of stone."

We are all born needing a heart transplant, of sorts. God wants to give us a good heart, a place worthy of Him to live in—a heart that is open and ready to see, hear, and love Him.

The good news is that we received our heart transplant the day we believed Jesus died for us. His death saved us from sin. It created within us a heart that beats to please God, a heart that loves and does good and kind things. This new heart changes everything! It is a heart that will beat forever—now and someday in heaven.

Thank You, Lord, for giving me a new heart, a heart so perfect in love that it will last me forever. Amen.

DAY 124

"God is not a man, that He should lie. He is not a son of man, that He should be sorry for what He has said. Has He said, and will He not do it? Has He spoken, and will He not keep His Word?"

NUMBERS 23:19

We can't fully understand God. Too often, we think of Him as if He's human. But He's not! God understands what it's like to be human, but that's where it ends. His thoughts and actions are unlike anything human.

God does not lie. He can't! If God lied, He would be an imperfect sinner. And everything about God is sinless. God is perfect in every way. He is not sorry for anything He has said, because all of His words are right and true. Best of all, God keeps His promises. When He says that He will do something, He does. God always keeps His word.

Because God is not human, His timing is not the same as ours. God will wait for the perfect time to act, and what He does might be far beyond our understanding. That's what makes Him our great God, not human, but amazing and awesome, our God who loves and cares for us in every way.

Father, when I think of You in human terms, remind me that You are God. Anything is possible. Amen.

DAY 125

"I tell you this: Do not worry about your life. Do not worry about what you are going to eat and drink. Do not worry about what you are going to wear. Is not life more important than food? Is not the body more important than clothes?"

MATTHEW 6:25

Today's verse is part of Jesus' Sermon on the Mount. As He spoke to the huge crowd, Jesus taught about the cares of life. His speech included five great ideas that—if followed—would bring people inner peace.

Picture those gathered on the mountainside, dressed in robes and sandals, nodding their heads as they identified with Jesus' words over two thousand years ago. His words are just as meaningful today. What if we turned our worries away from our stuff and focused instead on God? What would we be left with?

Jesus said we would be left with a treasure, one that never goes out of style! A treasure that moths and rust can't destroy and thieves don't break in and steal (Matthew 6:20). And the best part is—it's free. What we are left with is God's love and everything that comes with it! God will always make sure that we have what we need.

Heavenly Father, help those looking for happiness in their things to see that You are what they are searching for. Amen.

DAY 126

The Lord is near to those who have a broken heart.
And He saves those who are broken in spirit.
PSALM 34:18

There are many reasons for a broken heart. Can you name just a few? One of the most common reasons is disappointment.

Imagine this: You are planning to run with your older brother in a marathon. Every morning before school, you two get up early and run. Every day, for months, you train. Day by day you get stronger and stronger. And finally—you are ready.

It's race time. "Runners. On your mark. Get set. Go!"

You and your brother take off running. And then, you fall. You fall and break your leg! But that isn't all that's broken. So is your heart. Your disappointment fills every bit of your spirit, and nothing else seems important.

A doctor's help and time will fix your broken leg, but who will fix your broken heart? Jesus will! He promises to do so, and you know that you can count on Him.

Whenever you have a broken heart for any reason, ask God for help. Remember—He cares about you!

I am never alone, God. When I feel sad,
You are with me. You care for me and comfort me.
Oh what a loving Father You are! Amen.

DAY 127

I can have no greater joy than to hear that
my children are following the truth.
3 John 1:4

"Good job! Way to go! Nice going!" Everyone loves hearing praise when they've done something well. Parents love hearing praises about their children too.

Jesus' disciple John was no different. We see it in today's Bible verse. John was happy to learn that the people he had taught to love Jesus (John called these people his children) were continuing to follow in Jesus' footsteps and spreading the gospel. Hearing this, John said, brought him great joy.

Someone else loves hearing good things about His children. God! He loves hearing compliments about us, His kids. God loves when we do something Jesus-like, something kind, unselfish, and loving. He hears when someone says, "That was the right thing to do." Or, "I'm so proud of you!" Or, "You did a great job!" When the things we do are praiseworthy, it brings God great joy.

When you receive a compliment, imagine that it's coming right from the mouth of your heavenly Father. You are His child. Make Him proud with all that you do.

Dear God, I want everything I do to be praiseworthy. I will do my best every day to make You proud of me. Amen.

DAY 128

"Take my yoke upon you and learn from me."
MATTHEW 11:29 NIV

Jesus said, "Take my yoke upon you." To understand what He meant, you need to understand what a yoke is.

A yoke is a wooden bar, or frame, that connects two oxen at the neck. It is used when the animals carry a heavy load. The yoke balances the load and makes it easier to carry. A yoke is not worn by one animal—it unites two, to perform a task. For thousands of years, the yoke was a symbol of labor and hardship. Oxen carried their loads for miles, led by people walking with them. But Jesus offered a new meaning for the ancient ox collar. He said that if people thought of themselves as yoked together with Him, all of their troubles would feel lighter.

Taking Jesus' yoke means coming to Him and accepting His help. When you team up with Jesus, then you learn from Him how to handle any heavy problem that comes your way. Think about Jesus' words in Matthew 11:30 (NIV). He says, "My yoke is easy and my burden is light."

Jesus, sometimes I try to carry the load all by myself. I forget that by teaming with You the burden is light. Together, we can do anything! Amen.

DAY 129

Pilate wanted to please the people. He gave Barabbas to them and had Jesus beaten. Then he handed Him over to be nailed to a cross.

MARK 15:15

Pilate didn't want anything to do with this Jesus fellow. Even his wife had warned him not to get involved. So, he stalled. Then he released Barabbas, a murderer, and killed Jesus, an innocent man.

Was Pilate an all-around bad guy? No. He did it to please the crowd.

At first, a few people hated Jesus. They got more people to hate Him, and soon a whole crowd stood before Pilate shouting, "Crucify Him!"

Almost every day, we see unruly crowds, sometimes in the streets, sometimes at sporting events, and even in our own circle of friends. A crowd at school might be gathered around bullying someone. A crowd at a party might get kids to do things they otherwise wouldn't do.

Most of the time, it's fun to be in big groups. Usually they're harmless, and because of that it's often okay to go with the flow. But when the crowd laughingly suggests something that makes you uncomfortable, ask yourself: Are you choosing the wrong way, or are you choosing Jesus?

I choose You, Jesus! When the crowd presses in around me trying to drive me away from You and Your teaching—Jesus, I choose You! Amen.

DAY 130

Before the throne there was what looked like a sea of glass, shining and clear. Around the throne and on each side there were four living beings that were full of eyes in front and in back.

REVELATION 4:6

God allowed John a brief glimpse into heaven, and what he saw there amazed him.

Four creatures surrounded God's throne, almost like the stately lions some kings kept chained near theirs—only these beasts were unchained and far more majestic! One was like a lion, another like an ox, another like a man, and another like an eagle. Each had six wings and was covered with eyes all over its body—even under its wings!

God also allowed the prophet Ezekiel a peek at these creatures. Ezekiel called them cherubim and said they have humanlike bodies (Ezekiel 1:5; 10:1). Instead of six wings the cherubim had four, and each creature had all four faces: the face of a man, an eagle, an ox, and a lion (Ezekiel 1:5–10; 10:8–14).

These incredible heavenly beings are proof of God's creativity. Who knows what awaits us when we get to heaven? Certainly, it will be unlike anything we have seen here on earth.

God, Your creativity is beyond my imagination. I wonder what incredible things I will see someday in heaven. Amen.

DAY 131

Growing strong in body is all right but growing in God-like living is more important. It will not only help you in this life now but in the next life also.

1 TIMOTHY 4:8

Imagine this: What if God allowed Paul, the Bible's letter writer, to visit earth again for a day? Paul walks into a gym where he sees dozens of people running on treadmills, riding exercise bikes, and lifting weights.

Paul says to a man nearby, "What are you all doing?"

"Getting fit!" the man replies. "I'm working to strengthen my abs."

All of this is confusing to Paul. He says to the man, "Growing strong in body is all right but growing in God-like living is more important. It will not only help you in this life now but in the next life also."

Imagining Paul in a modern gym is make-believe, but even when he lived in ancient times, Paul understood that growing as a Christian is more important than growing a strong body. When you live a Christian life and follow Jesus, He will make you strong in character. Growing strong in your body is good, but Jesus makes you strong in *every* way!

Jesus, I am a Christian in training. You have given me all the training equipment I need: Your Word, prayer, and faith in You. Thank You! Amen.

DAY 132

"The Helper is the Holy Spirit. The Father will send Him in My place. He will teach you everything and help you remember everything I have told you."

JOHN 14:26

Jesus' time on earth was about to end and—in today's verse—He prepared His disciples for His departure.

The disciples were confused and frightened, so Jesus comforted them with words of assurance, peace, and hope. He said, "Do not let your hearts be troubled or afraid" (v. 27).

At first, Jesus' followers thought they would be left alone. But Jesus promised them He would send the Father's Helper to teach, direct, guide, and remind them of every word He had told them.

Jesus called the Holy Spirit "the Helper," but the Holy Spirit has other names, as well: strengthener, comforter, adviser, counselor, friend.

The Holy Spirit comes into our hearts to help, teach, comfort, and accomplish God's work here on earth. Through His presence inside us, we learn to know God. The Helper comforts us and helps us to understand the Bible. Because the Holy Spirit lives in our hearts, we are never ever alone!

Helper, strengthener, comforter, adviser, counselor, friend—oh, Holy Spirit of God! Thank You for living in my heart, guiding me, and drawing me near to the Father. Amen.

DAY 133

Even though I walk through the darkest valley, I will fear no evil, for you are with me; your rod and your staff, they comfort me.

PSALM 23:4 NIV

Do a rod and a staff sound comforting to you? If you've said the Twenty-third Psalm, then you've probably said these words and wondered what they mean. A rod and a staff are shepherds' tools.

Sheep traveled into valleys for food and water, but the valley also contained danger. The high ridges created perfect places for lions and coyotes to wait to snatch an innocent lamb. Searching for new grass, sheep often wandered away where they slipped into swamps or fell down steep cliffs. Tiny flies bit their ears.

But the shepherd was prepared. He constantly watched over his flock for any signs of danger. With his tall staff with a crooked end, he could snare a sheep from a swamp or guide it in fast-moving waters.

His rod, a short stick with leather strips on the end, kept the flies and mosquitoes away—and could be used in cleaning and grooming.

Like those sheep, we humans get into dangerous situations in the valleys of life. But the Lord stays with us, protects us, and saves us when we get into trouble.

Jesus, You are my shepherd. You direct me where I should go, steer me from danger, and rescue me when I stray. You never leave me, and I am so grateful. Amen.

DAY 134

"The blind are made to see. Those who could not walk are walking. Those who have had bad skin diseases are healed. Those who could not hear are hearing. The dead are raised up to life and the Good News is preached to poor people."

MATTHEW 11:5

Doubt is something all humans do. When we aren't sure, we ask questions. Jesus' cousin John the Baptist was no different.

John had always believed that Jesus was who He said He was—the Son of God, our Savior. Everywhere he went, John preached about Jesus. And it got him into trouble.

When John told King Herod about Jesus, he reminded Herod of his own sins, and that made the king angry. He had John thrown into prison.

Chained to a prison wall, John needed reassurance from Jesus. He sent a message: "Are You the one who was to come?"

Jesus replied reminding John of the miracles He had done: "The blind see. The lame walk. Skin diseases are healed. The deaf hear. The dead are raised up to life."

If you doubt, then remember Jesus' answer to John. Jesus is real! Everything He did, every miracle, was real. And Jesus is still with us today, in Spirit, helping us in every way.

Jesus, when I doubt, remind me of the great miracles You performed. Assure me that You are Jesus, my Savior, my God! Amen.

DAY 135

"Keep these words in your heart that I am telling you today. Do your best to teach them to your children. Talk about them when you sit in your house and when you walk on the road and when you lie down and when you get up."

DEUTERONOMY 6:6–7

God is speaking in today's verse, and the words He wants us to keep in our hearts are the Ten Commandments:

Put God first. He should be your one-and-only God.
Worship God only.
Be respectful when using God's name.
Remember the Sabbath.
Respect your parents.
Do not kill.
Be faithful to the one you marry.
Do not steal.
Do not lie.
Do not be jealous of what others have.

These are God's rules for living a good Christian life. They are so important that God told the Israelites, in ancient times, to be sure to teach them to their kids. God said, "Talk about them when you sit in your house and when you walk on the road and when you lie down and when you get up."

Get into the habit of discussing God's rules with your family. Memorize them, and do your very best to obey them every day.

God, I will remember Your Ten Commandments and do my best to obey them. Amen.

DAY 136

Jesus said, "Who is My mother? And who are My brothers?"
MATTHEW 12:48

When Jesus' family heard of the huge crowds following Him, they worried about His safety. They went to talk to Him.

"Someone said to [Jesus], 'Your mother and brothers are outside and want to talk to you.' Jesus said, 'Who is My mother? And who are My brothers?' He put out His hand to His followers and said, 'See, these are My mother and My brothers!' " (vv. 47–49).

It sounded harsh. Disrespectful even. But, Jesus wasn't excluding His mother and brothers—He was expanding the definition of family. He went on to say, "Whoever does what My father in heaven wants him to do is My brother and My sister and My mother" (v. 50). Jesus was reminding the crowd that we are all God's children. When we accept Jesus as our Savior, God adopts us into His forever family and promises us a place in heaven.

When we remember that we are all God's kids, then it becomes easier to lend a helping hand to strangers, like a new kid at school, or a kid no one likes, or a person in your neighborhood.

Whom in God's family can you help today?

I am honored to be a member of Your family, God. How can I help my sisters and brothers today? Amen.

DAY 137

Later God tested Abraham, and said to him, "Abraham!" Abraham said, "Here I am."

GENESIS 22:1

Then God said to Abraham, "Take. . .your only son, Isaac, whom you love. . . . Give him as a burnt gift on the altar in worship" (Genesis 22:2).

What? Was God *really* telling Abraham to allow his son to be killed as an offering? Back then, people gave their best farm animal to God by killing it and burning its body on God's altar. But Isaac?

Still, Abraham obeyed God. He trusted God to bring Isaac back to life. He was ready to follow God's command.

God did not allow Abraham to sacrifice his son. But it was a test of Abraham's faith. And Abraham passed God's test. He was ready to trust God with everything. Even his beloved son.

The word *test* appears ninety-five times in the New Life Version of the Bible. Throughout history, God has tested His people to see if their faith in Him is strong. God's tests not only measure our faith, but they help make our faith stronger. And remember this, God will never give you a test that is beyond your ability to pass.

Father God, if You decide to test me, then give me the strength and courage to pass Your test. Build my faith. Make it strong. Amen.

DAY 138

All the Holy Writings are God-given and are made alive by Him. Man is helped when he is taught God's Word. It shows what is wrong. It changes the way of a man's life. It shows him how to be right with God.

2 TIMOTHY 3:16

Some versions of the Bible use the phrase "God-breathed" instead of "God-given." We may hear these words and hardly give them another thought. It is as if God breathed His words into the Bible, and then they were there. If we dig deeper in the Bible, though, we learn that God's Word is alive. It is living and powerful (Hebrews 4:12)!

The Bible is as reliable today as it ever was! Scripture speaks to us in our current situations just as it did to people a few thousand years ago. . .and just as it will forever. His Word helps us to know right from wrong. It is a powerful teacher.

Everything changes throughout history, but God has been able to speak to people exactly where they are through His living Word. There is certainly no other book or any other thing in the world that can do that. Only the living Word, the Bible, continues to be God-breathed and up-to-date forever.

Dear God, all things pass into history except for You and Your Word. How wonderful it is that Your Word will live forever! Amen.

DAY 139

The death of His holy ones is of great worth in the eyes of the Lord.

Psalm 116:15

Nothing on earth is forever. Everything dies. New things take the old's place. God reminds us of this in Ecclesiastes 3:1–2: "There is a time for everything that happens under heaven. There is a time to be born, and a time to die."

We all will die one day. We don't know when or how, but God does. And He does not want us to worry about it or to be afraid. He wants us to wake up every morning expecting to live a long and happy life. Death should be the farthest thing from a kid's mind, except for one thing—to remember that when we die our souls keep on living in heaven with God forever.

When a Christian dies, that person's loved ones feel sad because that person is gone. But, at the same time, there is a great celebration in heaven. God celebrates being with His beloved child.

Don't worry about dying. Don't be afraid. Focus your thoughts on how much God loves you, and be happy that you will be with Him someday.

Lord, I am not just my body. My soul lives within it with You, and after my body dies I know I will live on in heaven as Your precious child. Amen.

DAY 140

There was no king in Israel in those days.
Each man did what he thought was right.
JUDGES 21:25

The ancient Israelites bounced from one disaster to another while ignoring God's Law. They only shaped up when they faced an enemy. Then they cried out to God. Hearing their cries for help, God would raise up a hero to rescue them. This hero, or judge, ruled over the people and kept them in line until he died. At that point the Israelites again "did what was right in their own eyes" and the cycle began anew.

We are a lot like those ancient Israelites. Too often we do what is right in our own eyes. We give in to temptation and sin, and that gets us into trouble. Then we cry out to God, "Help! Get me out of this mess!"

Ignoring God's rules didn't work for the Israelites, and it won't work for us today. It is wise to examine what we think of as right and wrong. Ask yourself, "Whose rules am I following?" Then do your best to follow God's rules.

I don't want to be separated from You, Lord, by going my own way. Remind me, please, to check what I think is right and wrong and make sure I'm following Your rules. Amen.

DAY 141

Until I come, read and preach and teach the Word of God to the church.
1 TIMOTHY 4:13

Before the days of television and radio, families shared books by reading them aloud. As they sat around the fireplace, they listened to the words and imagined themselves in settings in faraway lands.

But, since the invention of radio, television, and computers, families rarely read aloud anymore—except, of course, bedtime stories.

The Bible is a book that families should be sharing. It was never meant to be read only in silence. When God's Word is shared aloud, it gives people a chance to discuss what God is saying and to learn from each other.

Maybe you hear God's Word spoken aloud only in church and in Sunday school. Those are good places to share His Word, but you should also be sharing the Bible with your family and friends.

Get in the habit of reading the Bible aloud. Listen to its words, and imagine yourself in the situations God's people faced long ago. Think about what those words mean to you today. Discuss the Bible with each other. It's a great way to learn more about God and His teaching.

Dear God, I don't often think about reading the Bible aloud. Thank You for reminding me to do so. Amen.

DAY 142

I pray that your hearts will be able to understand. I pray that you will know about the hope given by God's call. I pray that you will see how great the things are that He has promised to those who belong to Him. I pray that you will know how great His power is for those who have put their trust in Him.

EPHESIANS 1:18–19

Today's scripture is part of Paul's letter to his church friends. In it, he prays for their hearts to understand about God. Some Bible versions use the words "eyes of your heart," and Paul might have been speaking from firsthand experience when he used those words.

Years before, God had made Paul blind—that was when Paul, then known as Saul, hated Jesus. But afterward, Jesus miraculously healed Paul. Not only did Paul receive a change of heart, but his eyes were literally opened to Jesus (Acts 9:1–19).

Your heart is important for not only your physical life but your spiritual life as well. It's the part of your soul containing all your thoughts, delights, and desires. Why was Paul so eager for his friends to be able to understand about God? Because he wanted them to experience what he had—a trusting heart filled with the love of Jesus.

Father, please open my heart to understand more about You. Amen.

DAY 143

Do not let yourselves get tired of doing good. If we do not give up, we will get what is coming to us at the right time.

Galatians 6:9

Thank you. Two little words that mean so much. How often do you say them?

What if you worked hard, day after day, doing the best you could, but you got nothing in return? Not even a thank-you. Would you feel like giving up? More important, *would* you give up?

In today's Bible verse, Paul is writing and reminding his friends not to get discouraged that their hard work went unrewarded. His friends had been telling everyone they met about Jesus. And often, that telling was met with hatred. These Jesus followers were doing their best to be kind and do good works, and they got nothing good in return. Paul told them not to give up. God would reward them when the time was just right.

Learn from Paul. Don't give up trying when no one seems to notice the good work you've done. God knows, and He will bless you! And remember to thank the people who are kind and work hard for you.

God, help me to never stop doing good work, even if I'm discouraged, and remind me to thank those who are kind to me. Amen.

DAY 144

The Lord has loving-pity on those who fear Him, as a father has loving-pity on his children. For He knows what we are made of. He remembers that we are dust.

PSALM 103:13–14

"The Lord has loving-pity on those who fear Him." What did King David mean when he wrote those words in today's Bible verse?

Imagine that you've messed up big-time. You're worried about what your dad might say when he finds out. But you don't have to worry! Your dad loves you. He has "loving-pity" on you. He's not pleased that you messed up. Still, he remembers that you are a kid and you're still learning how to behave.

God is our Father. He understands that humans, young and old, sin sometimes. They mess up and worry that Papa God might be angry and not forgive them. But they needn't be afraid! God made each of us. He knows all about us. He knows when we sin. He knows when we're sorry. And God will always have loving-pity on us—His kids. When we confess our sin and ask for His forgiveness, He wipes away that sin like it never happened. What a wonderful heavenly Father we have!

Heavenly Father, Papa God, I am not afraid to confess my sins to You, because I know You will look on me with loving-pity and forgive me. Amen.

DAY 145

My Christian brothers, you know everyone should listen much and speak little. He should be slow to become angry. A man's anger does not allow him to be right with God.

JAMES 1:19–20

Many teachers of the New Testament believe that James, the writer of today's scripture, was Jesus' half brother. If that's true, then we can see the influence Jesus must have had on His half brother's life.

James tells Christians to "listen much and speak little." Maybe he had watched Jesus in action and saw how people reacted to Him. Most of the time when Jesus spoke, people listened. But there were some, even leaders of the church, who closed their ears to His teaching and talked. . .and talked. . .and talked about themselves.

And James had likely seen how angry some people were with his brother. They hated Jesus for no reason other than He said He was the Son of God. Those people listened to the wrong words and ideas being spread by the haters. And that made them not right with God.

James learned from his brother to be wise about listening and about not becoming angry. Read his words aloud. Listen to them and let them sink deep into your heart.

Jesus, sometimes I talk when I should be listening. Teach me to be quiet and to learn from You. Amen.

DAY 146

Then Peter came to Jesus and said, "Lord, how many times may my brother sin against me and I forgive him, up to seven times?" Jesus said to him, "I tell you, not seven times but seventy times seven!"

MATTHEW 18:21–22

Jesus' disciple Peter asked Jesus a simple question: "How many times do I need to forgive someone?" And Peter likely thought he was being generous when he added, "Up to seven times?"

We wonder what was in Peter's head when he asked this question. Did he want others to admire his generosity at being willing to forgive seven times? Or maybe someone Jesus and Peter knew had been sinning against Peter, and Peter wanted the Lord to know that he had forgiven that person more than a few times—and he'd had enough.

Whatever Peter's reason for asking, Jesus' answer was probably not what Peter expected. Jesus answered, "Not seven times, but seventy times seven!" In other words, *keep on forgiving*!

God forgives us for every sin we confess to Him. Think about how many times we sin in a lifetime. That's generous forgiving, and that's how God wants us to forgive others.

Lord, my heart holds tightly to hurt feelings. But You have given me the ability to forgive even the worst of sins. So, help me to be generous when forgiving those who have hurt me. Amen.

DAY 147

Even if the fig tree does not grow figs and there is no fruit on the vines, even if the olives do not grow and the fields give no food, even if there are no sheep within the fence and no cattle in the cattle-building, yet I will have joy in the Lord. I will be glad in the God Who saves me.

HABAKKUK 3:17–18

Habakkuk was tired of the tough times he lived in. He wanted to know how long this would continue. He took his complaints to God. When would the trouble stop? Why hadn't God answered his prayers for help?

God answered. Yes, He was aware of what was going on, and yes, He would help, but it would come about in His timing.

Then Habakkuk's complaints switched to words of praise, which is amazing because nothing had changed. There still wasn't food or livestock in the fields or buds on the fig trees. How is it possible that Habakkuk could praise God in the midst of such trouble?

He understood that joy is found in Jesus alone. Situations change, people come in and out of lives, but Jesus is always with us, all the time, all the way.

Dear Jesus, when blessings don't come when I ask for them, when I wonder if they will ever come, thank You for being the only blessing I need. Amen.

DAY 148

For this reason, I ask you to keep using the gift God gave you. It came to you when I laid my hands on you and prayed that God would use you.

2 TIMOTHY 1:6

Look around your room. Are there toys or video games that you no longer play with? Books lying around gathering dust? Sports equipment shoved into a closet? Clothes you don't wear? Maybe your mom says, "If you're not going to use this stuff, then let's get rid of it!"

Some stuff we outgrow and give away, but we should never allow God's gifts to be tucked away somewhere, unused.

God gives each of us certain talents—things we are good at. They are His precious gifts to us, and we need to use them. God wants us not only to use His gifts but to share them and do good with them.

When we put God's gifts in action to serve Him, God knows that He can trust us with even more. His gifts to us will increase, strengthen, and multiply.

Are you using the gifts God has given you? Can He trust you with more?

God, You have given me special talents and inspiring gifts. I pray, open my eyes to sharing those gifts. Through faith and obedience I will use them to serve You. Amen.

DAY 149

No, Christian brothers, I do not have that life yet. But I do one thing. I forget everything that is behind me and look forward to that which is ahead of me. My eyes are on the crown. I want to win the race and get the crown of God's call from heaven through Christ Jesus.

PHILIPPIANS 3:13-14

Paul's past was not what you might expect from a Christian. He had belonged to a religious group that hated Jesus' followers. Back then, Paul was known as Saul. He talked much about how he would like to kill the followers of the Lord (Acts 9:1).

But after Saul met Jesus, raised from the dead, on a road leading to the city of Damascus, everything changed, even his name. Saul became Paul, one of the greatest Jesus followers ever.

By the time Paul wrote the words in Philippians 3:13-14 he had put thoughts of his past sins behind him. He focused only on serving God and the promise that one day he would live in heaven.

God forgives us for past sins, and Paul reminds us not to dwell on what we've done. Instead, we need to move on, living our lives for Jesus.

Father, allow me to focus just on today. What can I do for You? How can I spread Your Word where it is most needed right now? Amen.

DAY 150

He went away again the second time.
He prayed, saying, "My Father, if this must happen
to Me, may whatever You want be done."
MATTHEW 26:42

In this verse, Jesus was in the garden of Gethsemane just hours away from His arrest and crucifixion. He prayed, asking God if there was some different way to accomplish what God wanted Him to do. In fact, Jesus didn't ask it once—He made the request three times in Matthew 26.

Jesus' prayers show us the 100 percent human side of Him. In one of His darkest hours, Jesus was overwhelmed with human emotions. He asked God for something that God would not provide. But Jesus, perfect and obedient, ended His prayers by saying, "May whatever You want be done."

This is one of those times when we read about Jesus and discover that He had a human side that allowed Him to understand our feelings. He knows how it feels when God says no.

Do your best to follow Jesus' example. Remember that God knows best. When God says no to your prayers, focus on how much He loves you—even when His will doesn't match yours.

Father, I wonder why You refuse when I ask for what I think is right. But Your knowledge is greater than my understanding. So, Your will be done, God; Your perfect will be done. Amen.

DAY 151

If you know what is right to do but you do not do it, you sin.
JAMES 4:17

Today's world is very different from the way it was when Jesus lived. In His time, people were not as unsure about helping a stranger in need. But the world has changed. Sadly, people concerned for their own safety stand by watching when a stranger needs help. Those kinds of stories are common in the news today. And maybe when we see them, we say, "I would never stand by and do nothing."

Stepping in to help in a dangerous situation is heroic. But what about stepping in for the little stuff? How many times do we think, *It would be really nice if I did something for this person,* and then talk ourselves out of it? *They'll think this is silly. They won't even notice. I don't have time.*

James reminds us to stay focused on doing what's right. We never know what the future holds. We never know when we might need a good deed from someone else.

Dear God, today make me aware of little ways that I can brighten the lives of others. Where You see a need, Father, send me to fill it. Amen.

DAY 152

"He who is greatest among you will be the one to care for you."
MATTHEW 23:11

"If I had a million dollars," a boy said, "I'd hire a butler. Someone to do everything for me." That sounded a bit selfish, so the boy said, "Everyone could have one!" Then after a moment's thought he added, "Wouldn't it be cool if everyone in the world had a servant taking care of them?"

"And whose would *you* be?" his father answered. "If everyone had a butler or maid, then that would include the butlers and maids! The only way everyone could be taken care of like that would be if all the people with servants also were servants!"

Everyone taking care of everyone else—that's exactly what Christians are supposed to do. But it doesn't work when people think they are too important to be servants.

Jesus served us through His death and beyond. And God has already done everything for us by giving us this world, this life, and the next. We have already been served by the greatest.

So, whose servant will you be?

Jesus, I sometimes miss opportunities to serve You and others. Open my heart to the possibilities. Teach me to be a good servant. Amen.

DAY 153

"You are My Son. Today I have become Your Father."
HEBREWS 5:5

No one knows for sure who wrote the book of Hebrews in the Bible. But one thing is sure; its writer understood the power of God's Son, Jesus. The writer knew that some of the people who had halfheartedly accepted Jesus were soft in their faith. Some thought that Jesus, at some point, had been promoted by God to be His Son. Others thought that Jesus was just an important guy who did a good job talking about God. There were also those who didn't care about Jesus at all.

The author of Hebrews wanted everyone to know that Jesus was a part of God from the very beginning. Just like God, Jesus always existed.

Some of the most important passages in the Bible are when Jesus talks to His Father (Luke 22:42; 23:34, 46). To a Roman soldier, the Man on the cross "was the Son of God" (Matthew 27:54). In the heart of every believer is the truth that Jesus is God's "only Son" (John 3:16).

The Bible teaches that, without a doubt, Jesus is God's Son. He has been—always—and He is forever.

O Son of God, You are so wonderful! How amazing that God sent You to save me from sin. Jesus, You are in my heart. I love You. I praise You. Amen.

DAY 154

"I sent the hornets ahead of you. They drove out the people and the two kings of the Amorites from in front of you. You did not do it by your sword or bow."

JOSHUA 24:12

Throughout the book of Joshua, Israel's armies fought the Canaanites in one battle after another. You could certainly get the impression that their swords and bows had a lot to do with them taking Canaan, the Promised Land. But wait! Almost every battle came with a miracle: collapsing walls, hailstorms, prolonged daylight—even God inspiring them to go on night marches and launch surprise sunrise attacks.

In addition, just before Israel's armies showed up, God drove the Canaanites crazy and sent many fleeing from Canaan, driven out by massive plagues of hornets. No surprise. God had forewarned Moses twice, forty years earlier, that He would do that (Exodus 23:28; Deuteronomy 7:20), so when Israel entered the Promised Land, Canaan's armies were already small and weak.

Why did God do these miracles? He wanted Israel to understand that only *He* could give them victory and that they should respect and serve Him (Joshua 24:8–14; 2 Chronicles 20:12, 15). God still does miracles to help us reach our goals today, and His reasons are the same.

**You are always present in life's big moments.
Thank You, God, for Your greatness and Your love. Amen.**

DAY 155

Jesus was about thirty years old when He began His work. People thought Jesus was the son of Joseph, the son of Heli. Heli was the son of Matthat. Matthat was the son of Levi. Levi was the son of Melchi. Melchi was the son of Jannai. Jannai was the son of Joseph. Joseph was the son of Mattathias. Mattathias was the son of Amos. Amos was the son of Nahum. Nahum was the son of Esli. Esli was the son of Naggai.

LUKE 3:23–25

Have you ever wondered why God included such long and boring family histories in the Bible? To kids, and even grown-ups, these family histories sound dull. But we have to remember that the Bible isn't just for us. It is a book for all humankind.

In some world cultures, a person hasn't been properly introduced until that person's family history is known. The Bible's long lists of ancestors aren't boring to the people in those countries. Instead, Jesus, Mary, and Joseph are shown in their proper family setting.

Isn't it great that God thought of everyone when He gave the world the Bible?

Father, I think it's neat that You've included family history in the Bible. It reminds me that I have a long list of ancestors here on earth, but I am also a child of God! Amen.

DAY 156

"Heaven and earth will pass away,
but My words will not pass away."
MATTHEW 24:35

Jesus made that promise about two thousand years ago. Since then, the world has changed with breakneck speed. We live in an age when words zip around the globe in seconds and opinions can be broadcast to millions through television and the Internet. So, how does Jesus' promise, spoken before the invention of the printing press, hold up? Just like all His promises—His words are perfectly true.

If all the Bibles ever printed were still available, there would be one for every person alive today—with plenty left over. The New Testament has been translated into half of the world's languages. The Bible can be read in Braille, downloaded from the Internet, heard as audiobooks, and carried around in a cell phone. One hundred million copies are sold each year, and the average American home is estimated to contain four Bibles.

Heaven and earth are still around, but some people still haven't read or believed in God's Word. Pray that they come to believe.

Jesus, Your words are priceless. I pray for everyone in the world to come to believe in them as the truth and receive Your gift of forever life in heaven. Amen.

DAY 157

"We are not asking this of You because we are right or good, but because of Your great loving-pity."

DANIEL 9:18

Why do you think God blesses you? Is it because He saw you do something right or good? Certainly, God sees our good works. But nothing we do earns us His blessings, or even His forgiveness.

Daniel understood this. That's why when he prayed, asking God to get his people out of trouble, Daniel asked God for loving-pity.

Loving-pity is the same as mercy. Mercy is when God doesn't punish us for our sins as we deserve. Remember—Jesus took that punishment for us. He made it so God forgives all our sins as soon as we ask.

When Daniel asked for God's loving-pity, he knew that he had nothing to offer God except himself and the confession of his sins. There was nothing he could do to earn God's mercy and forgiveness.

Let's join Daniel in understanding that we bring absolutely nothing to God. But let's also know, like Daniel, that in God's great mercy, He chooses to hear, love, and forgive us.

O mighty God, Your great loving-pity is beyond my understanding. I have nothing to bring You, yet in my sinfulness You hear me, love me, and forgive me. Thank You, Father. Amen.

DAY 158

But many came and told false things about Him. At last two came to the front. They said, "This Man said, 'I am able to destroy the house of God and build it up again in three days.'"

MATTHEW 26:60–61

Have you ever played the telephone game? One person whispers something to the next person in line. That person passes it on. And by the time the message gets to the last person, it sounds entirely different!

That's the kind of thing that went on in the final days of Jesus' life. False information was passed around.

The rumor was that Jesus said He could destroy the local church—the temple, or house of God—and then rebuild it in three days! The people thought He was saying something crazy.

What Jesus had really said was "Destroy this house of God and in three days I will build it again" (John 2:19). He was talking about His body, His crucifixion, and resurrection.

We need to be careful when quoting Jesus' words or any other words in the Bible. They are written just as they are because they are the true, perfect words of God.

The Bible says add nothing to Your Word; the whole Bible is Your truth. When sharing Your Word with others, God, may I speak only Your words and Your truths. Amen.

DAY 159

I love the Lord, because He hears my voice and my prayers.

Psalm 116:1

Psalm 116:1 is a wonderful short verse that you should memorize. It is a strong message of hope.

Whether we are offering our praise to God or coming to Him with our troubles, we know from the few words in this verse that God hears us. Isn't that mind-blowing? The almighty God of the universe, who created and assembled every particle in existence, hears us when we come to Him.

Knowing that God hears us gives us hope. That hope comes from believing that God answers our prayers. How He answers them may not be what we expect, but we can be sure that the Lord knows what He is doing. He hears us, and He gives us what He knows is best.

Maybe we go to the Lord in song, praising. Maybe we spend some time reading and thinking about God's Word. Maybe we are praying to Him as we reach out for His comfort. Whatever we do, God hears us and is interested in what we have to say. Isn't that a great reason to love the Lord?

I have so many reasons to love You, God, so many reasons to worship and praise You. How grateful I am that You hear my voice! I love You, Lord. Amen.

DAY 160

Herod was afraid of John. He knew he was a good man and right with God, and he kept John from being hurt or killed. He liked to listen to John preach. But when he did, he became troubled.

MARK 6:20

John the Baptist's life was in King Herod's hands. Herod's wife wanted John dead, so her husband threw him in prison and later ordered him killed. John shouldn't have lived as long as he did, but Herod liked to listen to him. Why? Because there is a soul in each of us that pulls us toward God.

A tiny part of Herod must have hoped John would answer his questions and show him the way to the Lord. Sadly, it never happened. Herod was more concerned with his kingly position.

The Bible says that John's was a voice "in the desert" (Matthew 3:3). He didn't speak only to those who wanted to hear; he tried to reach those who said they couldn't care less—people like Herod.

God wants us to reach the "godless." They might struggle and fight against it—but their souls cry out to be saved.

Look around you. Whom can you tell about Jesus?

Dear God, lead me to the godless ones who You know that I can help. Give me the perfect words and actions to lead them to You. Amen.

DAY 161

Do not be joined together with those who do not belong to Christ. How can that which is good get along with that which is bad? How can light be in the same place with darkness?

2 CORINTHIANS 6:14

We don't know much about Paul's personal life outside his ministry for Jesus. But we do know that Paul understood the difference between believers and nonbelievers. He had been a nonbeliever himself when he was known as Saul. But Jesus came to him and changed all that.

Paul asks us to think about opposites, like good and bad and light and darkness. He reminds us that both cannot exist in the exact same place at the same time.

Imagine sitting in an absolutely dark room. If someone turns on a light, the whole atmosphere of the room changes. That's what it's like for a nonbeliever to believe! Jesus comes into that person's heart and lights it up with His love. Everything changes—for the better.

Paul warns us not to be joined together with nonbelievers. We need to be careful not to allow them to pull us away from Jesus.

I know it is possible for nonbelievers to turn believers away from You, Father. Give me the strength to steer clear from their ideas and turn my thoughts toward You. Amen.

DAY 162

"If the base of the building is destroyed, what can those who are right with God do?" The Lord is in His holy house. The Lord's throne is in heaven. His eyes see as He tests the sons of men.

PSALM 11:3–4

Jesus said, "In the world you will have much trouble. But take hope! I have power over the world!" (John 16:33). Just like everything else Jesus said, He spoke the truth. The world has trouble.

Some trouble is outside our control. We can't stop earthquakes, tsunamis, or hurricanes. Some trouble we bring on ourselves through greed, jealousy, anger, and disobedience.

We may never understand why God allows His people to suffer. But we do know that regardless of the way things appear, our loving God is still in control of our world and our lives.

Psalm 11:3 asks, "What can those who are right with God do?" The answer is we can help!

As Christians, we can help those in need. We can rebuild cities hit by natural disasters. And even more important, we can help rebuild lives by telling people about Jesus!

Yes, we have trouble in the world, but still, we trust that God is in control.

Heavenly Father, I am always increasing my trust in You. When bad things happen, I learn to trust You without understanding. It is enough that You are in control. Amen.

DAY 163

"I am the First and the Last. I am the beginning and the end."
REVELATION 22:13

Is Jesus God? Yes, He is! Jesus is a part of God equal to Him in every way. Our God is unique among the religions of the world. No other religion has a God whose Son is equal to the Father.

Over and over we find that the titles God gave to Himself in the Old Testament are being applied to Jesus Christ as well. In the Old Testament, God called Himself a shepherd, the beginning and the end, the Almighty, the first and the last. In the New Testament, we find the same titles given to Jesus.

The Bible is unique because in it God reveals who He is. Jesus is God come to earth as a man—but not like any human. Jesus is God Himself coming into the world to save us from sin. And God is also the Holy Spirit, the one called the helper who guides us every day. Our God is one perfect God with three equal parts, Father, Son, and Holy Spirit, now and forever.

Jesus, I learn how to live by Your human example, and I trust in You as my God—Father, Son, and Holy Spirit—three persons, one God, one perfect You! Amen.

DAY 164

We love Him because He loved us first.

1 JOHN 4:19

What is love? Maybe you said, "Hugs and kisses and all that mushy stuff!" Love for other humans is an unselfish and unconditional emotion that leads us to give beyond where common sense ends. But a greater love exists—our love for God. It makes us want to worship Him with praise and singing. It fills us up with joy because of His blessings.

Where does love begin?

The Bible tells us we love because God loves us first. Our love flows from God's bottomless well of devotion for us. He begins the relationship He wants with us, drenching us with His love as He adopts us as His children. The power of His love within us fuels our love when human love is running on empty. He plants His love within our hearts so we can share Him with others. We draw from His endless supply.

Love starts with God. God continues to provide His love to nourish us. God surrounds us with His love. We live in hope and draw from His strength, all because He first loved us.

Oh, God, the human love I know on earth cannot compare with Your love. When I feel empty, Your love fills me up. Your love is perfect. It never fails. Amen.

DAY 165

Children, as Christians, obey your parents. This is the right thing to do. Respect your father and mother.

EPHESIANS 6:1-2

Do you always obey your mom and dad? Be honest. Do you *always* obey? Everyone has bad days when they just want to dig in their heels and say no. Kids are no different. Most kids have times when they don't readily want to do what their parents say.

That's not what God wants, though. The Bible clearly says that children should obey their parents. And along with obedience, God uses the word *respect*. He wants you to respect your parents, as well. Respect means believing that your parents know best and will guide you with their wisdom.

Ephesians 6:1-2 is about the human relationship with our parents. But we can take it further and think about our relationship with God. All of us—our parents included—are God's children. And God expects obedience and respect when He teaches and guides us, through the Bible. Think about that today. In what ways can you show respect both to your parents and to God?

Father, please forgive me for the times when I disobey my parents and You. Help me to respect you both and to abide by your words. Amen.

DAY 166

A woman came from the land of Canaan. She cried out to Jesus and said, "Take pity on me, Lord, Son of David! My daughter has a demon and is much troubled."

MATTHEW 15:22

Some things Jesus said are difficult to understand. He told little stories that had a message, but He often made people think about what they meant. His conversations with others were sometimes puzzling too. There were those who said, "This teaching is too hard!" But always, Jesus had a reason for His words, and His reasons were perfect.

One day Jesus met a non-Jewish woman who cried out to Him, "Lord, Son of David"—a common name for the Messiah—and begged Jesus to drive a demon out of her little daughter. Jesus at first ignored her then finally told her that He was "sent only to the lost sheep of Israel" (the Jews) (Matthew 15:21–25 NIV).

Why would Jesus, who loved and accepted everyone, answer her this way? Because His first priority was carrying His message of forgiveness for sin to the Israelites, God's people—and *then* to the rest of the world. Jesus wasn't being mean. He was just telling her the truth. And afterward, Jesus healed her daughter, just as she asked.

Jesus loves us all.

Dear Jesus, thank You for loving us no matter where we come from, who we are, or where we live. Amen.

DAY 167

"As soon as you began to pray, an answer was given, which I have come to tell you. For you are loved very much."
DANIEL 9:23

Daniel is one of the better-known Bible people. You probably first think about God rescuing Daniel from a den of hungry lions. But there is much more to this man and his story.

Daniel was made a slave after the Babylonians conquered Jerusalem. Under King Nebuchadnezzar's rule, Daniel became one of the king's most trusted advisers. All the while he was in slavery, Daniel remained faithful to God. His heart broke for the sins of the people of Israel.

In the middle of praying one day, Daniel's prayer was interrupted by the appearance of the angel Gabriel. "Daniel," he said, "I have now come to give you wisdom and understanding. As soon as you began to pray, an answer was given" (vv. 22–23). Imagine that. As soon as Daniel began to pray, even before he asked God for what he wanted, God had already sent the answer!

As He did for Daniel, God knows our needs even before we ask Him in prayer. Even before the words leave our lips, God has already heard them, and He has already answered them.

Thank You, Lord, for answering my prayers. Before I ask, You already have the answer. How great You are, God! Amen.

DAY 168

He threw the money down in the house of God and went outside. Then he went away and killed himself.

MATTHEW 27:5

Judas is a key player in the story of Jesus' crucifixion. He was the disciple who betrayed Jesus and brought the Roman soldiers to take Him away. But another disciple also betrayed Jesus. Do you know who he is? Peter.

Peter denied he ever knew Jesus, not once but three times. In terms of betrayal, they were both horrible—yet Peter went on to do great works, while Judas died in embarrassment and disgrace. What made the difference?

Judas sold the Lord for greed. He took money for turning Jesus in. Judas, by taking control of the situation, ruined his own life. He was so ashamed that he killed himself.

Peter, on the other hand, owned his shame. He trusted Jesus to forgive him and was given great responsibility after Jesus rose from the dead.

When you mess up and take control over something you shouldn't, be like Peter and trust Jesus to forgive you. Then serve Him with gratefulness.

**I forget sometimes and try to control things.
Forgive me, Father. Remind me that You are in control.
My life and everyone else's are in Your capable hands. Amen.**

DAY 169

Then Job stood up and tore his clothing and cut the hair from his head. And he fell to the ground and worshiped.

JOB 1:20

People express sadness in different ways. Some people cry, others burst with fits of anger, and a few simply shut down and are quiet. In some cultures, people wear black as a sign of sadness. In other countries, they wear white.

How did Job express sadness when God allowed everything he owned to be taken away? He followed the traditional ways of mourning in his culture by tearing his clothes and shaving his head. But Job also worshiped.

Even with the terrible situation he was in, Job turned to God. He lay on the ground in front of the Lord, submitting his entire self. In his time of overwhelming loss and overpowering helplessness, Job opened his heart to the only one who fully understood and could help him in his time of deepest need—God.

We can learn from Job that when everything in life seems gone, lost, or out of reach, God is waiting. God understands our sadness and stays with us. As we turn our hearts to Him in worship, His healing Spirit will provide us comfort.

Sadness is a powerful emotion, Lord, but not nearly as powerful as Your love. I worship You for understanding, for comforting me, and for sharing my pain. Amen.

DAY 170

But the person who is not a Christian does not understand these words from the Holy Spirit. He thinks they are foolish. He cannot understand them because he does not have the Holy Spirit to help him understand.

1 CORINTHIANS 2:14

Paul divides humans into two classes: unbelievers and born-again believers—those who give God total control of their life.

Unbelievers may be smart but fail to understand God's Word because worldly desires fill their hearts. They are unable to comprehend the size of God's love and the power. Since they don't believe, the Bible's basic truths are hidden from them.

On the other hand, born-again believers focus on the thoughts and will of God. His Spirit lives in their hearts and leads, guides, comforts, and speaks to them.

Jesus said, "For sure, I tell you, unless a man is born again, he cannot see the holy nation of God" (John 3:3). Only when we accept Jesus into our hearts do we begin to find truth in the Bible. The moment we ask forgiveness for our sins and accept Jesus as our Savior, we become God's own. And from then on, we begin to understand His Word.

Heavenly Father, I know people whose hearts are closed to Your Word. Please open their hearts to be born again, to understand, and to trust in You. Amen.

DAY 171

Then Jacob gave Esau bread and vegetables, and Esau ate and drank. Then Esau stood up and went on his way. So Esau hated his birth-right.
GENESIS 25:34

In Old Testament times, the oldest son was promised a birthright. This meant when his father died, the son inherited all the father had. This was good news for Esau as the oldest son.

One day Esau came home hungry. His brother, Jacob, had a pot of stew simmering on the stove. Esau grabbed for a bowl.

Jacob shook his head. "First, sell me your birth-right" (Genesis 25:31).

The stew bubbled in the pot as Esau watched Jacob cut a thick slice of bread. His stomach growled. All he wanted was food. "See," he said, "I am about to die. So what good is my birth-right to me?" (Genesis 25:32). Then Esau sold his birthright to Jacob for stew and bread.

What did God think of this? "None of you should. . .forget God like Esau did. . . . For one plate of food he sold this right to his brother" (Hebrews 12:16).

Sometimes it's easy for us to trade our God-given treasures for temporary comfort and pleasure.

I'm tempted sometimes, Lord, to want worldly things that for a short while bring me comfort, joy, and peace. You are all those things now, always, and forever. Help me to remember. Amen.

DAY 172

"There is no way to be saved from the punishment of sin through anyone else. For there is no other name under heaven given to men by which we can be saved."

ACTS 4:12

Who was Jesus? Believers and nonbelievers answer this question differently.

Believers know in their hearts that Jesus is the Son of God. They believe that God sent His Son into the world to save us from sin. They understand that when Jesus rose from the dead, it was His guarantee to believers that after their bodies die, their souls will live on, at home with Him in heaven. Believers trust that Jesus is God, and they obey and respect Him as their Lord.

Most nonbelievers accept that Jesus did exist. There are historical facts to support it. But they do not believe that He was the Son of God. They explain away His miracles as tricks. They do not believe that after Jesus died on the cross, He came back to life. They don't believe that Jesus can save us from sin; many believe that they don't need saving.

What do you believe? Is Jesus your Lord and Savior?

Jesus, You are my Savior and also my Lord. I worship and praise You, believing that You are the risen Son who came to earth to save me. Thank You, Jesus! Amen.

DAY 173

Samson found a jawbone of a donkey and took it in his hand. He killed 1,000 men with it.

JUDGES 15:15

Samson was a big man with enormous physical strength. In the Old Testament book of Judges, we discover that God allowed Samson to aggravate and judge the Philistines, who were ruling harshly over the Israelites. At one point, Samson set their fields on fire. The Philistines fought back hard against Samson's family.

Samson's own people, afraid of further violence, came to arrest Samson and hand him over to the Philistines. Samson agreed to go with them, but at the moment of the handoff, the Spirit of God came to save him. Samson saw and grabbed a jawbone of a donkey and used it to kill a thousand Philistines! That never could have happened unless God made it so.

It was certainly God's power that allowed Samson to wipe out the Philistines. But Samson did not give the credit to God. He was a self-centered man who loved worldly things—and he bragged, praising his own strength and a donkey's jawbone for the victory, rather than the powerful Spirit of God.

God, You are the one who enables me to do what seems impossible. All of the credit and praise I give to You. Amen.

DAY 174

We came into this world with nothing.
For sure, when we die, we will take nothing with us.
1 TIMOTHY 6:7

What will you take with you to heaven? That's a silly question, isn't it? We all know that when we die we can't take anything with us. But more about that later. . .

Some people store up treasures here on earth, and sometimes those treasures become the most important things in their lives. Jesus had something to say about this: "Do not gather together for yourself riches of this earth. They will be eaten by bugs and become rusted. Men can break in and steal them. Gather together riches in heaven where they will not be eaten by bugs or become rusted. Men cannot break in and steal them. For wherever your riches are, your heart will be there also" (Matthew 6:19–21).

Later, Paul wrote the words in today's Bible verse to remind people that when they die they take nothing with them. That's true when it comes to worldly things, but there are two things that we *can* take with us: our love for God and the promise that we will live forever with Him in heaven.

Father, You are all that really matters.
My treasure is in heaven with You. Amen.

DAY 175

This is the day that the Lord has made.
Let us be full of joy and be glad in it.
PSALM 118:24

"Wake up! You are going to be late for school!"

Some mornings it's hard to get out of bed. You just want to snuggle under the covers, bury your head in the pillow, and sleep. But you know that you can't! You have to go to school, church, or wherever.

Part of growing up is facing your responsibilities, and one of them is getting yourself out of bed and ready for the day.

Getting up is easier when you remember the words in Psalm 118:24. God gives us each new day as a gift. He made that day for us, and what we do with it is up to us.

You can think of a new day like a blank canvas on which you can paint anything. God wants you to paint a picture full of joy and gladness. How can you do that? By getting up without grumbling, thanking God for His day, and then going out and spreading around kindness to others.

Give it a try today.

I forget to thank You in the morning for giving me a brand-new day. Thank You for all my days, God! Amen.

DAY 176

His loving-pity never ends. It is new every morning. He is so very faithful.
LAMENTATIONS 3:22–23

We all have days that start well and then end up being not so good. It's one of the facts of life that every day is not a good day. We humans mess up, and bad stuff happens. We cause a bad day, or someone causes it for us. But one bad day doesn't have to lead to another.

God understands! He sees our troubles. He knows when we mess up. And He is always ready to help us pick up the pieces and start again. Today's scripture reminds us that God's love and understanding have no end. He gives us the opportunity to put our bad day in the past and start fresh the next day.

Our God is always faithful. That means we can count on Him never to abandon us. Even when we get ourselves into a real mess, God hangs in there with us—and not to punish us but to help us!

Trust in His love today and every day. Allow Him to help you turn a not-so-good day into a good one.

Lord, You are my best friend. You help me through my troubles and brighten up my days. Amen.

DAY 177

Do not forget to be kind to strangers and let them stay in your home. Some people have had angels in their homes without knowing it.
HEBREWS 13:2

Hebrews 13:2 is a verse about *hospitality*—showing kindness to strangers.

Jesus and His disciples often relied on the hospitality of others for shelter and food. They traveled light, and they had few possessions. In the New Testament, Paul, Timothy, Peter, and John all wrote about the importance of hospitality (Romans 12:13; 1 Timothy 5:10; 1 Peter 4:9; 3 John 1:8). And the author of Hebrews 13:2, most likely Paul, reminded Christians to be kind to strangers. He suggested that some strangers might even be angels sent from God.

Today, most strangers to whom we extend generosity and hospitality are probably not angels. Still, we can't know if someday God will allow us to entertain an angel without us knowing it.

When you practice hospitality, God might be using you to minister to others. But in today's world, you need to be careful with strangers. Talk about this with your parents: What are some safe ways that you can show kindness to someone you don't know?

God, teach me to be wise when being kind to strangers. Teach me new ways to minister to others and show them Your amazing love. Amen.

DAY 178

"Power belongs to you, God, and with you, Lord, is unfailing love."
PSALM 62:11–12 NIV

Today's scripture is from a psalm written by King David.

David fully understood the power of God. He'd had much trouble in his life, and God helped him through it all. As a boy, David had faced the giant soldier Goliath, and with God's power, David brought Goliath down with just a slingshot and a stone. And when an angry king was chasing David, God kept David safe. Even when all his friends had turned against David and wanted him killed, God remained his friend and helper.

David was well aware of God's power and love, and he did his best to honor God with worship and praise. He pleased God, and in return God made him a great king. He called David "a man after my own heart." God said, "He will do everything I want him to do" (Acts 13:22 NIV).

God's power belongs to you too! His love for you is greater than any other love. The strength He gives you isn't necessarily muscle strength. Instead, He gives you a spirit strong enough to smash whatever trouble gets in your way.

Father, strength isn't about muscles and physical power; it's about the power You give me to conquer all of life's problems. You are my strength. Without You, I am weak. Amen.

DAY 179

Always listening. . .But they are never able to understand the truth.
2 TIMOTHY 3:7

The amount that mankind has learned since the Bible was written is mind-boggling. Take what you know about how people lived back then and compare it to now.

Today we have 24-7 access to the Internet, television, and radio. We have phones that go with us wherever we go. Medical breakthroughs provide humans with artificial knees, transplanted organs, and laser surgery. Modern medications treat conditions ranging from an annoying headache to an unusual heartbeat. New technologies have allowed us to peer deep into outer space.

Scientific discoveries have helped us to see the world like never before. And the truth is—God's fingerprints are everywhere.

Some people reject the ideas that God created the universe and that He allows us to learn new things. Learning is good, but learning apart from God's will is not.

We need to give God the thanks but also be careful that as we learn we keep our minds on His rules for what is right and good—and not on our own.

Dear Father, I praise You for all the good things You have allowed us to learn and do. Help us all to follow Your will as we learn. Amen.

DAY 180

Jesus got into the boat. The man who had had the demons asked to go with Him.

Mark 5:18

There was a man filled with demons who cried out to Jesus to help him. Jesus did! He told the demons to come out of the man and to go into a herd of pigs nearby. The demons did what Jesus said. They entered the pigs, and then the pigs ran into the sea and died!

Seeing what Jesus had done, the man wanted to go with Jesus and follow Him.

Jesus said no—and yes!

The man lived among nonbelievers who hated Jesus. He didn't want to go back and live with them. He wanted to live only with those who loved Jesus.

But Jesus had something else in mind. He told the man no; he couldn't come along and follow Him. Instead, Jesus sent him back to the nonbelievers.

Then, something wonderful happened. That man told all the people about the incredible thing Jesus had done for him, and all of them were amazed. In that way, the man *did* follow Jesus. He became like a disciple spreading God's Word.

Look around—at school, your friends, your family—and ask, "Whom can I tell about Jesus today?"

Jesus, sometimes I feel uncomfortable with nonbelievers. Teach me not to be shy about sharing Your Word. Show me what to do and say. Amen.

DAY 181

"For I know the plans I have for you," says the Lord, "plans for well-being and not for trouble, to give you a future and a hope."
JEREMIAH 29:11

Because of their sinfulness, the Jews were held hostage by Babylon. After seventy years, Jeremiah, the prophet, told them God said they would be released soon. God promised that if the people would pray and seek Him with all their heart, He would listen and be with them (vv. 12–14).

In Jeremiah 29:11, the prophet's reassuring words of hope must have been comforting to the Israelites. The same is true today. When God promises something, He delivers!

Sometimes hope comes in the form of a second chance when we think we have failed. Or in the words of a doctor who has a cure for an illness. Hope often comes with a loving gesture, a warm hug, or an encouraging word. Hope is one of God's most precious gifts.

God wants to forgive our sins and lead us on to a good future—just as He did for the Israelites. He has great plans for you. That's His promise!

Father, You provide hope when things seem hopeless. Trusting in Your plans for me brings me joy. My future is in Your hands, so how can it be anything but good? Amen.

DAY 182

"All of you bring trouble instead of comfort."

Job 16:2

Job speaks the words in today's verse. He tells his three friends—Bildad, Eliphaz, and Zophar—who had come to comfort him that all they were doing was making him feel worse.

Days before, Job had lost everything but his wife in a series of "accidents" caused when Satan tried to break his faith. Job lost all seven thousand of his sheep, three thousand camels, at least one thousand oxen, five hundred female donkeys—and worst of all, ten children. Now his health was being taken away.

When his friends arrived, they sat silently with Job for a while, but then they began to question why Job had suffered. Finally, they decided that Job must have done some terrible sins to get himself into this mess. That's when Job told them what bad comforters they were.

Some versions of the Bible call them "miserable comforters," "sorry comforters," "painful comforters." Of course, none of those adjectives—*miserable*, *sorry*, or *painful*—actually go with the word *comforter*.

When our friends are going through hard times, we should do our best to be loving and godly comforters.

Father God, when I am suffering, You know the perfect ways to comfort me. Please teach me to comfort others with true, godly love. Amen.

DAY 183

"I say to you now, stay away from these men and leave them alone. If this teaching and work is from men, it will come to nothing. If it is from God, you will not be able to stop it. You may even find yourselves fighting against God."

ACTS 5:38–39

Peter and his friends were preaching about Jesus. This didn't sit well with a group called the Sadducees. Peter and friends were arrested and brought before the high court. They were sentenced to die after Peter bravely spoke of Jesus' resurrection. He said he would continue to preach about Jesus: "We must obey God instead of men!" (Acts 5:29).

Gamaliel, an important and respected man, addressed the court. He reminded them of other men who had started movements. Once those men were killed, their followers fell away. Gamaliel's advice was to set Peter and the others free. He said that if Peter's actions were inspired by man they would fail. But if inspired by God, nothing would stop them. The judges, realizing they'd lose in any fight against God, released Peter and the others.

When we face obstacles while doing God's work, we can carry on, trusting that God's plan will always win.

Dear God, I won't worry when obstacles get in my way. You have a perfect plan for me, and nothing can stop it. Amen.

DAY 184

"See, I have marked your names on My hands."
ISAIAH 49:16

Have you ever had a bad day turn into a bad week. . .turn into a bad month. . .turn into a bad year? The Israelites found themselves in those times. As their sin increased, God was preparing to hold them accountable. They struggled thinking that maybe God had forgotten or abandoned them.

But God would never do that! He said, "See, I have marked your names on My hands."

The Israelites probably had no idea what God meant, except that having their names marked on His hands meant that they were His. But God had a greater meaning to His message. He was comparing His hands to the nail-scarred hands of Jesus. The name of everyone who believed that Jesus died for their sins would be with God, and they would have a place saved for them in heaven.

In the middle of troubling times, it's tempting to think that God has forgotten us. But He hasn't! It is His nail-scarred hand that reaches down from heaven and holds our own.

Jesus, the scars on Your hands are because of my sin—a reminder of my salvation. My name is written in heaven as a child of God. Oh, thank You, Lord Jesus! Amen.

DAY 185

"You put away the Laws of God and obey the laws made by men."
MARK 7:8

If you break the law, you get into trouble. Can you name two laws that people commonly break? Maybe you said speeding and littering, or something else. Those laws are man-made laws. There are tons of them meant to keep us happy and safe.

Most people try very hard not to break any man-made laws. They live as law-abiding citizens and are respected by their neighbors.

Obeying the law is a good thing, something everyone should do. But what about God's laws? Do most people obey them?

The Ten Commandments are God's most well-known laws, but there are others. Entire books of the Bible are dedicated to God's laws. It is almost impossible for a person to know all the laws written in the Bible. And it *is* impossible for a person to keep all of them. If someone did, that person would be perfect like Jesus, and no human is as perfect as Him.

Although it's impossible to follow every law in the Bible, we can be careful to follow the ones that we do know. We try hard to follow man-made laws, and we should try just as hard—no, even harder!—to follow God's laws.

Teach me Your laws, Father. Then remind me to follow them as best I can. Amen.

DAY 186

"Honor your father and your mother, so your life may be long in the land the Lord your God gives you."
EXODUS 20:12

Every parent has rules for their kids to follow. Let's see how good you are at remembering your house rules. How many can you list?

Your list might be long. There might even be rules on there that you think are unnecessary. But you should remember that parents make rules for a reason. They've been around for a long time, and they understand that without rules, kids—everybody even!—can get hurt or into trouble.

God says to honor your mom and dad. One way to honor them is by willingly obeying their rules. *Willingly* means being respectful while doing what you are told. If there is a rule that you disagree with, then ask to quietly discuss it. And if your parents still say no, then accept their answer with respect.

Someday you may be a parent too. By then, you will have been around a long time and will understand the importance of house rules. In the meantime, follow God's law and honor your parents.

Dear heavenly Father, forgive me for not respecting some of the rules my parents have set for me. Help me to obey and honor my parents with respect. Amen.

DAY 187

Give great honor to the Lord with me.

PSALM 34:3

You should honor God above all others and in everything you do. Here are some ways to honor Him.

Honor God when you play by sharing with your friends. Be a good sport, be honest and fair when you play games, and don't grumble if you lose.

Honor God with your words. Watch your language so that everything you say will be right with God. Don't swear. Be careful that your words don't hurt someone.

Honor God with your thoughts. Keep your mind focused first on God and then only on good things—things you know He approves of.

Honor God with your attitude. Do your best every day to have a positive attitude. Be patient and kind. Smile and encourage others to smile with you!

Honor God with your friendships. Make friends with other kids who love God. Don't give in to peer pressure. Help each other to do what is right.

One of the best ways to honor God is by setting a good example for others by the way you live.

Can you think of more ways to honor the Lord? How can you honor Him in your community? At school? At church?

God, teach me ways to honor You. I want You to be pleased with everything I do. Amen.

DAY 188

Have a true love for each other. Love covers many sins.

1 Peter 4:8

The greatest act of love ever was Jesus' death on the cross. He suffered embarrassment and awful pain because He wanted us to be free from sin so we can go to heaven when we die. His love threw a cover of forgiveness over our sins.

Jesus is our example of true love. He could have chosen not to care about our need for forgiveness. But He didn't. Jesus understood the importance of forgiveness. When He died, God made a way to forgive us for our sins and give us a new life in heaven.

We should be a reflection of Jesus' true love by forgiving others. Think about this: if you forgive someone for something they've done, your forgiveness can breathe new life into that relationship.

If you and your best friend have a fight, you both feel terrible. The only thing to fix that is forgiving each other. And when you do forgive, your broken friendship comes back to life again. Your love for one another wins over the sin that broke you up.

Memorize today's Bible verse so you will have it in your heart whenever you need to forgive. And remember too Jesus' great act of love.

Dear Jesus, please help me to love others the way that You do. Amen.

DAY 189

"For My people have done two sinful things: They have turned away from Me, the well of living waters. And they have cut out of the rock wells for water for themselves. They are broken wells that cannot hold water."

JEREMIAH 2:13

In ancient times, people dug wells into the earth or rock to receive rainwater for their daily use. But sometimes the wells cracked, leaving mud and filth behind. In Jeremiah 2:13, God uses this as an example to remind His people to follow Him.

The people had turned away from God. They were worshiping false gods, idols. They were all caught up in worldly things, selfishly wanting for themselves. It was as if they had dug a well and filled it up with all this bad stuff. God said that sooner or later this "well" was going to crack, leaving nothing but sin in their lives. Then there would be no way for them to go to heaven.

But God reminded them that His "well" would not crack. He called Himself "the well of living waters." God meant if they turned from sin and followed Him, they could live forever with Him in heaven.

Ask God, today, for some of His living water! There's plenty for everyone.

Dear God, fill me up with Your living water. Forgive me for my sins, and lead me in all my ways. Amen.

DAY 190

He came to a cave, and stayed there. The word of the Lord came to him, and said, "What are you doing here, Elijah?"

1 KINGS 19:9

Isn't it surprising when God, who knows everything, asks us a question?

In 1 Kings 19:9, God already knew what had brought Elijah to the point of such misery that he prayed to God to take his life.

God knew that Elijah was in serious trouble and was running in fear for his life. Despite knowing all this, God still asked Elijah why he was hiding out in a cave.

Elijah isn't the first person God has asked a direct question, knowing the answer. God asked Adam and Eve where they were, even though He knew they were trying to conceal themselves from Him (Genesis 3:9). In their case, as well as Elijah's, fear and hopelessness had driven them to a place of hiding and shame.

Sometimes we live in a way that causes God to ask us the question He asked Elijah. God sees and knows everything we do. Listen for His voice inside your heart. He might be asking you to stop and think about what you are doing.

Aren't you thankful He cares enough to ask?

Father, You always see me. Help me to stop, think, and act according to Your will. Amen.

DAY 191

Jesus was full of the Holy Spirit when He returned from the Jordan River. Then He was led by the Holy Spirit to a desert.

LUKE 4:1

After Jesus was baptized, He went into the desert. But He wasn't just going for a walk—He was led there by the Holy Spirit to face Satan.

For forty days, God allowed Satan to tempt Jesus to see if His human side might rebel and give in. Jesus was out there for almost six weeks, and the human part of Him must have been afraid. God tested Him, and Jesus passed. He never gave in. He used scripture verses to answer Satan, and after Satan tempted Him in every way, he left Jesus alone.

Those forty days, when Jesus might have struggled to remain true to His Father, give hope to the rest of us. He might have been scared, perhaps tempted—and there might have been doubts and the possibility of failure. But because of that experience, the Lord is able to stand right beside us, understanding us when we face testing times.

You can always turn to Jesus, because He knows what it's like—He understands you.

Jesus, You understand what it's like to be human and face worldly temptations. Sometimes it's hard to resist! Please give me strength to stand up to Satan. Amen.

DAY 192

Your eyes saw me before I was put together. And all the days of my life were written in Your book before any of them came to be.

Psalm 139:16

God knows everything about us, where we are at all times, and what we are going to say before we open our mouths. In fact, He has planned out all of our days.

God has a special plan for everyone. The Bible talks about several people God set apart for greatness: Moses, who led the Israelites out of Egypt; David, Israel's great king; John the Baptist, called to prepare the way of the Lord.

But God also knows the days of ordinary people. Every day, He is moving you forward in His plan for you. Your relationships with family and friends, your education and special talents, all that He gives and takes away are part of God's plan. King David wrote, "All You know is too great for me. It is too much for me to understand" (Psalm 139:6). Although you might not understand the path God has planned for you, you can be sure that the plan is perfectly in line with His will.

God, how can You know all about everyone who has or ever will live? Your ways are so far beyond my understanding, and yet You love me. You are so wonderful! Amen.

DAY 193

For our God is a fire that destroys everything.

HEBREWS 12:29

The Bible often uses comparisons to help us understand. Today's verse compares God to fire. Fire is a powerful image in the Bible. It represents the presence, judgment, and holiness of God.

When Moses led the Israelites out of slavery, God went ahead of them in a pillar of fire to light their way. In ancient times, an Israelite ready to make the perfect offering to God would bring the best lamb to sacrifice on the altar. The holy ritual of burning the animal's fat in an all-consuming fire symbolized the cleansing of the worshiper's sin.

A fire can destroy everything. After a fierce forest fire, there appears to be nothing left. But watch, and soon you will see signs of rebirth appear with shoots of green growth and the return of life. What was destroyed comes back to life—a comparison to Jesus' body and His resurrection!

When we trust God, we allow Him to burn away our selfishness, pride, and anything that blocks His light from shining through our lives. His love burns away our sinfulness and gives us a fresh new start.

Lord, cleanse me of my sin. Burn away my old ways. Create in me a new and more holy life. Amen.

DAY 194

Then He began to say to them, "The Holy Writings you have just heard have been completed today."
LUKE 4:21

Jesus declared Himself the Son of God in front of a hometown audience. More than a few jaws would have dropped, but the listeners were quite civil about it—until He didn't do things the way they wanted. Then they tried to throw Him off a cliff! These people knew Jesus' parents, and they had known Him as a child. Now He was shaking their world with unfamiliar ideas and what seemed to be miracles. Some doubted that He was, indeed, the Messiah.

As Christians, we often are among nonbelievers (perhaps in school, at sporting events, and even in the neighborhood). It's difficult to stand up in front of people who know you and say, "I am a child of God." Some will think you've flipped; others will poke fun. Is it worth the hassle? Wouldn't it be easier to stay quiet?

But that isn't what it's all about. Jesus spoke up—and God wants us to do the same. Face others and tell them who you are. It won't be easy, but God will provide the courage.

Dear God, take away any shyness I have about sharing You with my family and friends. You are my Father, and I am proud to let others know. Amen.

DAY 195

He will not let your feet go out from under you.
He Who watches over you will not sleep.
Psalm 121:3

Maybe you have been to sleepovers where you try to stay awake all night. Sooner or later, you become so tired that you can't stay up any longer. With only a few hours sleep, you'll still feel tired the next day, and maybe even the day after that, until your body catches up on the rest it needs.

Today's Bible verse tells us that God does not sleep. He watches over us, never once taking His eyes off us even for a few quick moments of rest. God guards us all the time, 24-7.

The Lord stays up all night, looking after us as we sleep. He patiently keeps His eyes on us even when we sleep away from home. He always comforts us when fear or illness makes us toss and turn at night.

Like when your mom or dad tiptoes into your room to check on you while you sleep, God surrounds you even when you don't realize it.

You can sleep well every night because God is watching over you.

O God, how grateful I am that You never sleep. When I am asleep, You guard me because I am Your child. I love You, Father! Amen.

DAY 196

"For sure, I tell you, unless a seed falls into the ground and dies, it will only be a seed. If it dies, it will give much grain."

JOHN 12:24

Before a wheat seed is sown, it lies lifeless on the barn floor. But there is life hidden deep within it. When planted, the seed's waterproof coating breaks down. Soon, roots emerge and tiny shoots jet upward. Before long, the seed blossoms into a towering stalk filled with countless grains of wheat.

In one of His parables, Jesus compared Himself to a wheat seed to emphasize the necessity of His death, the power of His resurrection, and the idea that many souls would be saved because of Him.

His parable applies not only to Jesus but to every believer. When Jesus comes into your heart, it is as if He plants Himself within you. When you put your faith and trust in Him, your love for Him grows. It's no longer hidden deep inside. Others see your love for Him too. And every time you share Jesus with others, your actions and words might plant His seed in their hearts too!

Jesus, I want Your love to grow within me. Help others to see it grow and to want You in their hearts too. Amen.

DAY 197

"But the one who stays true to the end will be saved."
MATTHEW 24:13

There are many Bible stories about people who stayed true to God in the worst of times. Daniel, for example, was thrown into a den of hungry lions because he refused to stop worshiping God. Abraham was so true to God that he would sacrifice his own son, if that's what God wanted. Think about Noah. If he hadn't stayed true to his faith in God, he wouldn't have built the ark. And Paul went through shipwrecks, beatings, and prison, but he always stayed true to God.

"Staying true" means hanging on to your faith. In good times, it's easy to have faith in God. But when times get hard, we have to be careful that our faith doesn't slip away. It's in those times that God will grow our faith even stronger if we stay true to Him.

God makes an important promise at the end of today's Bible verse: "But the one who stays true to the end *will be saved.*"

Hang tight to your faith in Him. Stay true. And when bad times come, remember God's promise—He will save you.

Dear God, I know I can count on You to save me from trouble. Help me, please, to stay strong in my faith and true to You always. Amen.

DAY 198

Then the angel of the Lord went farther. He stood in a narrow place where there was no way to turn to the right or the left.

NUMBERS 22:26

Imagine this: You and your friends decide to go exploring in the woods. For a while, you follow a walking path, but then you decide to go off the path on your own. As you walk deeper into the woods, obstacles get in your way—rocks to climb over, bushes covered with burrs that stick to your clothes, logs that make you trip. The way becomes so narrow that you can't turn to the right or to the left. Do you think, maybe, God is telling you to stop?

Sometimes in life we head in the wrong direction. We start walking down a path that God knows will get us into trouble. That's when God might start putting obstacles in our way. It's Him saying, "Stop. Think about where you are going. Is it the right direction?"

When your plans don't seem to be working out, stop and pray. Ask God to show you whether you should go on or go a different way.

God, if I head down the wrong path in life, make me stop. I want to follow the way that You have set for me. Amen.

DAY 199

If anyone thinks he is important when he is nothing, he is fooling himself.

GALATIANS 6:3

A grandfather asked his grandson, "What do you think you want to do when you grow up?"

"I *know* what I want to do," the boy said. "I'm going to be president!"

"Why do you want to be president?" his grandfather asked.

"Because then I can rule over all the people. I'll command the army and all other branches of the military. I'll have all kinds of people ready to serve me whenever there's something I need. I'll even tell leaders of other countries what I think they should do. Best of all, I'll be the most important man in the world!"

"And how important are you right now?" the grandfather asked.

His question took the boy by surprise. He thought and then answered, "I don't know. I'm just a kid."

In God's eyes, the boy was just as important now as he would be if he were president. No matter how important we think we are, what matters to God is just that we understand we are nothing without Him. Every good thing we accomplish is because of Him.

Heavenly Father, You have blessed me with accomplishments here on earth—but what I have achieved is nothing without You. All the glory and honor belongs to You. Amen.

DAY 200

Every word of God has been proven true. He is a safe-covering to those who trust in Him.
PROVERBS 30:5

Some people say that you can't prove much of what's in the Bible. And because of that, they reject God. If it can't be proven, they believe, then it doesn't exist.

The Bible is ancient. We know that because some of those ancient Bibles have been discovered, and the words in those Bibles say the same things. Can you think of any other book that has existed for thousands of years and still remained popular?

Archaeologists have discovered things that prove the existence of people, places, and things in the Bible. Maps and names and messages carved into stone were found to support what's in the Bible. A section of the ancient wall of Herod's temple exists in Jerusalem, and many other places mentioned in the Bible still exist.

But, what's important isn't the physical proof that the Bible is 100 percent true—it's that God requires His people to trust in Him. He wants us to have so much trust in Him that we believe without proof that He exists and that His words are true.

Do you trust God enough to believe that the Bible is perfectly true?

I believe the Bible as truth, Lord. I need no evidence. My proof is in You, the one who cannot lie. Amen.

DAY 201

It is bad for those who are taking it easy in Zion, and for those who feel safe on the mountain of Samaria, you great men of the most important nation, to whom the people of Israel come!

AMOS 6:1

Amos was a shepherd who also grew sycamore figs, a poor man. But God called him to be a prophet and carry His words to the rich leaders of Israel (Amos 7:14–15).

God was disgusted with these leaders, and He wanted them to know it! He had blessed them greatly, and what did they do? They took so much pleasure in those blessings that they forgot God. They slipped into a time of lazy self-centeredness in which all they cared about was themselves.

Amos went to Zion, where they lived, and gave them God's message: "It is bad that you great men of God's most important nation are taking it easy." In other words, "Wake up! Get with it! God gave you these blessings. Now put them to work for Him!"

Remember Amos' words. When God blesses you, don't just be satisfied and take it easy. Get busy and put those blessings to work!

Lord, it means nothing when I am satisfied with myself but everything when You are satisfied with me. Wake me up! Send me out to work for You. Amen.

DAY 202

Lot looked and saw that the Jordan valley was well watered everywhere like the garden of the Lord.

GENESIS 13:10

Have you heard someone say, "Maybe it's too good to be true?" A man named Lot should have thought about those words.

Their pastureland wasn't big enough for the huge flocks and herds that belonged to Abram and his nephew, Lot. Abram offered Lot first choice of the surrounding areas. Wanting the best land, Lot moved onto the beautiful plains of the Jordan Valley.

But soon Lot discovered that the people who lived there were wicked and sinning against God. When their evil ways grew to the point of no return, God destroyed the place with fire and brimstone. Only Lot and his two daughters escaped the destruction.

Proof of the fire exists today in the Jordan Valley. Still-recognizable city walls and buildings have been transformed into calcium sulfate and calcium carbonate ash, both by-products of intensely burning limestone and sulfur.

Lot took what looked like the best. But he ended up losing everything except what he and his daughters carried while fleeing their city.

Sometimes there's wisdom in holding back and wondering: Is it too good to be true?

Father God, help me to carefully weigh what looks too good to be true. Before I make a decision, remind me to hold back and seek Your will. Amen.

DAY 203

Then He turned to His followers and said without anyone else hearing, "Happy are those who see what you see!"

LUKE 10:23

Jesus' disciples were blessed men. It wasn't that they were particularly special—not until Jesus chose them—but no man or woman before them or since them has been as blessed. Why? Because they were able to see Jesus in the flesh, to live, talk, eat, and walk with Him as a human being, something none of us will get to do. And they paid dearly for the privilege. Many hated them for loving the Lord.

Jesus' earthly mission wasn't finished when His body died. He would appear again to the disciples and guide them as they spread the good news in foreign lands, and He had also taught them to look for Him in "the least of these."

What does that mean? It means that we still get to see Jesus! Until we join Him in heaven we will see the Lord at work in others as they help the humble, the hungry, the lonely, and the poor.

Jesus, allow me to see You through the world's people. Open my eyes to Your gentle compassion, the truths of Your teaching, Your amazing forgiveness, and Your deepest love. Amen.

DAY 204

"Look among the nations, and see! Be surprised and full of wonder! For I am doing something in your days that you would not believe if you were told."

HABAKKUK 1:5

"O Lord. . .I cry out to You, 'We are being hurt!' . . . Why do you make me see sins and wrong-doing? People are being destroyed in anger in front of me. There is arguing and fighting. The Law is not followed. What is right is never done. For the sinful are all around those who are right and good, so what is right looks like sin" (Habakkuk 1:2–4).

The prophet Habakkuk said those words about 2,600 years ago, but they might sound familiar today. We live in a world with problems similar to those in Habakkuk's time.

God answered Habakkuk, "If I told you how I'm going to fix this, you wouldn't believe me."

Habakkuk had to trust that God was in control, and He would work everything out for the good of His people (Romans 8:28).

God is just as much in control today. He has a good plan for those who love Him. We might not understand right now why bad things are happening in the world. But God sees, and He understands.

God, I worry that nothing seems to be going right, but then I remember—You are in control, working it all out for good. Amen.

DAY 205

The Lord turned and looked at Peter. He remembered the Lord had said, "Before a rooster crows, you will say three times that you do not know Me."

LUKE 22:61

Jesus had just been arrested, and Peter, afraid for his own life, lied and said that he didn't know Jesus.

What do you think Peter saw when he looked into the eyes of the Lord? In Jesus' time of greatest need, He turned to Peter—His friend—and heard him lie, heard him put his own safety before Jesus'. The expression on Jesus' face made Peter run away. Not to hide, but to weep bitterly because, undoubtedly, he would have seen only love and understanding on Jesus' face.

Some Christians today are like Peter. They are afraid to say that they know and love Jesus, afraid that others might make fun of them, or worse. So, they blend in with the crowd and keep quiet about their faith.

Imagine the expression on Jesus' face as He sees you pretending that you don't know Him. He loves you! Don't disappoint Him by lying about your faith.

Dear Jesus, forgive me when I don't share You with nonbelievers who I think will make fun of me. Give me courage to stand up and say that I'm proud to call You my Lord! Amen.

DAY 206

Whatever your hand finds to do, do it with all your strength.
ECCLESIASTES 9:10

Today's Bible verse is a call to action. It tells us to put all of our effort and strength into everything we do.

Instead of thinking that you have to clean your room because your mom told you to, act like you're doing it for God. The same goes for homework–do it to please the Lord. Help with the dishes, take out the trash, go to bed on time without complaining–do it as if God Himself had asked you to. Whatever you do, think of it as something you are doing for Him. And remember, God sees everything. He knows if you do it willingly or if you rebel.

Your best effort should go into staying away from what you know is wrong. But if you do mess up, ask God to forgive you. Depend on His wisdom to give you strength not to make the same mistake again.

When you give, give your best; when you work, do your best work; when you pray, pray with all your heart. And when you've done the best you can, leave the rest up to God.

Lord, please keep the thought fresh in my mind that whatever I do I am doing it for You. Then help me to do my best. Amen.

DAY 207

Some are weak. I have become weak so I might lead them to Christ. I have become like every person so in every way I might lead some to Christ.

1 CORINTHIANS 9:22

Jesus is for everyone. There is plenty of room in the kingdom of heaven for everyone ever born. And Jesus went out of His way to reach people wherever they were.

Jesus did everything that could have been done to offer hope. He performed miracles one after another. He healed the sick. He made the blind see and the lame walk. His teaching caused enormous crowds to gather as word of who He was spread from region to region. He showed kindness to people, whether or not others were around to witness it. Certainly Jesus knew how to reach people!

It may seem difficult to imagine that anyone could relate to the Son of God. How amazing is it to think that while He was so far above everyone else, He humbled Himself and was able to relate to all people on a level that no one else in history ever could?

You can help lead others to Jesus! Show kindness and be at peace with everyone so that they can see the love of Jesus shine through you.

O Jesus, let Your perfect love shine through me, especially in hard times and in difficult situations. Amen.

DAY 208

Show Your great loving-kindness. You save by Your right hand the people that come to You for help from those who hate them.

PSALM 17:7

David certainly wasn't feeling loved when he wrote the words in today's scripture verse—he was on the run! His prayer in this verse is for forgiveness and protection. While running from his enemies, David called out to his God of unfailing love. Giving in to misery and frustration must have been tempting, but David kept his focus on God in the middle of a dangerous situation.

We may never find ourselves running from murderous enemies, but all of us have moments when everyone seems to be against us. Sometimes the situation is because of our actions and at other times circumstances beyond our control. Whatever the situation, we have a choice—like David—to remember God's unfailing love.

Today, look for the ways God shows His love for you. It may be in a sunrise that takes your breath away, in something fun that you hadn't planned for, or in an unexpected compliment from a friend. God's unfailing love is at work in your life in wonderful ways.

Father God, remind me today of all the little ways that You love me. You are so good to me. I love You too! Amen.

DAY 209

Pleasing words are like honey. They are sweet to the soul and healing to the bones.

PROVERBS 16:24

There's an old saying that goes "Sticks and stones may break my bones, but words will never hurt me." It may be one of those rhymes that has lasted a long time, but it's simply not true. Unkind words spoken by another person do hurt, cutting deep into our spirits. They find their way into our hearts and make us want to cry. If you imagined those words as food, they would taste awful.

But think about how sweet kind words would taste. Encouraging and loving words sink into our hearts and make us feel happy!

Today's Bible verse compares kind words to honey. Honey is a symbol of happiness and health in the Bible. It is a good food. The Bible says that John the Baptist ate lots of honey. It's basically all that he ate!

We often forget that the power of our words can make someone feel good or cut deep into the heart and cause pain.

Choose your words carefully today—coat them with honey. Pass on an overheard compliment, say "I love you," or write a note of appreciation to share God's love through your words.

Lord, from now on, I will think before I speak and choose my words wisely. Amen.

DAY 210

Wear shoes on your feet which are the Good News of peace.
EPHESIANS 6:15

What was Paul thinking when he wrote these words in Ephesians 6:15? Perhaps he had another scripture verse in mind, one he had read in the Old Testament book of Isaiah: "How beautiful on the mountains are the feet of him who brings good news, who tells of peace and brings good news of happiness, who tells of saving power, and says. . .'Your God rules!' " (Isaiah 52:7).

Good footwear was important to people in Bible times. They often walked wherever they needed to go, sometimes walking for many miles wearing leather sandals on their feet. Paul might have been thinking of Jesus and His disciples walking from city to town preaching God's Word. Or, he might have been thinking of the sandals worn by Roman soldiers, sandals with spikes that sunk into the ground and allowed them to stand firm in battles.

Whatever Paul had in mind for shoes, his message in Ephesians 6:15 is clear. Wherever you go, go peacefully and spread the good news about Jesus. Tell others that Jesus came to save them from sin and make a place for them in heaven.

Where will your shoes take you today?

God, I want my feet to help me carry the good news and to always be ready to defend it. Amen.

DAY 211

Take away the waste from the silver, and a silver pot comes out for the workman.
PROVERBS 25:4

Silver is rarely found in the earth in a pure state. Usually, when silver is dug out of the rocks, it's mixed with the sulfide ore of lead or other less valuable minerals. It then must be put through a refining process to remove the waste.

The ancient method of doing this, in Bible times, was to melt the ore containing the silver in a furnace and add lead to the mix; the lead decomposed and worked to draw out the waste. The result was pure silver, which could then go to the silversmith to be made into articles of beauty and value fit for kings.

The Bible describes God's people as silver and the Lord as a "purifier of silver" who puts them through the refiner's fire to remove the impurities (Malachi 3:2–3 NIV).

In other words, God is always working on us to remove the bad and useless stuff from our hearts. His goal is to make us pure, good, and ready for heaven. Jesus is the one who removes the sin from our lives. Because of Him, we are like the best silver—fit for God, our King.

Jesus, please work on me. Make me pure for God, like the finest silver. Amen.

DAY 212

Then Jesus said, "Father, forgive them. They do not know what they are doing." And they divided His clothes by drawing names.

LUKE 23:34

They never accepted Jesus; they worshiped false gods; they weren't even very nice guys. There were many reasons why the soldiers who drove nails through Jesus' hands and feet and then lifted His cross high should never have met God personally. But Jesus asked His Father to forgive them, even as they killed Him. If ever anyone felt the need for forgiveness, it would be those soldiers.

No human will ever be as forgiving as Jesus. That's a fact. But God wants us to try.

Take a few minutes to think about the people who've hurt you or those you won't trust. Are they any worse than the soldiers who killed Jesus? Do you think Jesus would forgive them if He were in your place?

Forgiveness is one of the biggest tests we face in life—and one of the blessings we need the most.

Jesus died so we would be forgiven for every sin we ever do. Let's try to be like Him as much as we can and be forgiving toward others.

Father, help me to forgive those who have hurt me, the way You have so generously forgiven me. Amen.

DAY 213

"For I am the Lord your God Who holds your right hand, and Who says to you, 'Do not be afraid. I will help you.'"

ISAIAH 41:13

"Fear not!" "Do not be afraid!" "I am with you!"

Hundreds of Bible verses address our emotions of fear, anxiety, and worry. Fear is nothing new. People have been afraid of one thing or another since the beginning of time. Maybe that's why, in verse after verse, God reminds us of His presence and offers us peace, as He did for countless others.

God gave Moses and Jeremiah the right words (Exodus 4:12; Jeremiah 1:9), David the strength (1 Samuel 30:6), Solomon the wisdom (1 Kings 3:12), and Mary the courage (Luke 1:30) to rise above their fears. But when you're afraid, how do you learn from them to trust God and rise above it?

Reread today's verse. God is so loving toward us with His words. He holds our hand and says four important words: "I will help you." It's His invitation to hold on to His hand and accept His help.

When you feel afraid, do what those others did. Take God's hand!

Take my hand, Lord, and help me. Allow Your strong yet gentle touch to take away my fear. Amen.

DAY 214

A day was set aside. On that day Herod put on purple clothes a king wears. He sat on his throne and spoke to the people. They all started to speak with a loud voice, "This is the voice of a god, not of a man."

ACTS 12:21–22

King Herod understood God's rules, but pride got in the way. He put his own need to be kingly above God's commands—and that got him into trouble.

Herod set up a festival of games to be played in the kingdom's stadium. Of course, he had to be at the center of attention! He put on his kingly purple robes, sat on his throne, and spoke to his subjects.

The crowd began to shout, "This is the voice of a god, not of a man."

As they worshiped Herod, he accepted their claim that he was a god, knowing that God's commandment says "Have no gods other than Me" (Exodus 20:3). According to the Jewish historian Josephus, God's angel infected Herod with parasites, and he died five days later.

Herod's story is a good reminder not to let pride or anything else get in the way of doing your best to follow God's rules.

Lord, please forgive me for those times when I've done what I know is wrong. Help me to do my best to remember and follow Your rules. Amen.

DAY 215

Keep your heart pure for out of it are the important things of life.
PROVERBS 4:23

When was the last time your heart got a checkup? When you went to the doctor, he or she probably used a stethoscope to listen to your heart. Maybe you got to listen to it beat. *Thump-thump. Thump-thump. Thump-thump.* Everything checked out. Your doctor said that you have a strong, healthy heart. That's great. But there is another kind of heart checkup, one better than any doctor can perform.

God wants you to do a check of your own heart. What's in there? Along with those even thumps, is there some sin clanking around?

Whatever is in your heart will come out in how you behave. When your heart is pure, only good things will come out of it. When sin creeps in, your words and actions will reflect that too.

Think about it. How have you been behaving lately? Is there some sin in your heart that you need to get rid of? No problem! Tell Jesus all about it and ask Him to give you a pure heart that's pleasing to God.

Lord Jesus, I've checked my heart and there's sin in there. I want it gone. Please forgive me for my bad behavior and help me to have a good and pure heart. Amen.

DAY 216

When Jesus had said this, He showed them His hands and feet.

Luke 24:40

Promises are easy to make—and to break. If you don't manage to keep one, and you don't care about your word, you might even say something to make it seem like that wasn't what you meant in the first place.

Think about Jesus, though. He could have summoned thousands of angels to save Him from the cross, but instead He suffered an awful death. He came to us to keep a promise. Jesus, the Son of God, came to earth to save us from sin and lead us to heaven. He was the promise that God would never abandon us. He loved us all in spite of our sin.

When Jesus rose from the dead, He showed His followers the nail marks in His hands and feet. The torn flesh spoke without words: *Do you see how much I love you?*

Jesus kept His promise to us. Let's do our best to honor Him in such a way that when we get to heaven, God will say, "I saw how much you loved Me."

Jesus, You were true to Your word. You never backed out. You always did what You promised. Help me to show my love for You by keeping my promises too. Amen.

DAY 217

A voice is calling, "Make the way ready for the Lord in the desert. Make the road in the desert straight for our God."
ISAIAH 40:3

An ancient custom in Bible times required that a representative be sent ahead of an important person to prepare the road. He removed obstacles like rocks and boulders and filled in the potholes. Travel was easier when the crooked road became straight and even.

People wanted to get through the hot, parched desert quickly. Travelers were sometimes injured while walking on the rocky ruts in the road. If they found the straightest route, they arrived more quickly at their destination, often an oasis. Here they found cool, refreshing water and much-needed rest to regain their strength to complete their journey.

Our journey in life sometimes leads us down rocky paths. We need someone to lead the way to get us out of trouble. We want to do what is right, but we stumble. God prepares our way for us. If we rely on Him as our representative, He will remove all the obstacles that get in our way. He makes the crooked road straight and gives us strength to keep walking.

Dear God, You go on ahead of me, clearing the obstacles and lighting my way. Thank You, Father! Amen.

DAY 218

Do not worry. Learn to pray about everything.
Give thanks to God as you ask Him for what you need.
PHILIPPIANS 4:6

In the Sermon on the Mount, Jesus told the crowd, "Do not worry about your life." He went on to explain that we shouldn't worry about where our food and drink is coming from or where we'll get the money to buy new clothes. Jesus also said, "Do not worry about tomorrow" (Matthew 6:25-34).

"Do not worry" sounds like great advice, but at times most of us have the feeling that it only works for some people but not for us. We worry about today's troubles, like moving to a new place, taking a test in school, and whether we will play well in Saturday's game to help our team win.

The key to not worrying is taking our problems to God in prayer, thanking Him for solving past problems, and trusting Him to work out the new ones. When we do that, we can stop worrying. We've handed our problem over to God, and we can follow where He leads us.

Father, worrying makes me tired. Today I ask You to take all my problems and work them out for my good. Show me the way, Lord, and I will follow You. Amen.

DAY 219

The Light shines in the darkness. The darkness has never been able to put out the Light.

JOHN 1:5

When God created the universe, He set the stars and planets in the sky. He gave Earth its sun and moon. We don't know what lies beyond what man has discovered about the universe, but God knows what's there.

If you look at the night sky on a clear night, you will see the moon and stars. But what about on a dark, cloudy night? Has God taken away the stars and the moon? No! They are still there but hidden from our sight.

It's like that with Jesus sometimes. He says, "I am the Light of the world" (John 8:12). But a dark cloud of sin can keep us from seeing Jesus at work in our lives. Beyond that cloud, He is still there—as mighty, powerful, and loving as ever. Jesus also said in John 8:12: "Anyone who follows Me will not walk in darkness."

We can't keep clouds from blocking out the stars, but we can remove that cloud of sin from our lives in order to see Jesus. He's there waiting for us. Nothing, not even the darkness, can keep Him away.

Jesus, please remove anything that keeps me from following You and seeing Your work in my life. Amen.

DAY 220

God makes a home for those who are alone.
He leads men out of prison into happiness and well-being.
But those who fight against Him live in an empty desert.
PSALM 68:6

God understands what it's like to be lonely. That's why He has put people around you who love you! And who loves you more than anyone on earth? God does! His love for you is perfect and forever.

There are times when a person can be surrounded by loving people but still feel alone. That lonely feeling might be caused by a bad choice the person made or maybe because someone else caused their feelings to be hurt. Whatever causes the loneliness, God doesn't want it! He promises to never leave us alone. He wants to lift us up, dry our tears, and make us feel happy and safe.

God has a way of bringing people into our lives exactly when we need them. If you feel alone, don't keep it to yourself. Reach out to someone—a family member, teacher, or friend. Then trust God with the rest.

Thank You, God, for the people who love me. Thank You too for Your perfect love. Whenever I feel alone, bring people into my life to help me. In Jesus' name. Amen.

DAY 221

Joseph went to have his and Mary's names written in the books of the nation. Mary was his promised wife and soon to become a mother.

LUKE 2:5

Caesar Augustus ruled that a census be taken of the entire Roman world, and everyone went to his own town to register. Joseph and Mary traveled from Nazareth to Bethlehem, where she gave birth to Jesus (Luke 2:1–7).

The Bible doesn't tell us that the journey from Nazareth to Bethlehem was almost a hundred miles. The route would take the couple through rugged land, up and down steep hills. The trip would take a minimum of five days on foot, and at night, Joseph and Mary would need safe places to camp. That Mary made the trip is in itself a miracle because she was about to have her baby.

Mary and Joseph aren't the only ones who face life's ups and downs. Everyone has times when they feel as if they are on a journey that never ends. God understands! When we're tired of trying, He gives us strength to keep on going.

Lord, life's journey is sometimes like climbing up a steep hill. I know that You understand. Take my hand and walk with me. Give me strength to go on. Amen.

DAY 222

Even if an army gathers against me, my heart will not be afraid. Even if war rises against me, I will be sure of You.

PSALM 27:3

Although King David was a man of many faults, his love for and trust in God was firm. This love and trust came from a close and ongoing relationship with God.

In Psalm 27, David was thinking about what might happen. There were people who hated and had tried to kill him. Yet as David wrote this psalm, he recognized God's presence and power at work in his life. David pledged that no matter the circumstances, he would trust God—because he knew it was safe and wise to do so.

Overconfidence can be a problem, but godly confidence is necessary in our lives. Without it, our faith begins to fail. Trusting God completely is an expression of faith and the most important step to winning when Satan tries to put obstacles in our way.

The more we seek God, the more our faith grows! David is proof of that.

Father God, I am doing my best to trust You completely. My faith grows stronger as I learn to trust You not only with big things but with the small things in my life. Amen.

DAY 223

You have never been tempted to sin in any different way than other people. God is faithful. He will not allow you to be tempted more than you can take. But when you are tempted, He will make a way for you to keep from falling into sin.

1 CORINTHIANS 10:13

Is there something you know you shouldn't do, but it's hard to keep from doing it? Maybe you find it hard to avoid sneaking an extra cookie from that package in the cabinet. Or maybe your friend wants you to go into the neighbors' yard and swim in their pool when they aren't home. You know you shouldn't—but it's tempting.

Satan is the one who tries to get you to sin. You might think that he is tempting you more than he tempts others. But today's verse says that there is nothing unusual about what tempts you.

Satan works very hard on Christians. But we know from 1 Corinthians 10:13 that God steps in to help us. No matter how weak we may feel, with God on our side we can walk away from anything Satan wants us to do. Isn't it great to know that God is here for us?

Lord, it's hard to resist sinning sometimes. Please help me to be strong and do what is right. Amen.

DAY 224

But they who wait upon the Lord will get new strength. They will rise up with wings like eagles. They will run and not get tired. They will walk and not become weak.

Isaiah 40:31

Imagine yourself in this story: You are hopelessly lost in the mountains. For days you have been wandering rocky paths, eating whatever berries you can find and looking for a way out. Finally you are too tired to go on. So, you sit down quietly and wait to be rescued. And then—the shadow of a great winged creature comes into view. As it gets closer, you see that it is a giant eagle! It swoops down, picks you up with its talons, and carries you home!

Of course, that only happens in fairy tales, but today's Bible verse tells a similar story, a true one.

God says that when you feel lost, tired, and weak, you should stop! Rest, listen for His voice, and wait for Him to rescue you. When you put all your faith and trust in Him, He will arrive at just the right time and bless you with the strength you need to go on.

Dear God, quietly I wait for You. Remove all distractions that might keep me from hearing Your voice. Speak to me, Father. I'm listening. Amen.

DAY 225

"We believe and know You are the Christ.
You are the Son of the Living God."
John 6:69

Many of Jesus' followers found His teachings too difficult to understand and left. So, Jesus asked His disciples where they stood. Would they leave Him too?

Peter answered, "We believe and know You are the Christ. You are the Son of the Living God."

Staying with Jesus meant the disciples went against their society's rulers. It made them enemies of the greatest military empire the world had known. They had left their homes and families to follow Jesus. What would cause them to walk away from all that? Read today's verse again.

The disciples did not just *believe* that Jesus was the Son of God. They *knew* it! They knew in their hearts that Jesus was who He claimed to be.

Simply saying that you believe in Jesus isn't enough. You need to know in your heart that He is real and alive today. His Spirit is with you all the time, helping you, leading you, and loving you.

Where do you stand? Do you know who Jesus is?

Lord, teach me to know that You are God—real in every way, my Creator, my Savior, and my hope. Amen.

DAY 226

"The time is coming, yes, it is here now, when the true worshipers will worship the Father in spirit and in truth. The Father wants that kind of worshipers."

JOHN 4:23

What does it mean to worship? It means to honor God in all that we do, to see ourselves as nothing when compared to Him, and to love Him not for what He does for us but because He is God, our Creator.

How should we worship? Jesus tells us.

In John 4:23, He speaks about the kind of worshiper God wants. Isn't that an interesting idea: God tells us how to worship Him. There is a certain kind of worshiper dear to His heart!

Jesus said that true worshipers worship in spirit and in truth. We know that Jesus is truth (John 14:6), and we know that the Holy Spirit lives in us when we accept that Jesus came to save us from sin (Ephesians 1:13). So, when we worship in spirit and truth, we come to honor God with our hearts filled with love for Jesus. That kind of worship gets God's attention.

Think about it: Does your own worship reflect spirit and truth?

O God, when I worship You, send the Holy Spirit to lead me in worshiping You in truth. Amen.

DAY 227

"You are sad now. I will see you again and then your hearts will be full of joy. No one can take your joy from you."

JOHN 16:22

Do you feel sad sometimes? Of course you do! All humans have times when they feel unhappy.

Nonbelievers who know you are a Christian might say unkind things to you when you feel sad—things like "If you really believed in Jesus, you would be singing and dancing all the time!" or "Maybe if you believed harder, you wouldn't feel so sad." Satan loves comments like those because if you aren't careful, they can knock down your faith.

Life on earth isn't always happy. Some days, we cry. And that will continue all our days until we get to heaven. That's when we get to sing and dance and be happy forever! Jesus makes this promise: "I will see you again, and your heart shall rejoice."

Until then, if you feel a bit down, don't allow the words of others to beat you up. Remember this: Jesus cried too. He cried when He saw how sad Mary and Martha were when their brother, Lazarus, died (John 11:35). If Jesus, the Son of God, cried, then surely it is okay for you to cry too.

It is part of being human, Lord, to cry. But I am glad that You understand sadness and comfort me. Amen.

DAY 228

For You are my hope, O Lord God.
You are my trust since I was young.
PSALM 71:5

One of the best things you can do right now is to give all of your hopes and dreams to God. Tell Him where you hope to be when you grow up. Would you like to be a parent? What sort of work would you like to do? And tell God all of your hopes for now—you hope you will get good grades in school; you hope you will make new friends at camp—stuff like that.

When you start giving your hopes and dreams to Him when you are young, then it becomes a habit for your lifetime.

Trust is a part of giving your hopes and dreams to God. Maybe He has something different and better waiting for you. When you give your hopes and dreams to Him, you also trust Him to give you what is best according to His plan for your life.

Spend time every day telling God about your hopes and dreams. Then, someday, many years from now, you can say to Him, "You are my hope, O Lord God. You are my trust since I was young."

Father, I trust You with my hopes and dreams for now and the future. Amen.

DAY 229

"David was a good leader for the people of his day. He did what God wanted. Then he died and was put into a grave close to his father's grave."

ACTS 13:36

David began life as the annoying baby brother to his siblings. None of them—no one—could have known God's amazing plan for David.

In his first act of greatness, David brought the giant soldier Goliath down with his slingshot and a stone.

Surely God had designed a special purpose for David's life.

He gave David a natural talent for music and poetry, which David used to write many of the Bible's psalms. His God-given leadership abilities gave David success on the battlefield and later as king of Israel.

David desired to obey God but failed miserably at times. Yet God looked deep into David's soul and said, "David. . .will please My heart. He will do all I want done" (Acts 13:22). Despite the ups and downs, David accomplished God's plan for his life.

God has a tailor-made plan for you too, and He's designed you with the talents and abilities needed to complete it. Isn't that exciting?

Thank You for the talents and abilities You have given me, Lord. I know they are part of Your plan for me. Help me to use them wisely and according to Your purpose. Amen.

DAY 230

Then the follower whom Jesus loved said to Peter, "It is the Lord!" When Peter heard it was the Lord, he put on his fisherman's coat. (He had taken it off.) Then he jumped into the water.

John 21:7

"When Peter heard". . .in other words, he hadn't actually recognized Jesus at that point. But when Peter understood it was Jesus, risen from the dead, standing there on the shore, he couldn't get off his fishing boat and to shore fast enough!

He grabbed his coat before jumping into the water. Why? It wasn't going to help him swim faster. The heavy woolen garment was more likely to drag him down. So why did he take it with him? Because Peter had no idea of ever returning to the boat. He was all about getting to his Lord!

After the resurrection, the disciples never knew when or where they might meet Jesus—and that's pretty much the situation today.

If Jesus came back right now, would you ask for all kinds of proof and look around to see who is watching? Or would you follow Peter's example and "dive in headfirst" to meet Him?

Jesus, call to me, "Here I am," and I will come to You. I come in faith, wanting to be near You, wanting to learn all that You have to teach me. Amen.

DAY 231

Then the Lord said to him, "Who has made man's mouth? Who makes a man not able to speak or hear? Who makes one blind or able to see? Is it not I, the Lord?"

EXODUS 4:11

God asked Moses to complete some pretty tough jobs. Throughout Exodus chapter 4, we repeatedly hear Moses tell God why God's plan won't work, finally stating, "Uh, Lord, you've picked the wrong guy for the job. . .You see, I'm not good enough" (v. 10).

Did Moses really think this was news to God? In Exodus 4:11, God scolds Moses.

Like Moses, when God asks us to do something, we sometimes have a similar response. We doubt, ignore, get angry, or even laugh (like Sarah in Genesis 18:10–14). In our attempts to tell God why He's wrong, God's response would surely be something like "I know you, better than you know you, so get on with it. . . . Oh, and don't forget. This isn't a solo mission" (Exodus 3:12).

Often, what we label impossible and imperfect is God's perfect way to execute His plans. It's up to us to make ourselves available, remembering we're not alone.

Father, I know that the impossible is possible when You and I tackle it together. If You think I'm good enough, then I am. I'm ready. I'm willing. Let's go! Amen.

DAY 232

Even more than that, I think of everything as worth nothing. It is so much better to know Christ Jesus my Lord. I have lost everything for Him. And I think of these things as worth nothing so that I can have Christ. I want to be as one with Him. I could not be right with God by what the Law said I must do. I was made right with God by faith in Christ.

PHILIPPIANS 3:8–9

Paul gave up everything to follow Jesus. He could have remained a powerful Pharisee, an enemy of Christ, admired by the other Pharisees. But instead, Paul chose Jesus. He traded a lifetime of riches and comfort for Jesus' promise of forever life in heaven.

Paul gave up everything willingly. In fact, he thought none of his past stuff and the admiration of others was worth anything anymore. All he wanted was Jesus. And Paul understood that Jesus was all he needed. He wasn't made right with God by following the Jewish laws. Instead, he pleased God through his solid faith in Christ.

Think about it: Is your faith in Jesus strong, like Paul's, or do you put more faith in whatever you have right now?

Lord, everything I have is worthless compared to You. But I am the wealthiest kid on earth because I have You in my heart and the promise of eternal life. Amen.

DAY 233

Let no one show little respect for you because you are young. Show other Christians how to live by your life.

1 TIMOTHY 4:12

Most of the time, age has its privileges. The older you become, the more responsibilities you are allowed until you're all grown up and you can do whatever you choose.

It doesn't work that way with faith. Think about how Jesus said we should come to Him—like little children!

Some people could live to be 150 and still not understand God the way a little child does. Little kids are really good at believing what they are told. Sadly, as they get older, Satan chips away at their faith and makes it harder for them to believe.

As a young believer, you likely still remember what it's like to believe without any of Satan's obstacles getting in your way. Hold on to that memory and keep believing that way! Then, do your best to remind the grown-ups in your life what it is like to have faith without doubt. You will be doing them a favor!

Dear God, help me to hold on to my little-kid faith, that simple kind of faith without doubt. It is in that purest form of belief that I am nearest to You. Amen.

DAY 234

Jesus was surprised when He heard this. He turned to the people following Him and said, "I tell you, I have not found so much faith even in the Jewish nation."

LUKE 7:9

It's hard to imagine Jesus being surprised. Yet Luke 7:9 says that's exactly what happened.

A soldier had sent for Jesus to come to his house and heal his dying servant. Before Jesus could arrive, however, the soldier sent another message. He told Jesus he wasn't worthy to have Jesus come to his home and that he believed Jesus had the power to heal his servant from where He was. Jesus was surprised by the soldier's faith. He was moved so much, in fact, that He spoke of it to the crowd gathered around Him.

The soldier wasn't the only one whose faith Jesus celebrated. There was the woman who begged Jesus to heal her daughter (Matthew 15:22–28), the four men who tore through the roof of a house to get their paralyzed friend inside to see Jesus (Mark 2:1–5), and a woman who believed that by touching Jesus' cloak she'd be healed (Matthew 9:20–22).

Each one approached Jesus in a different way, but all came to Him with a faith that surprised Him.

Would Jesus be surprised by your faith?

O Jesus, I have faith in You, but I want even more. Increase my faith! Amen.

DAY 235

When I am afraid, I will trust in You. I praise the Word of God. I have put my trust in God. I will not be afraid. What can only a man do to me?

PSALM 56:3–4

King David was forced to fight many wars. First King Saul's armies hunted him. Then the Philistines arrested him. After David became king, his land was attacked several times. Even after David had conquered all his outside enemies, his land was troubled by civil war. His enemies were eager to end his life.

David had many powerful enemies, and he was often tempted to lose hope. He didn't say that he was never afraid, because that wasn't true. There were times, when war loomed and his armies were vastly outnumbered, when he was afraid. But David's key to success was this: "When I am afraid, I will trust in You." When he trusted God would be with him, David's courage returned and he could say, "I will not be afraid."

Most of us today don't have enemies out to kill us, but the idea that helped David survive three thousand years ago works just as well for us today.

God, in You I trust, and I will not be afraid. Trusting You is the key to overcoming my fear. Trusting You makes me strong. Yes, God, I put my trust in You. Amen.

DAY 236

They were surprised and wondered how easy it was for Peter and John to speak. They could tell they were men who had not gone to school. But they knew they had been with Jesus.

Acts 4:13

In Bible times, the priests and the Sadducees were among the most educated men around and probably thought themselves the wisest. Yet, here were two uneducated men, Peter and John, speaking about Jesus and leaving them lost for words.

How did Peter and John come to have such an impact? It wasn't because of something they read in textbooks, although they did study Old Testament scrolls. It wasn't that they learned from their parents what to say. It was Jesus who opened their minds to what was real in the world!

Unlike Peter and John, we don't get to be with Jesus face-to-face, but we do get to invite Him into our lives, and with Him comes the kind of understanding He gave Peter and John.

So, when you are faced with a problem, consider not only what you've learned in books and school and what others think you should do. Ask Jesus what to do. When you do things His way, others will notice.

Jesus, my Teacher, how wonderful it is that You are willing and eager to share Your wisdom with me. Amen.

DAY 237

"He must become more important. I must become less important."
JOHN 3:30

God had His plan in place. He had chosen Jesus' cousin John the Baptist to preach to the people and prepare them for Jesus' ministry.

When John's disciples complained that a new preacher, Jesus, was drawing followers from their group, John said, "He must become more important. I must become less important."

John understood that his job was to prepare the way for the Messiah. It was his time, now, to move aside. John prepared the path for Jesus and then stepped out of the way, taking the focus off himself and shifting it to Jesus.

Maybe you feel like you're not good enough to be one of Jesus' helpers. Not everyone can preach—like John did. But there are so many other things that you can do. Be kind to everyone. Give food or clothing to the poor. Pray for others. Every time you help someone, you act as Jesus' helper.

Step aside from what you want to do and focus on Jesus. He wants to be greater—more important—than anything else in your life.

Lord, I am Your helper ready and excited to serve. Put me where You need me most. Amen.

DAY 238

You should think about the kind of life you are living.

2 PETER 3:11

Try this. List three things that describe your life right now.

Maybe you chose to answer with adjectives, like *happy* or *excited*. Or maybe you listed things that are important to you, like playing sports or dancing. Often, people describe their lives by the ways they feel and the things they do.

But God wants us to look at life through His eyes.

Second Peter 3:11 says that you should think about the *kind* of life you are living. In other words, are you living a life pleasing to God? Or would the way you live make Him shake His head and say, "Oh no. I need to help this kid turn toward Me"?

Everyone, kids and grown-ups, needs to think about how their lives look to God.

At bedtime each night, take a few minutes to think about the way you lived that day. Are there a few things for which you need to ask God's forgiveness? Did you do something good for others? What can you do tomorrow that will please God? The more you think about these things, the more likely you will live in a way that makes the Lord happy.

Dear God, I want to live a life that pleases You. Please show me the way. Amen.

DAY 239

How long, O Lord? Will You forget me forever?
How long will You hide Your face from me?
PSALM 13:1

Little children love playing hide-and-seek. But what if the hider hides too well? After a while, a child can feel forgotten, left alone, and afraid.

Of course, you would never play with a younger brother or sister that way, but you can imagine how frightening it would be to feel abandoned and alone.

That's how King David felt when he wrote Psalm 13. His heart was filled with sadness. His enemies succeeded while David failed, and worse, they let him know that they were happy about it. And with all that stuff going on, as long and as hard as David prayed, God seemed to have left him alone.

Have you ever felt that way? It's difficult to believe that God still loves you when your prayers go unanswered. But, you should remember that God asks us to wait for His answer and to trust that He will answer when the time is just right.

While writing, David remembered this, and he ended his psalm with these words: "But I have trusted in Your loving-kindness. My heart will be full of joy because You will save me" (v. 5).

Father, I know that You will never leave me alone and afraid. I trust You. Amen.

DAY 240

I have fought the good fight, I have finished the race, I have kept the faith.
2 TIMOTHY 4:7 NIV

In 1992, Derek Redmond was determined to win the Olympic 400-meter dash. But less than halfway around the track his hamstring tore, and Redmond collapsed in pain. Thousands of spectators and a worldwide television audience watched the other runners leave Redmond in their dust. But he picked himself up and hobbled after them.

The runner's tears and suffering were too much for his father, who ran out of the stands onto the track to help his son cross the finish line.

We'll never know if Derek Redmond could have finished that race on his own. In his moment of need, he didn't have to depend on his own strength; he leaned on his father.

Our lives are like a race. We might set out with our eyes on a prize. But there are traps and obstacles along the way. Our faith will take a beating—it might be in shreds as we approach the end. We might have to hobble, hop, and crawl, but we know this—leaning on our Father, God, is our guarantee of crossing the finish line.

Lord, I've done my best. There's such a short distance to cross that line. Carry me, please; I can't get there on my own. Amen.

DAY 241

Then little children were brought to Him that He might put His hands on them and pray for them. The followers spoke sharp words to them. But Jesus said, "Let the little children come to Me. Do not stop them. The holy nation of heaven is made up of ones like these."

MATTHEW 19:13-14

Everyone crowded around Jesus. They wanted healing, and they wanted Him to pray for their needs. One by one, Jesus put His hands on them and prayed. Some mothers had brought their children to see Jesus. They wanted Him to bless their little ones. But when they tried to get through the crowds, some of Jesus' followers told them to go away. The Bible doesn't tell us why. But maybe those followers didn't think that the kids were as important as the grown-ups.

In the middle of that big crowd of people, Jesus saw what was happening. He called out, "Let the little children come to Me. Do not stop them."

Kids are important to Jesus. They always have been and always will be. Jesus is never too busy to spend time with you and hear your prayers.

Dear Jesus, You always have time for me. You make me feel special and important. Thank You, Jesus. I love You! Amen.

DAY 242

Then Eliakim. . .said to Rabshakeh, "Speak to your servants in the Aramaic language, for we understand it. Do not speak with us in the language of Judah. The people on the wall might hear it." But Rabshakeh said to them, "Has my ruler sent me to speak these words to your ruler and to you, and not to the men sitting on the wall?"

2 KINGS 18:26–27

Today's verses might be confusing unless you focus on the idea of language. In this time of ancient kings, the rich and important spoke Aramaic while the lower class—the people sitting on the wall—spoke Hebrew. What good was it to the lower class if the ancient Old Testament writings weren't translated into their language?

Over thousands of years, the Bible has been translated into thousands of languages. Pretty amazing! But, even so, several hundred of those don't include *all* the books of the Bible. And millions of people today do not have a single verse of the Bible translated into their language.

Pray today for those who still have not heard the complete Word of God. Ask God to find ways to get Bibles to them in languages they can understand.

God, please! The whole world needs to know all about You. Get Bibles into the hands of all the people. Amen.

DAY 243

"For we must tell what we have seen and heard."

ACTS 4:20

One of the men speaking here is Peter. He is addressing the religious leaders in the same temple where, a short time before, he had denied that he knew Jesus. Now Peter stands there accusing the priests of nothing less than the murder of his Lord. He isn't scared, and he isn't backing down. What made Peter so brave?

Fear isn't important to him anymore. Peter can't help but speak because he had seen and heard the amazing things Jesus had done. He saw Jesus, walking and talking, risen from the dead. The Peter who denied Christ would never have spoken like this to the priests if he didn't know that Jesus had sent him help. The Holy Spirit, the helper, was behind, around, and inside Peter.

Our world can be troublesome. Sometimes you might be afraid, like Peter had been. But if you believe, like Peter did, that the Holy Spirit is always in and around you, you can stand up to anyone—or anything.

I believe it, Jesus! You are the Son of God, the risen Christ, the one who sent the helper through whom I have strength to carry out God's will. Amen.

DAY 244

"Be strong and have strength of heart. Do not be afraid or shake with fear because of them. For the Lord your God is the One Who goes with you. He will be faithful to you. He will not leave you alone."

DEUTERONOMY 31:6

Deuteronomy 31:6 is part of a speech that Moses delivered to the Israelites just before they entered Canaan, the Promised Land. Moses told them that he would not be traveling with them into Canaan. God had chosen to replace Moses with a new leader, Joshua. The Lord Himself would go on ahead with Joshua to take possession of the land (Deuteronomy 31:1–7).

The Israelites worried that fighting might occur with the Canaanites. But Moses encouraged them to be strong and trust that the Lord would be with and protect them. Many times, Moses reminded the Israelites that they needed to trust in God. God's words are even repeated in the New Testament in Hebrews 13:5: "I will never leave you or let you be alone."

Even today, trouble exists in the part of the world known as the Promised Land. But God continues to promise the Israelites—and us too—"I will never leave you or let you be alone."

O God, You are the one who gives me courage when I am afraid. Thank You for promising to never leave me. Amen.

DAY 245

So Ananias went to that house. He put his hands on Saul and said, "Brother Saul, the Lord Jesus has sent me to you."
ACTS 9:17

Ananias was a follower of Jesus. This kind and faithful man had heard of Saul of Tarsus and was afraid to meet him.

Saul (later known as Paul) had murdered Christians—that is, until Jesus visited him on the road to Damascus. That event left Paul blinded and terrified. He hid in the dark of someone's spare room and didn't eat or drink for three days.

To Ananias, Paul must have seemed a wild and extremely dangerous man, very different from himself. But because Jesus was now in Paul's heart, the first word Ananias spoke to Paul was "Brother."

How can people so different from us ever be enough like us that we call them "brother" or "sister"? Maybe you know someone who you consider different from you. Maybe that difference has made you avoid that person. No doubt, Ananias felt the same about Paul. But we need to look at others through Jesus' eyes and treat everyone with loving-kindness. Why? Because we believers are all God's children!

Lord, open my eyes to see how other kids and I are alike. Help me to love them because we Christians are all brothers and sisters in God's big family. Amen.

DAY 246

The Lord said, "These people show respect to Me with their mouth, and honor Me with their lips, but their heart is far from Me. Their worship of Me is worth nothing. They teach rules that men have made."

ISAIAH 29:13

Are there certain prayers that you recite at mealtime, at bedtime, or in church? You probably know the words very well and say them with ease. But when was the last time you really thought about those words and what they mean?

From God's viewpoint, the actions of our hearts speak louder than our words. If our prayers consist of mindlessly repeating words, then we are missing out on connecting with our God who loves us and wants a relationship with us through our praying. In other words, God wants us to be thinking of Him and loving Him when we pray.

Isaiah 29:13 is a reminder that God looks beyond the words of our prayers and considers the heart that says them. When you pray, remember that God is listening. The next time you recite a prayer from memory, think about its words. Feel them, and speak them from your heart.

Father, thank You for reminding me to think about my prayers. When I pray a familiar prayer, I will pray from my heart. Amen.

DAY 247

But God showed His love to us. While we were still sinners, Christ died for us.

ROMANS 5:8

We didn't deserve Jesus. If you read the Old Testament, you'll discover that time after time, from the very beginning, people turned against God and did what was wrong. And still, God loved us all so much that He sent His only Son to die for us, a bunch of sinners. Nailed to a cross, Jesus accepted the punishment for our sins—past, present, and future. And all God asked in return was for us to come to Him for forgiveness and accept Jesus Christ as our Savior.

No, we didn't deserve Jesus. But He gave His life for us anyway.

We will continue to sin, and God will continue to forgive us and love us, thanks to Jesus.

What can we do to show Jesus our appreciation? When someone asks for help, we can lend a hand readily and without complaining. Maybe they don't deserve our help. But we should help anyway, remembering that Jesus helped us, a bunch of sinners.

Jesus, You generously gave Your life for me—someone undeserving of Your sacrifice. When someone who I feel is undeserving asks for my help, I will remember what You did for me. Amen.

DAY 248

The Lord is slow to anger and great in power. The Lord will be sure to punish the guilty. The way He punishes is in the strong-wind and storm. The clouds are the dust under His feet.

NAHUM 1:3

Clouds always point to God's power. He created the clouds, and today's verse tells us that God is so huge, the clouds are merely the dust under His feet. He lives within and beyond the heavens.

By watching clouds, we see hints of God's presence. We see Him as Creator when we imagine the different shapes the clouds resemble: animals, funny faces, flocks of sheep.

Storm clouds remind us of God's power. He commands the raging winds, the crashing thunder, and the flashes of lightning. Nahum 1:3 says, "The way He punishes is in the strong-wind and storm."

But God is very patient and slow to punish His people. He waits for us to acknowledge Him as our King and Savior and to ask for His forgiveness. Then, He welcomes us into His arms.

Look up at the clouds today and remember, they are just dust under God's feet. He towers high above them, looking down at us from heaven.

Lord, I look up and see You in the clouds, the sunshine, and the stars. What wonders lie beyond them? Someday I will see You in Your heaven. Amen.

DAY 249

Do not have anything to do with a man given to anger, or go with a man who has a bad temper. Or you might learn his ways and get yourself into a trap.

PROVERBS 22:24-25

The book of Proverbs, in the Old Testament, is filled with good advice. Today's scripture passage warns about the kind of people we hang out with. It tells us that someone's bad behavior can rub off onto us, if we aren't careful.

Proverbs 22:24-25 says not to hang with angry people. But, you could replace the word *anger* with any other sin. In other words, you should choose your friends wisely and stay away from those who willingly do what is wrong.

It can be easy to fall into a trap. For example: If someone speaks angry words to you, then you might speak angry words back. If someone sneaks an extra piece of candy when they should take just one, you might be tempted to take an extra piece too.

King Solomon, the author of Proverbs 22, says we shouldn't hang out with people who are always angry or those who behave badly. Their behavior can be catching, like a cold or the flu. Wise words from a very wise king!

Heavenly Father, please help me to choose friends who love You and do their best to live by Your rules. Amen.

DAY 250

I do not understand myself. I want to do what is right but I do not do it. Instead, I do the very thing I hate.

ROMANS 7:15

"I can't do anything right."

"I failed."

"I should have done better."

People can be so hard on themselves! They get it into their heads that they need to be perfect or do things perfectly. With those thoughts in mind, when they don't live up to their own expectations, they feel like failures.

The truth is that everyone is a failure. Why? Because our example of perfection is Jesus, and no one can be as perfect as He is.

Paul was one of Jesus' strongest followers, and yet he thought of himself as a failure. When he wrote the words in today's verse, he hated it that as much as he loved God, he still continued to sin.

Paul also wrote, "There is not one person who is right with God. No, not even one" (3:10). "For all. . .have sinned and have missed the shining-greatness of God" (3:23).

No one is perfect. No one can be perfect. So—stop being hard on yourself. Your best is good enough.

I struggle with perfection, Lord. I try my best and still I fail. But my best is good enough for You! Teach me not to be so hard on myself. Amen.

DAY 251

The heavens are telling of the greatness of God and the great open spaces above show the work of His hands.

PSALM 19:1

The universe. Outer space. Called by any name, it's an amazing place filled with stars, comets, black holes, and our home planet, Earth.

The first verse of the Bible clearly states that God created the universe. Scientific observations agree that our universe did indeed have a beginning, just as the Bible says.

But science goes much deeper than the birth of the universe. It shows an Earth fine-tuned for intelligent life, an amazingly rare possibility even in the vastness of space. The evidence points to a planet designed by a Creator.

With the heavens displaying the Creator's glory, it shouldn't surprise us that scientists also discovered that the conditions that make life possible on Earth provide a perfect setting to study our universe, as well.

Stand outside on a clear night and look into the sky. Think about the magnificence and greatness of God's creation. Only a mighty and powerful God could create all the wonders you see.

Father, I see what Your mighty hands have made, nothing out of place, the whole universe in line with Your perfect will. You are so awesome! Amen.

DAY 252

For this reason, we always pray for you. We pray that our God will make you worth being chosen. We pray that His power will help you do the good things you want to do. We pray that your work of faith will be complete.

2 THESSALONIANS 1:11

Paul, the Bible's greatest letter writer, is at it again in this verse, this time writing to his church friends in Thessalonica, a city in ancient Greece.

Paul spent much time praying for his friends in various churches. For the Thessalonians, he prayed that God would make them worth being chosen. In other words, give them all they needed to do what God wanted them to do. Paul's words suggest that his friends already had in mind their calling—God's plan for them. He asked that God use His power to help the Thessalonians stay strong in their faith and keep working toward their goal.

The prayer Paul prayed for the Thessalonians can also apply to us. God has a plan for everyone, and through His power God helps us to complete His plan.

When you pray tonight, ask God to increase your faith so, like Paul's friends, you can do the good things God has planned for you to do.

By faith, I believe that You will fulfill the plans You have for me. Thank You, Father! Amen.

DAY 253

For I know that nothing can keep us from the love of God. Death cannot! Life cannot! Angels cannot! Leaders cannot! Any other power cannot! Hard things now or in the future cannot! The world above or the world below cannot! Any other living thing cannot keep us away from the love of God which is ours through Christ Jesus our Lord.

ROMANS 8:38–39

Lots of things try to separate us from God—way more things than you can think of. Why? Because God's love is a great prize! Otherwise no one on this earth (or below it) would care.

Jesus warned us. He said, "In the world you will have much trouble" (John 16:33). And then He added this comforting thought: "But take hope! I have power over the world!"

It's a tough battle to stand firm against trouble, but in Romans 8:38–39, Paul tells us to stay strong.

If you'll only hold on to Jesus, He'll wrap His arms and His love around you. Any trouble you can think of—earthquakes, meteor strikes, storms, whatever!—can never break His embrace.

**Wrap Your strong arms around me, Jesus.
Embrace me in love whenever evil tries to separate us.
I know that I will be safe resting in Your arms. Amen.**

DAY 254

Your Word have I hid in my heart, that I may not sin against You.
PSALM 119:11

God allowed Jesus to be tempted by Satan, but He didn't give in, because the Word of God was in His heart.

It must have been difficult even for Jesus. The Bible says that He had been in the wilderness for a long time. He hadn't eaten for forty days and nights, and His human side must have been in a weakened state. It's difficult for anyone to function well after experiencing that kind of hunger.

But Jesus knew the Word of God, the Bible, very well. Each time Satan tempted Him, Jesus was able to ward off trouble by using God's Word as a weapon.

This same weapon is available to us today. By reading and thinking about God's Word, we become much stronger in our faith. It becomes easier to battle temptation. The Bible says that we will never be tempted beyond that which we are able to handle (1 Corinthians 10:13). And Psalm 119:11 reminds us that we can win against temptation by filling our hearts and minds with God's Word.

Dear God, when I face trouble, I will rely on Your Word. I will find comfort, refreshment, and strength in its everlasting power. Amen.

DAY 255

And he broke in pieces the brass snake that Moses had made. For until those days the people of Israel burned special perfume to it. It was called Nehushtan.

2 KINGS 18:4

The Israelites became impatient with Moses and God and complained bitterly against them, so God sent poisonous snakes that bit many of them. When the people repented, God told Moses to hammer out a bronze snake and hold it up on a pole, and "if a snake bit any man, he would live when he looked at the brass snake" (Numbers 21:9).

The Israelites hung on to this symbol of God's power for hundreds of years. Maybe they thought it still had healing powers many years later. But somewhere during the centuries the Israelites began to worship the bronze snake and burn incense to it.

It was King Hezekiah who began destroying the idols. He named the snake Nehushtan, which means "unclean thing." Then he smashed it into pieces.

God gives us many helpful things, good things, but if we begin to worship those things instead of God Himself—or give them too much of our attention—then they become idols and need to be destroyed.

Heavenly Father, I'm grateful for the good things You have given me, but open my eyes if I have turned any of them into idols. I want to worship only You. Amen.

DAY 256

Now that which we see is as if we were looking in a broken mirror. But then we will see everything. Now I know only a part. But then I will know everything in a perfect way. That is how God knows me right now.

1 CORINTHIANS 13:12

Some carnivals and fairs have fun houses with mirrors that make your reflection look strange. They might make you extremely tall or wide or even wiggly. One thing is for sure—if someone didn't know you, they would never recognize the real you just by seeing you in one of those broken mirrors.

In 1 Corinthians 13:12, Paul says we see the world as if we are looking into a broken mirror. He meant that we can't see the world through God's eyes and know everything about it perfectly, the way God does. We can't even know everything about ourselves the way that God does.

But Paul adds that when we get to heaven, then we will see things with godly eyes. Imagine how perfect, beautiful, and wonderful everything will look. And that includes us! Then we will see ourselves the way God made us—perfect in every way.

There is so much about the world and myself that I can't know, God. I'm looking forward to heaven someday so I can see things the way that You do. Amen.

DAY 257

The Lord said to Moses, "Say to the people of Israel, 'These are the special suppers of the Lord, which you will keep for holy meetings. These are My special suppers.' "

LEVITICUS 23:1–2

Holidays ("special suppers") in ancient Israel combined celebrations with worship to honor God's amazing blessings.

The weekly Sabbath, although a day for rest and worship, served as a time for Israelites to remember that God had saved them from slavery in Egypt (Deuteronomy 5:15).

At the feast of harvest, or Pentecost, loaves of bread were presented as an offering from the wheat harvest, along with sacrificial animals. Jewish tradition also links this feast to the day God gave Moses the Ten Commandments on Mount Sinai.

During the Feast of Booths, the Israelites camped out in fragile shelters for seven days as a remembrance of God's care and protection following their escape from Egypt. This joyous feast took place at the end of the harvest season and included a time of thanksgiving to God for the year's crops.

Like the Israelites, we should use all our holidays to celebrate God's goodness and remember the blessings He has given us.

Can you think of ways to include God in all your celebrations?

Father, I'm sorry that so many people forget to honor You on holidays. I will remember to worship You on holidays and every day! Amen.

DAY 258

The eyes of those who do not believe are made blind by Satan who is the god of this world. He does not want the light of the Good News to shine in their hearts. This Good News shines as the shining-greatness of Christ. Christ is as God is.

2 CORINTHIANS 4:4

In this verse, the "god of this world" is Satan. "Those who do not believe" are those who think they are too wise for faith. The "eyes" are their hearts. Satan blinds their hearts to the good news that Jesus died so they can go to heaven someday.

The idea that they can't understand the good news breaks the Lord's heart. But there is something that we can do! We can show nonbelievers Jesus in how we speak and act. We can make them notice that we are always kind, even when others are not kind back. We can speak softly and gently and avoid getting angry. In other words, we can do our best to be like Jesus and hope they will see.

God is more powerful than Satan! He has a way of making blind hearts see. And often He uses us—His children—to open a nonbeliever's "eyes."

Heavenly Father, even where my faith is not welcomed, I will honor You and do my best to be like Jesus. Amen.

DAY 259

They turned away from the Lord and did not serve Him. The anger of the Lord was against Israel.

JUDGES 10:6–7

Does God get angry? Yes, He does. God is good, loving, compassionate, patient, truthful, faithful, just, and slow to anger. But He does become angry—not in an imperfect human way but with a holy anger against evil.

Jesus expressed this kind of holy anger when He sent the greedy and ungodly merchants out of God's temple (Matthew 21:12–13). In the same way, after the Israelites returned to idol worship, God allowed neighboring nations to bully them for eighteen years (Judges 10:8).

From the beginning of time, God has expressed His anger against all forms of wickedness and idolatry. But—think about this—His anger toward evil is also an expression of love for those of us who are good and love Him.

Anger is best left to God.

Paul taught believers, "If you are angry, do not let it become sin. . . . Do not let the devil start working in your life" (Ephesians 4:26–27).

If you become angry, get over it! Let God deal with your problem before Satan sneaks in and makes you do something you'll regret.

Help me to control my anger so I will not sin. Thank You, Lord. Amen.

DAY 260

So the missionaries went away from the court happy that they could suffer shame because of His Name.

ACTS 5:41

The missionaries in this verse were Jesus' disciples. With the Holy Spirit's help, they did many miracles among the people, and because of that, many more people believed in Jesus.

Those in the ancient Jewish court didn't like all the attention the disciples got. So, they arrested the men and punished them with a whipping. Then they let them go and told them to stop speaking about the Lord.

As the disciples limped away in pain, they rejoiced that God had allowed them to suffer for Him.

How could suffering be cause for celebration?

The Bible says, "But even if you should suffer for what is right, you are blessed" (1 Peter 3:14 NIV). God sees, and He will bless you for doing what is right.

When Jesus was arrested and taken to the cross, He continued to be gentle and respectful to those who hurt Him. The Bible also says this is how we should be. Then others will be ashamed when they see how we react (1 Peter 3:16).

Even if someone makes fun of you, stand strong for Jesus. God will see and bless you.

Dear Jesus, sometimes I am bullied because of my Christian faith. Surely You understand how that feels. Help me to stand strong and focus on Your blessings. Amen.

DAY 261

He answered me, "I am all you need. I give you My loving-favor. My power works best in weak people." I am happy to be weak and have troubles so I can have Christ's power in me.

2 CORINTHIANS 12:9

Eric Liddell was a missionary to China. He wrote a prayer telling God that whatever terrible things happened to him, he would not lose his faith. He said nothing would cause him to stop loving God and others. He would have "a heart full of gratitude."

He didn't mention that he was in a Japanese prison camp, not knowing if his family was safe. Also, he was dying of a brain tumor.

But Eric's certainty that God loved him—and that Jesus had died for him—was enough to prove that his blessings still outweighed his problems. He accomplished work that left others in the camp thinking of him as something like a saint.

Eric's story reminds us that our bad times don't have to be hopeless times. When we are weak, God still can do great things through us. When you think you have nothing else going for you, if you lean on God, you'll have more than enough.

Lord, in my weakness You give me strength, and You are my comfort in times of trouble. With You in my heart, I have all that I need. Amen.

DAY 262

The Lord was sorry that He had made man on the earth. He had sorrow in His heart.
GENESIS 6:6

Some people point to Noah and the flood and say, "I can't trust a God who got angry and wiped everyone out!"

But God was not angry. He was sorry.

God did everything possible to avoid the flood. He gave people plenty of time to turn from their wickedness. He patiently waited until there was only one good man left—Noah.

God didn't send the flood without warning. Noah warned the world for a hundred years (the time it took the ark to be built), but no one believed him. By the time the rain began, the world was out of control with sin. No one cared about God.

Now we see the flood in a whole new way—God was sorry that His people had filled His world with sin. He had to do something to stop them.

God is good to those who love Him. So good that He sent Jesus to save us from sin. The Bible gives us every reason to put our whole life into His hands, today and forever.

My loving and forgiving God, You knew that humans would continue to sin, so You sent Jesus to save us. Your love for us is greater than any other love! Amen.

DAY 263

Nothing should be done because of pride or thinking about yourself. Think of other people as more important than yourself.

PHILIPPIANS 2:3

What is the first thing you notice about someone you don't know? Maybe it's the way that person looks. But first impressions based just on appearance don't tell us much about a person. The way people behave shows us so much more!

Jesus didn't dress in fancy clothes. He looked just like an ordinary guy dressed in a robe and sandals. But when people looked at Jesus, they saw love. They saw it in how He looked at them, the way He spoke to them, and even how He said their names. Those who met Jesus during the short time He was on the earth must have truly been filled with His love. The proof of this is the huge crowds that followed Him. The people knew that Jesus truly cared about them and would heal and help them.

The way Jesus behaved made every person feel important. And that is how we should behave too. Think of yourself as Jesus' disciple. With everyone you meet, let His love shine through you.

Jesus, I want to be like You. Extend Your love to others through my smile, my words, and my acts. Amen.

DAY 264

"Call to Me, and I will answer you. And I will show you great and wonderful things which you do not know."
JEREMIAH 33:3

Today's verse is the word of God spoken directly to the prophet Jeremiah.

For forty years, Jeremiah had been sharing God's warning that the cities of Judah and Jerusalem would be destroyed because of their people's sinfulness. Now God's and Jeremiah's words were coming true: the Babylonian army was ready to attack.

King Zedekiah, Judah's king, accused Jeremiah of siding with the Babylonians and had him thrown into prison. But while Jeremiah was there, God told him to pray. "Call to Me," God said, "and I will answer you." Then God promised to give Jeremiah wisdom about things he did not know.

Proverbs 2:6 says, "For the Lord gives wisdom. Much learning and understanding come from His mouth."

If we pray to God, He will answer us and also "show [us] great and wonderful things which [we] do not know." Just as God gave Jeremiah wisdom when he prayed, He will do the same for you.

God, I need Your help. I've been struggling with a problem, and I'm still not sure what to do. But You know! Please, God, guide me with Your wisdom. Amen.

DAY 265

"It is bad for you who are rich. You are receiving all that you will get."
LUKE 6:24

Did Jesus dislike rich people? It might seem that way from His words in Luke 6:24. And if you remember, in Matthew 19:12, Jesus said that a camel could more easily step through a needle's eye than a rich person could make it through the gates of heaven. But, no, Jesus did not dislike the rich.

He didn't dislike the rich, but He reminded them that everything they owned on earth was short-lived. In other words, they could not take their wealth with them to heaven. And forever life in heaven is worth far more than anything on earth.

Jesus' message is for all people. Be content with what you have (Hebrews 13:5). "Do not gather together for yourself riches of this earth. They will be eaten by bugs and become rusted. Men can break in and steal them. Gather together riches in heaven where they will not be eaten by bugs or become rusted. Men cannot break in and steal them" (Matthew 6:19–20).

Remember: if you have Jesus and His promise of forever life, then you have everything you need.

Lord Jesus, thank You for Your many blessings. I am grateful for them all, but nothing compares to my relationship with You. It is always first in my heart. Amen.

DAY 266

As Jesus went from there, He saw a man called Matthew. Matthew was sitting at his work gathering taxes. Jesus said to him, "Follow Me." Matthew got up and followed Jesus.

MATTHEW 9:9

God often uses the most unlikely people to carry out His plans. Think about David, the young shepherd boy in the Old Testament. God chose him to become Israel's greatest king. And in the New Testament, we read about Saul, the angry man who murdered Christians. He became Paul, one of Jesus' greatest followers.

Jesus chose the unlikely to be His disciples. At least seven were fishermen. Jesus said He would make them fishers of men, meaning that He had chosen them to recruit others to follow Him. And Jesus chose Matthew, a tax collector, who worked in a business known to take advantage of people and their money. And Judas Iscariot. Jesus chose him knowing that Judas would betray Him and turn Him over to soldiers to die on the cross.

We might not always understand why God uses unlikely people to do His work, but we trust that He knows what He's doing.

Do you wonder if God might choose you to do something great? Pray and ask Him to lead you.

God, You know the plans You have for me. How can I serve You? Show me the way. Amen.

DAY 267

When Peter came, Cornelius got down at his feet and worshiped him. But Peter raised him up and said, "Get up! I am just a man like you."

ACTS 10:25–26

The disciple Peter loved Jesus, but he was human and made mistakes. His faith was sometimes weak, he spoke "sharp words" to Jesus, and he even denied that he knew Jesus (Matthew 14:28–31; 16:21–23; 26:69–75). Who would ever imagine that anyone would mistake Peter for a god and worship him?

After Jesus rose from the dead and the disciples were filled with the Holy Spirit, Peter became a powerhouse and a miracle worker. He prayed, and the sick were healed and the dead were raised to life. Even his shadow healed people (Acts 3:1–8; 5:15; 9:32–42)!

So, when Peter entered Cornelius' house, this Roman soldier bowed down to worship him. Peter quickly grabbed Cornelius, pulled him to his feet, and set him straight—he was to bow down and worship no one but God!

This is good advice for us when we're tempted to bow to and worship some leader, entertainer, sports figure, or any other person or thing. God is the only one worthy of our worship.

Father, You are my only God, and I worship only You. I will not bow down to any person or anything on earth. Amen.

DAY 268

Then He said to me, "Son of man, eat what is in front of you. Eat this book, then go and speak to the people of Israel."
EZEKIEL 3:1

"Eat this book"! What in the world was God telling the prophet Ezekiel to do?

He wasn't *really* telling Ezekiel to start chomping on the book set before him. The "book" was the Word of God, the scriptures, and God wanted Ezekiel to know very well what God wanted him to say to the Israelites. God's message to them was in that book (back then, a scroll) set before him.

When Satan wanted Jesus to turn stones into bread, Jesus said, "Man is not to live on bread only. Man is to live by every word that God speaks" (Matthew 4:4). God's Word, the Bible, is the healthiest "food" we can "eat." Its words nourish us and give us strength.

The prophet Jeremiah said, "Your words were found and I ate them. And Your words became a joy to me and the happiness of my heart" (Jeremiah 15:16).

The Bible brings us joy, life, hope, peace, comfort, encouragement, and so much more. It also helps us to preach the good news of Jesus Christ.

Have you eaten God's Word today?

**Nourish me with Your Word, God.
Fill me up with Your scriptures. Amen.**

DAY 269

"Do something to let me see that you have turned from your sins. Do not begin to say to yourselves, 'We have Abraham as our father.' I tell you, God can make children for Abraham out of these stones."

LUKE 3:8

To understand today's verse, you need to remember God's promise to Abraham:

"I will give you many children. . . . You will be the father of many nations. . . . Many will come from you. . . . Kings will come from you. I will make My agreement between Me and you and your children after you through their whole lives for all time. I will be God to you and to your children's children after you" (Genesis 17:2, 4, 6–7).

God honored His promise, and Abraham became the father, grandfather, great-great-grandfather. . .of all the people of Israel.

Then after a while, the Israelites thought they were more important than others. They became lazy, and their faith in God was weak. It was John the Baptist, many, many generations later, who spoke the words in Luke 3:8 warning God's people to get up and get busy working for the Lord.

How about you? Are you working for Jesus?

Jesus, put me to work. What can I do to spread Your Word? I am ready and willing. Amen.

DAY 270

Now there was no one to be found in all the land of Israel who made things of iron. For the Philistines said, "The Hebrews might make swords or spears." So each one of the Israelites went down to the Philistines to get his plow, his pick, his ax, or his grain cutter sharpened. He had to pay two-thirds part of a piece of silver to have the plows and picks sharpened, and one-third part of a piece of silver to have the axes and grain cutters sharpened. So on the day of battle there was no sword or spear in the hands of any of the people who were with Saul and Jonathan. But Saul and his son Jonathan had them.

1 SAMUEL 13:19–22

Technology in Old Testament days was all about who had the strongest spears and swords. The Philistines planned to use their advanced technology in metal making against the Israelites. But God had another plan.

Surprisingly, not much has changed since then. Nations still compete for the best technology and use their technology against other nations.

The lesson is that even the most advanced twenty-first century technology can't stop God's plans. Just as He provided for the Israelites to win their battle back then, He provides for us now.

You set Your plan in action, and man-made technology can't stop it. How great You are, Lord! Amen.

DAY 271

"No one can have two bosses. He will hate the one and love the other. Or he will listen to the one and work against the other. You cannot have both God and riches as your boss at the same time."

MATTHEW 6:24

Jesus reminds us in today's verse that we should use our possessions and money for God's purpose. If we let our stuff be our boss, then we'll have no time or space in our hearts for God.

Do this: make a list of the five most important things in your life, in their order of importance.

Was God at the top of your list? Was He on your list at all?

Some of the things we think are important—family, friends, pets, school, hobbies, and games—are good things, but we place them out of order in our priorities. God is our boss. The boss above all other bosses! And He wants to be number one in our hearts.

So, when you find your stuff getting in between you and God, stand up to it and say, "Hey! You're not the boss of me!"

God, I am so busy with school, friends, and other things that often my priorities shift away from You. Forgive me, please. I will try to do better. Amen.

DAY 272

But the fruit that comes from having the Holy Spirit in our lives is: love, joy, peace, not giving up, being kind, being good, having faith, being gentle, and being the boss over our own desires. The Law is not against these things.

GALATIANS 5:22-23

This is part of Paul's letter to the churches in Galatia.

The Galatians had been trying to follow the laws set forth in the Old Testament. While there was nothing wrong with that, they were forgetting that Jesus came to save them from the sins they committed. Paul reminded them that Jesus was more important than the Law, or anything else.

True faith in Jesus changes how a person acts. When His Spirit, the Holy Spirit, comes into a person, He takes control of the person's desires. He gives them a clear idea of right and wrong. When the Holy Spirit lives inside someone, it shows on the outside through how a person behaves. Paul calls those behaviors the "fruit" of the Holy Spirit.

Love, joy, peace, not giving up, being kind, being good, having faith, being gentle, and being the boss over our own desires are the fruits of the Spirit.

Does the Holy Spirit live in your heart? How do you know?

God, I want the way I behave to show the world that the Holy Spirit lives in my heart. Amen.

DAY 273

If a man has not worked to be saved, but has put his trust in God Who saves men from the punishment of their sins, that man is made right with God because of his trust in God.

Romans 4:5

Do you know the Opposite Game? When the leader says, "Step forward," you step back. When she says "green," you say, "red." It's hard, because you have to think before you act.

Some people play a sort of opposite game with God. Today's verse reminds us that God does not provide a ticket to heaven based on good work. Still, people think they will get to heaven through working hard! They say, "I've worked hard at being a good person. I hope God will let me into heaven."

It isn't about work—it's all about trust. Trusting Jesus is the only way to get to heaven. A person can do good work, but if they have not accepted Jesus as Savior, then they won't get there.

Work to please God, yes, but remember that the only thing that will get you into heaven is trusting your Savior, Jesus.

Jesus, I understand that the only way to heaven is by believing in You and Your gift of salvation. Thank You for leading me there. Amen.

DAY 274

My body and my heart may grow weak, but God is the strength of my heart and all I need forever.

PSALM 73:26

You may not have heard of Asaph. He is the man who wrote Psalm 73. Asaph was King David's music director and author of twelve of the psalms.

In Psalm 73, Asaph wonders, if God is good, then why do some good people suffer and some bad people don't? He says, "I have kept my heart pure and have not sinned. [Yet] I have suffered all day long. I have been punished every morning" (vv. 13–14). Asaph confesses that he sometimes feels like giving up and joining the bad guys (vv. 2–3).

Filled with anxiety, Asaph cries out to God. In prayer, he realizes that while the bad might do well for a while, God will punish them in His own way and in His own time. Asaph ends up praising God, "[You are] the strength of my heart and all I need forever."

When our bodies feel tired and sick, when we feel as if nothing we do is right, Psalm 73:26 reminds us that God is our everything.

Help me to be patient when seeking punishment for the bad guys. In Your time, Lord, and in Your way, You will deal with them. Amen.

DAY 275

Put yourselves through a test. See if you belong to Christ. Then you will know you belong to Christ, unless you do not pass the test.

2 CORINTHIANS 13:5

Here's a little test to find out if your faith in Jesus is strong.

Hanging out with other Christians (maybe your friends from church or your family) is important. When you are with them, you feel comfortable talking about Jesus and praying and sharing your faith with each other. But what happens when you step outside that comfort zone and you find yourself in a crowd of nonbelievers?

Satan will do his best to try and trick you into doing what you know is wrong. You need to keep your eyes and ears open and test your behavior. Ask yourself, "Would Jesus approve?" If you answer yes, then you've passed the faith test. But if your answer is no, you've failed.

But don't worry! There's good news.

Everyone fails the test sometimes. The good news is you can take the test again and again. If you open your heart to Jesus, then He will strengthen your faith and help you to pass.

Jesus, whenever I head the wrong way, pull me back. My heart is open to You. Please boost my faith and make it strong. Amen.

DAY 276

Be careful that no one changes your mind and faith by much learning and big sounding ideas. Those things are what men dream up. They are always trying to make new religions. These leave out Christ.

COLOSSIANS 2:8

There is a Sunday school song that goes "Be careful little ears what you hear." Today's verse echoes that thought. It warns against another of Satan's traps.

Some people twist God's words in the Bible. They make them sound like they mean something other than what God meant. Our ears have to be fine-tuned to pick up those twists when we hear them.

God's Word is perfectly perfect. That's why memorizing scripture word-for-word is important. When you do that and learn the true meaning of God's words, then you are less likely to fall into Satan's trap.

Satan was the serpent who convinced Adam and Eve that it was okay if they ate fruit from the one tree God said was forbidden. Because they listened to what they thought was good advice, sin came into the world forever!

So, be careful that no one changes your mind about what God's Word says. Ask Jesus to help you decide whether what you hear is real and true.

Dear Lord, keep me focused on the truth of Your Word. Remind me to study the Bible and trust You to help me understand it. Amen.

DAY 277

*"But where are your gods that you made for yourself?
Let them come if they can save you when you are in trouble.
For you have as many gods as cities, O Judah."*

JEREMIAH 2:28

The Bible has much to say about false gods. In the first of His Ten Commandments, God said, "Have no gods other than Me" (Exodus 20:3).

But the people didn't listen. Even while Moses was up on Mount Sinai receiving the Ten Commandments from God, the Israelites were worshiping a calf made of gold. Because Moses had been gone from them so long, they had lost faith in God and in Moses—and they made their own god to worship.

Years later, King Solomon built altars where each of his wives could go to worship their false gods. How many wives did Solomon have? Three hundred! And each worshiped a false god.

The prophet Jeremiah saw, and in today's verse we see him warning the people to stop.

Even today, people worship false gods—money, celebrities, things. But there is only one God, and He demands our attention.

Father, many things distract our attention from You—the Internet, television, books. Open my eyes to false gods. The only God I want to worship is You! Amen.

DAY 278

Jesus said to them, "The Day of Rest was made for the good of man. Man was not made for the Day of Rest."
MARK 2:27

In His fourth commandment, God said, "Remember the Day of Rest, to keep it holy. Six days you will do all your work. But the seventh day is a Day of Rest to the Lord your God" (Exodus 20:8-10).

God's reason for this command is found in Genesis 2:2-3: "On the seventh day God ended His work. . . . And He rested on the seventh day from all His work. . . . Then God honored the seventh day and made it holy, because in it He rested." If the Creator chose a day off for rest, after six days of creation work, who are we to ignore His command that we rest too?

How does your family honor Sunday? Together, decide how to make Sunday special. Plan what you could do for others. Decide on activities you won't participate in. Make it a day of rest that God will approve of, a day in which you remember and honor Him.

Lord, in our family, Sunday will be a day of rest and remembrance of You. Show us ways that we, as a family, can honor this day and spend it with You. Amen.

DAY 279

In the morning, O Lord, You will hear my voice. In the morning I will lay my prayers before You and will look up.

PSALM 5:3

Most kids, and grown-ups too, pray at bedtime. But what about the rest of the day? Other than mealtime prayers, do you pray all day long?

God loves hearing your voice as you go about your day. He wants you to speak to Him when you are in school. Invite Him to give you wisdom when you take a test. Ask Him to provide you with understanding in math, science, or any subject you struggle with. Speak to God when you play sports. Ask for physical strength and for Him to help you be a good sport. Get in the habit of looking around and thanking God for all the blessings you see.

Psalm 5:3 reminds us that it's important to start every day with some quiet time with God. Beginning tomorrow, get up a little earlier than usual and start your day with the Father. He's waiting to hear from you.

Dear God, thank You for listening to my prayers and knowing exactly what I need. I will meet You in the morning so we can talk before I start my day. Amen.

DAY 280

Do you think I am trying to get the favor of men, or of God? If I were still trying to please men, I would not be a servant owned by Christ.

GALATIANS 1:10

"And they lived happily ever after." That's how fairy tales end. The prince and his princess ride off into the sunset on a beautiful white horse. The end.

Everyone loves a happy ending, but the truth is that in this world some endings aren't happy. Parents divorce, people die, dreams don't always come true, and those who are supposed to love us sometimes let us down. That all sounds very negative, doesn't it? But there's good news.

There is someone out there who makes our happily ever after a reality. His name is Jesus! He loves us all the time, no matter what. He can heal broken relationships and comfort us when we are sad. He knows our wishes before we make them.

When we focus on Jesus, He makes all the world's problems seem easier to handle. And when He died for us, He gave us the most special gift of all—the gift of happily ever after in heaven.

Jesus, You must really love me to have suffered and given Your life for me. You loved me before any human did, and Your love for me lasts forever. I love You too. Amen.

DAY 281

Jesus Christ is the same yesterday and today and forever.

HEBREWS 13:8

Close your eyes and imagine Jesus when He was on earth. What do you think He looked like? We can only guess. There were no cameras back then, and the men who wrote the Bible did not include drawings of Jesus. We suppose He had olive skin, long hair, and a beard. We picture Him wearing a white robe and sandals. That is how most artists have painted Him.

But what Jesus looked like is not at all important when compared to who Jesus is: God's Son, the Savior, the Messiah—the one God sent to earth to die for our sins.

The Jesus who lived back then is the same now, and He will be forever! Jesus spoke the truth, and His truth lives on in the Bible and in us. The things He said and taught will not change. He said it Himself in Malachi 3:6: "For I, the Lord, do not change."

Jesus is, and forever He will be, and all that He was and is, is yours! Isn't that awesome?

Dear Jesus, I've gotten to know You through the Bible, and I'm grateful that You won't ever change. I know I can always count on You, because the Bible tells me so. Amen.

DAY 282

Jesus said, "I am the Way and the Truth and the Life. No one can go to the Father except by Me."
JOHN 14:6

Jesus made a statement when He was here on earth, one simple sentence that describes who He is and why He came here. Jesus said, "I am the Way and the Truth and the Life. No one can go to the Father except by Me."

Jesus is our way to heaven. Our *only* way! His death on the cross cleared a path for us that wasn't there until Jesus arrived. Until He came, no one had a sin-free heart pure enough for heaven.

Everything Jesus said here on earth was the truth. We can count on His words in the Bible being 100 percent true, now and forever.

It is Jesus who took the punishment for our sins so our hearts will be pure and ready for heaven. He is our promise that life goes on for Christians when they die—eternal life, forever life, in heaven.

And finally, Jesus is the one who brings us to Father God face-to-face. It is Jesus who, when you get to heaven, will take you by the hand and introduce you to the one who made you.

**You mean everything to me, Jesus.
Without You, I would be totally lost. Amen.**

DAY 283

Great is our Lord, and great in power.
His understanding has no end.
PSALM 147:5

God has amazingly great power. Genesis 1:16 tells us that He created all the billions upon billions of stars. Psalm 147:4 says He knows the exact number of stars. And there's more. God calls every one of them by name—as if they were His pets! Remember that the next time you wonder if God is big enough to answer your prayers.

The second half of this verse says God's "understanding has no end." When you are praying for wisdom in a complicated or worried situation, fix that thought firmly in your mind. You may have no clue as to the right answer, but God certainly does! His understanding is endless.

At times, we don't understand why God allows us to go through troubled times, but He certainly knows—and He cares deeply for each one of us. He not only knows every star by name, but He knows your name too.

Psalm 147:5 is one of the most powerful verses in the Bible. When we think deeply about its words, they can fill our minds with comfort and peace.

God, who am I among all the stars in the universe? But You know their names, and You know mine too! You know me, You understand me, and that brings me peace. Amen.

DAY 284

When they say, "He went up," what does it mean but that He had first gone down to the deep parts of the earth?
EPHESIANS 4:9

Paratroopers, in World War II, jumped out of planes in the dark of night into enemy territory. They took weapons and as much ammunition as they could carry. Then they loaded canvas bags with more weapons and equipment and tied them onto their ankles before they jumped!

Now, imagine this: Your enemy controls the land below. On the way down, the jumpmaster takes away all your weapons. He says there are some good people below who might help—though they don't have many weapons themselves. Oh, and you will definitely die down there.

Would you make the jump?

Jesus was somewhat like those paratroopers. His crucifixion and ascension—the day He went back to heaven—are well known. But the key part of His journey was the beginning. He had to come down to earth—"enemy territory"—before He could complete God's plan of salvation and go back up to heaven to be with His Father.

Remember this: Jesus weighed all the risks of coming down to earth. He knew He would die. But He loved us. Love won—and down He came!

Love came down. I will remember that, Jesus. Because You love me, You came down to save me. Thank You! Amen.

DAY 285

They got up early in the morning and went up to the top of the hill country, saying, "Here we are. It is true we have sinned. But we will go up to the place which the Lord has promised."

NUMBERS 14:40

Before entering the land God promised to Israel, Moses sent out twelve scouts to explore the region.

After forty days, the men returned and reported, "It is indeed a bountiful country. . . . But the people living there are powerful" (Numbers 13:27–28 NLT).

Two scouts, Caleb and Joshua, urged the Israelites to go at once and take possession of the land. But the other scouts spread fear, saying, "We can't go up against them! They are stronger than we are!" (Numbers 13:31 NLT). Hearing this, the Israelites turned against Moses and wanted to kill Caleb and Joshua.

During the riot, God showed up. For their unbelief, God sentenced the Israelites to wander forty years in the desert.

Ignoring God's words, the Israelites still tried to take the land, but the enemy attacked and soundly defeated them.

Sometimes opportunities God gives us disappear, never to return. That's why it's important to listen for His voice and act on His instructions.

Father, sometimes Your voice whispers to my heart, but I don't listen. Forgive me. Help me to always tune in to Your words and follow Your instructions. Amen.

DAY 286

You know that only one person gets a crown for being in a race even if many people run. You must run so you will win the crown.
1 CORINTHIANS 9:24

In his letter to the Corinthians, Paul compared living life the way Jesus wants us to with the intense training of a runner.

Paul's advice brings images of runners, sprinters, and marathoners stepping over the starting line, aware of others on the course who may cause a trip up. They keep their eyes on the goal and their minds on the commitment that helps them put one foot in front of the other, no matter what.

Paul reminded the Corinthians that they should live as if they were running toward heaven. He told them to keep their mind on Jesus, because Jesus would give them the strength to work hard and keep their eyes on the prize.

For runners in a race, the prize is a trophy—Paul called it a crown—but the prize for living the way Jesus wants us to live is forever life in heaven. That's the greatest prize of all!

Jesus, please help me to work hard to live a good life and to keep my eyes fixed on You and heaven. Amen.

DAY 287

Take lies and what is false far from me. Do not let me be poor or rich. Feed me with the food that I need.

PROVERBS 30:8

King Solomon wrote most of Proverbs, but the wisdom offered in today's verse comes from a common man, a laborer named Agur.

In verses 7–8, he offered his "wish list" to God: "Two things I have asked of You. . .before I die: Take lies and what is false far from me. Do not let me be poor or rich. Feed me with the food that I need." He continued by saying a rich man was likely to take credit for his own success and forget God; but a poor man faced the temptation to steal to meet his needs (v. 9).

Agur asked God to keep sin away from him. He did not want to be rich so his riches became more important to him than God. Nor did he want to be poor and have to steal to eat. He asked God to provide everything that he needed.

What would be on your wish list to God? Would your wishes bring you closer to Him?

Dear God, guide me in the things I wish for. Lead me to ask only for those things that will strengthen my relationship with You. Amen.

DAY 288

Hate starts fights, but love covers all sins.
PROVERBS 10:12

The word *hate* appears in the Bible (NLV) 757 times—676 in the Old Testament, and 81 in the New Testament. The word shows up in Genesis, the first book in the Bible, proof that hate has existed for a very long time.

Throughout history, in ancient times and today, people suffer because of hate. Jesus was hated by nonbelievers and killed. His followers were hated and punished because they talked about Jesus. Wars have begun, killing innocent people, because of hate. Hate starts fights between people who disagree about politics. Hate, for no reason, causes bullies to pick on others. Hate seems to have taken over the world—but wait—that's not true!

Proverbs 10:12 says that love covers all sins. And what is love? God is love! His love is more powerful than all that sinful hate, and love will win over hate every time.

When you pray tonight, ask God to keep hate far from you. Ask Him to fill your heart with love and forgiveness, the way that He loves you.

Father, help me not to fall into hate's sinful trap. I want to always be loving and forgiving toward others, the way that You are toward me. Amen.

DAY 289

After he had seen this, we agreed that God told us to go to Macedonia to tell them the Good News.

ACTS 16:10

Paul didn't stay in one place very long. He was a missionary. His goal was to spread the good news to those who had not heard.

Paul teamed up with a guy named Silas, and they mapped out the route they wanted to take. They traveled northward through Syria and into the southern provinces of Asia Minor. But God stopped them from preaching there. So, they traveled to their next destination—but God stopped them from preaching there too!

Discouraged, they went to the seaport town of Troas. There, in a dream, a Macedonian man appeared to Paul saying, "Come over to the country of Macedonia and help us!" (Acts 16:9). Without delay, Paul and Silas sailed from Troas to the region of Macedonia, which was exactly where God wanted them!

Do you listen for God's direction in all areas of your life, or do you go your own way? Seek His guidance and make adjustments to stay on track with Him. Don't miss out on God's best for you.

God, so often I go my own way and miss out on Your best for me. Help me to listen for Your guidance so I can stay on course. Amen.

DAY 290

Greet Mary. She worked hard for you.

Romans 16:6

Some people wonder if the Bible is true or if it is some sort of ancient novel, a kind of fairy tale.

As you study the Bible and line up its events with history, you will discover facts that prove that the Bible is true. Some will amaze you, and others might confuse you.

Think about this: If you wrote a novel, would you create multiple characters all with the same name? One proof that the Bible is a record of true-life events is how many people carry the same name: five to seven are called Mary, three or four James, three John, and two Judas!

The Bible reads more like a history book than a novel. It is all about real people and real events, and sprinkled throughout are God's thoughts and His advice to us.

Read it and judge for yourself. Do you think the Bible is the true Word of God?

Father, I believe the Bible as truth. Some people say that some or all of it is fiction. But I know better. The Bible is the Word of God. The Bible is You! Amen.

DAY 291

"Those who are wise will shine like the bright heavens. And those who lead many to do what is right and good will shine like the stars forever and ever."

DANIEL 12:3

An angel appeared to Daniel and told him what would happen at a time far into the future. The angel said that, someday, the bodies of those who have died will rise up from the grave, like Jesus' body did! But not all people, only Christians who had lived their lives for God. Those who were wise in life and believed in Jesus will rise with beautiful new bodies that glow with light. Because they lived to please God and led others to do the same, they will shine like the stars, forever and ever.

Look up at the stars. Our Creator made them all. He put them in place exactly where He wants them. He even arranged some in constellations for our enjoyment (Job 9:9). The stars are the work of His hands, and so are we!

If we shine brightly for Jesus now, by doing our best to be like Him, then He will see to it that, someday, in our new bodies, we will shine brightly forever—like the stars!

Mighty God, I will lead others to Jesus, and together we will light the way to You and heaven. Amen.

DAY 292

For if a man belongs to Christ, he is a new person.
The old life is gone. New life has begun.
2 CORINTHIANS 5:17

In today's Bible verse, Paul describes what happens to any person who enters into a relationship with God's Son, Jesus Christ. As soon as people accept Jesus into their hearts, it is as if their old lives are gone! They begin a new life living to please God and looking forward to the promise of heaven someday. Their old ways are ancient history. They show others by their words and actions that now they are living for Jesus.

All new believers begin learning how to live with Jesus ruling their hearts. They begin welcoming other Christians into their lives. They stop beating themselves up for mistakes they made in the past. They start to see themselves through God's eyes and love themselves the way that God loves them. They begin a lifetime of learning from and living by God's Word.

You can help others to give up their old lives and get a fresh start. How can you help? Tell them about Jesus!

Jesus, my Savior, You've made me brand-new, and I thank You! I want to help others get a new life too. Please teach me how. Amen.

DAY 293

"It is the smallest of seeds. But when it is full-grown, it is larger than the grain of the fields and it becomes a tree. The birds of the sky come and stay in its branches."

MATTHEW 13:32

Little beginnings can lead to big finishes.

Jesus picked up the tiniest of all seeds—a mustard seed—to show His disciples. Once planted, the seed grows slowly. The seedling takes days or even weeks before it gives any sign of breaking through the ground. Why does it take so long to grow?

A mustard plant requires deep roots. The plant grows its roots three times faster than the stalk in order to be well grounded. Mustard trees grow up to twenty-one feet tall with the roots reaching down to sixty-three feet in the ground.

God plants mustard seed-sized faith inside each of us. In times of trouble, our faith may seem so small we no longer think it exists. But God keeps working on us, pushing the roots of our faith deeper.

Ask God to grow your faith big and strong. You can help your faith grow through prayer and by studying the Bible.

Your greatest work in me, Father, comes when I'm completely unaware. Even when trouble comes and I feel separated from You, You nourish and strengthen the roots of my faith. Thank You, Father. Amen.

DAY 294

"Eye for eye, tooth for tooth, hand for hand, foot for foot."
EXODUS 21:24

Some verses in the Bible seem cruel, like this one from the book of Exodus. It seems to mean that if someone injures one of your body parts, then you are perfectly within your rights to injure that part of them, as well. But that's not at all what it means!

The words are not about revenge but fairness in judgment. God told the people of Israel that when two fighters came before the court, a judge was to order a punishment that fit the crime. If the victim lost an eye in a fight, for example, the judge was not to order that the other guy be put to death. Judges today follow similar laws so the punishment a person receives is fair for the crime that they commit.

God wants us to be fair too. He holds us to an even higher standard. When someone hurts us, we are to forgive them and allow God to be their judge. He will see to it that the punishment fits the crime.

God, give me grace to forgive my enemies. I have been hurt by others, but so was Jesus, and He readily forgave! Help me to be more like Him. Amen.

DAY 295

Their minds are in darkness. They are strangers to the life of God. This is because they have closed their minds to Him and have turned their hearts away from Him.

EPHESIANS 4:18

Has stubbornness ever kept you from doing something you really wanted to do? Maybe you felt awkward, afraid, or unwanted, so you said, "I don't want to go," or "I don't care." Nothing could make you admit that you really wanted to go or that you cared—a lot.

Some people are just as stubborn about not accepting Jesus into their hearts. The consequences of that are far worse than missing out on a good time. Hardening their hearts to Jesus could mean that those people will never get to heaven. They will miss the wonderful opportunity of forever life with God.

The stubborn ones who won't accept Jesus have no idea what they are giving up. And God does not want us to leave them behind.

Do you know people who refuse to accept Jesus? Then pray every day that they will give up their stubbornness. Ask God to show you if there's something else you can do to help lead them to Christ.

Lord, I reach out to You in prayer asking You to soften the hearts of those too stubborn to come to You. Open their hearts to receive You, Lord. Amen.

DAY 296

He makes the winds carry His news.
He makes His helpers a burning fire.
Psalm 104:4

To understand today's verse better, read Hebrews 1:7. There, Paul explains what the first part of Psalm 104:4 means. He says, "[God] said this about the angels, 'He makes His angels to be winds.'" Then Paul continues in Hebrews 1:14 telling us that angels are spirits who work for God. They are sent by Him to help save us from sin.

The second part of Psalm 104:4 can be explained through one of the references to fire in the Bible: God became a pillar of fire that led the Israelites out of Egypt (Exodus 13:21–22). God was in the fire, commanding it to go on ahead and light the way for the Israelites when they traveled by night.

So, Psalm 104:4 teaches us that God sends His angels, like the wind, all over the earth. It is their job to help us stay away from sin. Psalm 104:4 also reminds us that God is in control. He goes ahead of us lighting the way, just as He did for the Israelites when He led them out of Egypt.

Angels are proof that You love us and want to protect us. Thank You, Father, for sending Your angels. Thank You for Your love. Amen.

DAY 297

Whatever work you do, do it with all your heart.
Do it for the Lord and not for men.
COLOSSIANS 3:23

There are times, like when we're watching a beautiful sunset or having a fun time with our friends, when we think about God's gifts to us. Most of the time, though, we are busy with everyday tasks, and our minds are far from God. We need to remember that those everyday tasks are His gifts to us too. The only difference is in how grateful we are.

Brother Lawrence, a seventeenth-century priest, practiced something called "the presence of God." Believing God was always with him, Lawrence turned the washing of the dishes and the repairing of shoes into acts of worship. While doing his everyday tasks he would give thanks to God.

It's easy to think you are working for the Lord when you are helping others or doing something important. But it's much more difficult when you are taking out the trash or doing homework.

Try being like Brother Lawrence. Get into the habit of thanking God for whatever work you do.

Jesus, everything You did, You did for God and for me. You never complained or refused to do something. I want to be like You—ready and willing whatever the task. Amen.

DAY 298

For as he thinks in his heart, so is he. He says to you, "Eat and drink!" But his heart is not with you.

PROVERBS 23:7

Some people think that all they have to do is wish for something and God will make their wish come true. Of course, God is completely able to do anything at all, but the wishes in our hearts might not line up with what God wants for us.

Getting what we want is not about having faith that God can do it for us. It is more about having faith that God will give us what He knows we need, what is best for us.

Imagine a kid wishing for a castle to play in. God wouldn't make a castle appear mysteriously in the backyard, but He might put the thought in a dad's head to build a tree house, which ends up being much more fun than a castle anyway.

When you pray and ask God for something, do so knowing that you might not get what you ask for. Have faith, though, that God will always give you what you need. You can count on it.

God, thank You for Your gifts. Teach me not only to have faith in Your generosity but to be worthy and accepting of whatever You choose to give me. Amen.

DAY 299

"Heaven and earth will pass away,
but My Words will not pass away."
MARK 13:31

If there is anything we can be sure of, it is that what God says is true. Jesus said that even the earth will eventually be no more, but His words will continue to be as true as ever—forever.

As humans, we change our minds as we go through our lives. As kids grow up, they change the way they think. They learn different ways of seeing a particular issue. With their minds constantly learning new information, they can make better choices with how they feel about things.

That's not how it works with God, though.

He didn't start out like a child having to learn. God has been perfectly wise and right forever. And because of His perfect wisdom, His Word will never change. He has already made up His mind about everything that will ever happen.

We can be sure, as Mark 13:31 shows us, that what God says will still be true tomorrow, next week, next year, and forever.

O God, I can always count on Your Word. What You have said is the truth and the same today as it will be forever. I trust in You, Father. Your wisdom never fails. Amen.

DAY 300

"The men of God say things that are not true, and the religious leaders rule by their own thoughts. And My people love to have it this way! But what will you do in the end?"

JEREMIAH 5:31

There are false prophets just waiting to trick you. What does that mean? It means that some people will try to tell you things about God that just aren't true. It's important that you learn to spot a false prophet when you see one.

The first thing you need to do to identify a liar is to read and learn what is in the Bible. The Word of God is your handbook. All of God's rules and His best advice are found in the scriptures. The more you know about what is in there, the easier it will be to know when someone is lying to you about God.

The next thing you should do is pray. Ask God to help you spot false teachers and not allow any of their words to seep into your mind and heart.

And, finally, don't try to stand up to those false prophets alone. Arm yourself with the Bible and be ready to answer any false teaching you hear.

Lord, I don't want to be tricked by people spreading lies about You. Teach me to identify their false teaching. I want to be true to Your perfect Word to the end. Amen.

DAY 301

Anyone who hears the Word of God and does not obey is like a man looking at his face in a mirror. After he sees himself and goes away, he forgets what he looks like.

JAMES 1:23–24

Imagine there was a mirror that showed your true nature—the kind of person you really are inside. Would you look? What would you expect to see?

James tells us there is such a mirror. It's the Bible. When we know what's in there, we can compare what we look like inside with the way God wants us to be.

Some people can quote many Bible verses and know where all the books are in the Bible, but they pretend not to see the faults that the Bible points out to them.

The Bible does more than show us our faults; it shows us the way God created us to be. When we walk away from the mirror, we need to remember the image of how God made us.

When God looks at you, He sees the wonderful one He created. God always looks at you with love, and He wants to see you living your life trying to be like Jesus.

Dear God, when I look in the mirror, I want to see Jesus. Help me to be a reflection of the life He lived and the things that He taught. Amen.

DAY 302

"See, I have put in front of you today life and what is good, and death and what is bad."
DEUTERONOMY 30:15

Choices. We face them every day. Some are easy, like do you want to stay home and help Dad clean the garage, or would you rather go with your mom and sister to the movies? Some choices are hard, like when you have to choose one of three awesome places to have your birthday party. Choices can be unimportant—do I want another piece of pizza or not? Or important—should I find out why my little brother is crying, or should I keep on playing my video game?

Today's verse is about the most important choice of all: choosing between God and Satan. Moses is speaking to the Israelites. He's telling them that choosing God leads to a good life but choosing Satan leads only to what is bad. The Israelites listened halfheartedly to Moses, and because of that, they allowed Satan to trap them into doing what they knew was wrong.

Listen to Moses' words in Deuteronomy 30:15. Memorize them so you can remember them when you need to choose between right and wrong.

Then, choose wisely.

Lord, bless me with the wisdom to choose the right way. Help me to follow the path that leads away from Satan and brings me to You. Amen.

DAY 303

God does not change His mind when He chooses men and gives them His gifts.

ROMANS 11:29

Think about it: There is a holiday or special occasion for pretty much every month of the year. And don't forget to add birthdays!

Many holidays include gift giving, and much thought goes into choosing a gift the receiver will like. You might even change your mind a few times about which gift to choose.

God is not like humans when He gives gifts. He doesn't need a special occasion. He blesses us with His gifts every day for no reason other than He loves us. God always knows what we need, so we'll never have to return His gifts. And never will He take a gift back because He thinks we don't deserve it.

God's gifts are all around you: family, friends, pets. . .how many more can you name?

Thank Him for His gifts. Use them wisely. And remember to share them whenever you can.

Father, thank You for all those "just because" gifts—priceless one-of-a-kind gifts just because You love me. Help me to take good care of them and use them to please You. Amen.

DAY 304

"I will have shepherds over them who will care for them. And they will not be afraid any longer, or filled with fear, and none of them will be missing," says the Lord.

JEREMIAH 23:4

When disasters happen—events like storms, floods, and fires—we might wonder: Why did God allow that to happen? Why doesn't He do something? We can't know why God allowed a tragedy to take place, but we can be sure that He sends help when it happens.

Jeremiah 23:4 shows us how God often works in the world—He works through people.

Repeatedly in the Old and New Testaments we find God using people to reach out to a hurting world. He used shepherds and kings, men and women, children, and even a baby—Jesus—to save the world from trouble.

God still works through people. When a disaster strikes, He sends help through churches, hospitals, food pantries, disaster-relief workers, and a crowd of other volunteers who help in many ways.

God works through people today just as He did in ancient times when the Bible was written. You can be sure that if disaster strikes, God's helpers will show up right away. They always have, and they always will!

God, every day I see You working through good people in the world. I want to volunteer! How can I help? Amen.

DAY 305

But you, man of God, turn away from all these sinful things. Work at being right with God. Live a God-like life. Have faith and love. Be willing to wait. Have a kind heart.

1 TIMOTHY 6:11

Paul loved his young friend Timothy as if he were his son. Timothy was becoming a strong follower of Jesus, the way that Paul was. Paul wanted to help the younger man succeed in his life and ministry, so Paul wrote Timothy two letters full of advice.

"I write to you, Timothy. You are my son in the Christian faith. May God the Father and Jesus Christ our Lord give you His loving-favor and loving-kindness and peace" (1 Timothy 1:2). That is how Paul began his first letter. Then he went on giving Timothy advice:

"Turn away from all these sinful things," Paul wrote. "Work at being right with God. Live a God-like life. Have faith and love. Be willing to wait. Have a kind heart."

The to-do list for Timothy was long, but Paul knew that the young man would need to do those things if he were to be a powerful servant for God.

Paul's advice is good for all of us! Do your best to follow it, and you will surely please God.

Dear Father, help me, please, to follow Paul's advice. I want to serve You well. Amen.

DAY 306

This is what the Lord says to Cyrus, whom He has chosen, whose right hand He has held, "I send him to put nations under his power, and to take away the power of kings. And I will open doors in front of him so that gates will not be shut."

ISAIAH 45:1

Who will be president in 2030? Will you be married in twenty years? Will you have kids?

God knows. He has always known. In the Bible, we see God speaking through His prophets. He tells them in advance what will happen many years into the future. Today's verse is an example. Through the prophet Isaiah, God tells Cyrus why He made him a king and what will happen to him in the future.

We can believe that what the prophets said in the Bible is the absolute truth given by God. But we have to be very careful about people today who say that they are prophets and know the future, people like psychics and fortune-tellers.

Always turn to the Bible to help you with decisions about your future. Pray and ask God to lead you where He wants you to go. Then you will be sure that you are on the right path.

Heavenly Father, keep me from false prophets. I know that I can always trust Your answers to my prayers and the truthfulness of Your Word. Amen.

DAY 307

Only God can say what is right or wrong. He made the Law. He can save or put to death. How can we say if our brother is right or wrong?

James 4:12

Have you ever "gotten even" with someone over something? Have you ever reacted unkindly to someone else's unkindness?

We've all done it. It's our way of passing judgment on others. This is what we think they deserve, so we give it to them.

Does that kind of judgment make us better people? No, never! So, what should we do instead? We should love others, like the Bible tells us to.

Sometimes the love option makes us think we'll look foolish and weak. Wouldn't it be better to stand up, get in the other person's face, and tell them what we really think? The answer to that is to ask ourselves what would Jesus do.

Jesus taught us to love God and one another. It's the answer to every problem. It's the way Jesus lived when He was on earth.

Judging others usually only makes us deserving of a harsh judgment in return. Don't judge—love. And keep this in mind: God loves us even when we aren't so loving toward Him!

Jesus, I am no better than anyone else, so who am I to judge others? Help me, Jesus. Help me not to judge them but to love them instead. Amen.

DAY 308

I praise You seven times a day, because Your Law is right.

PSALM 119:164

In the Bible, the number seven shows up more than a few times. God created the universe in seven days. Major festivals such as the Passover and wedding feasts lasted seven days. In Pharaoh's dream, there were seven good years followed by seven years of famine. In the New Testament, seven churches are mentioned in the book of Revelation. King David prayed seven times a day. He lifted up praises to God throughout the entire day, every day. He filled the minutes of his life with thankfulness and paying attention to God.

The Bible tells us to pray all the time. But how is that possible?

You can set up times during your day to pray. Say a prayer when you get up in the morning and before you go to bed. Pray before each meal. You can pray just before you start your homework or before a sports event.

Write down a prayer schedule for tomorrow so you pray at least seven times. Use it to help you get into the habit of praying little prayers throughout the day.

God, sometimes I forget to pray. But I can change that! I will set times throughout my day to pray and praise You. Amen.

DAY 309

Tell your sins to each other. And pray for each other so you may be healed. The prayer from the heart of a man right with God has much power.

James 5:16

When something is troubling you, do you keep it to yourself, or do you tell someone? James, the author of today's verse, says that you should share your problems with others. If your problem is because you have done something wrong, that shouldn't keep you from talking about it. When you share your sins with others, they can pray for you, help you to feel better about yourself, and lead you to do better next time.

Be careful who you choose to share with. It should be someone who knows and loves Jesus, like you do. A family member is best, or a trusted friend. You don't have to feel afraid when sharing your sins with people who love you. God has put them in your life to help you.

And don't ever be afraid to talk with God about your sins. He already knows if you have done something wrong, and He is ready to forgive you. You are His child, and He loves you.

Heavenly Father, there are things that I am keeping to myself that bother me. Help me to share them with the right Christian family member or friend. Lead me, Lord. Amen.

DAY 310

Joshua said, "So put away the strange gods that are among you. Give your hearts to the Lord, the God of Israel."

JOSHUA 24:23

The Israelites knew that God performed many miracles, like dividing the Red Sea, providing food for them in the wilderness, and destroying Jericho's walls with blasts from a few trumpets. You would think their faith in God would be strong. But no. Many Israelites worshiped false gods—idols—as they wandered through the desert looking for the Promised Land.

Joshua saw and was troubled by all the false-god worship that was going on. He told his friends to stop it. "Put away the strange gods that are among you. Give your hearts to the Lord, the God of Israel," he said. Then Joshua ordered them to show God their faith in Him by destroying their idols. The Israelites listened and threw away their false gods. They followed the one true God to the end of their lives.

Is anything getting in the way of your relationship with God? Maybe there are some things you need to throw out or stay away from. Think about it. Is anything more important to you than God?

Dear God, make clear to me the things in this world that have become my idols. You are my God, and I choose to serve only You. Amen.

DAY 311

He said to the Jews who believed, "If you keep and obey My Word, then you are My followers for sure."
JOHN 8:31

Jesus taught us how to live in two ways. His wise words made clear what God expected of us. But more importantly, Jesus taught by example.

Think about Jesus, and list three words to describe Him. Maybe you said *kind*, *forgiving*, and *loving*. You recognize these qualities in Jesus by how He lived.

Jesus wants us to live like He did, doing what God expects of us. He wants us to live like Him—not just on Sunday when we worship Him in church and Sunday school, but every day.

Jesus said that we are truly His followers if we are faithful. That means we act like Christians every day, all day long. We do our best to do what God wants every day and learn what He wants by reading the Bible. Faithfulness also means trusting God to forgive us when we mess up and do something wrong.

Remember—Jesus is faithful to you all the time, so do your best to be faithful to Him.

Jesus, Your faithfulness to me is so great. You've set the perfect example for living, and You are so patient with me while I try to be like You. Thank You, Jesus. Amen.

DAY 312

Punish me when I need it, O Lord, but be fair. Do not punish me in Your anger, or You will bring me to nothing.

JEREMIAH 10:24

What did Jeremiah mean in this verse? Let's look at the last part first.

Jeremiah was upset with himself because, as hard as he tried to obey God, he still messed up. He knew that God had every right to be angry with him for his sins. If God gave Jeremiah the punishment he knew he deserved, Jeremiah would have nothing left—think about if your parents got angry with you and took away everything you had!

In the first part of the verse, Jeremiah begs God to be fair with His punishment. He needn't have worried, though, because God is always fair!

God sent His Son, Jesus, to take all the punishment that Jeremiah and everyone else deserved for their sins, and not just in Bible times, but forever. As long as we believe in what Jesus did for us, God will forgive us, and we don't have to worry about His anger.

Now that's more than fair, don't you think?

Dear God, thank You for always being fair with me. I know that when I confess my sins to You, You will be gentle and loving toward me and say, "I forgive you." I love You, God. Amen.

DAY 313

Jesus said to him, "Thomas, because you have seen Me, you believe. Those are happy who have never seen Me and yet believe!"

JOHN 20:29

Soon after Jesus rose from the grave, He appeared to some of His disciples. One of them, Thomas, had not been part of those first Jesus sightings. When others told him, he refused to believe—he wanted proof that Jesus was alive.

One week later, Thomas got his proof when Jesus walked through the locked doors of a room where the disciples were staying. He invited Thomas to feel where the nails had been in His hands and to touch His side that had been stabbed with a sword. Jesus mildly scolded Thomas, saying, "Do not doubt, believe!" (v. 27).

How about it? Do you believe? Do you believe in Jesus even though you can't see Him?

Jesus is in heaven with His Father, but the fact is that He does appear to us—through His words in the Bible and His Spirit that lives in us every day. Jesus says to all of us, "Happy are those who have never seen Me and yet believe!"

Dear Jesus, You are all around me. I see You in the sun, the moon, the stars, and many other ways. Sometimes there are moments when I doubt You. Forgive me for that, Jesus. Amen.

DAY 314

He Who sits in the heavens laughs. The Lord makes fun of them.
PSALM 2:4

Do you ever wonder whether God has a sense of humor? It shouldn't surprise you to discover that He does. After all, He made us in His image, and *we* laugh. Psalm 2:4 in the Bible says it clearly: "He Who sits in the heavens laughs." And you know that everything in the Bible is true. So—God laughs!

But what's that about God making fun of people?

Imagine God looking down at us. He sees people trying to hide from Him, or at least trying to hide their sins from Him. Of course that doesn't work, because God sees and knows everything. He looks down and sees some scientists and other people believing that there is no Creator, when they haven't yet figured out everything about our human bodies and how to fix them. Everywhere God looks, people think they can outsmart Him.

It is funny, when you think about it. No one can outsmart God or change His plans for our lives. So, God sits up there in heaven looking down at all of the ridiculous things people say and do.

"Those silly people!" He says. And He laughs.

O God, how foolish we humans are! I'm glad that You can look at us with a sense of humor. No one can outsmart You, ever. Amen.

DAY 315

We are pressed on every side, but we still have room to move. We are often in much trouble, but we never give up. People make it hard for us, but we are not left alone. We are knocked down, but we are not destroyed.

2 CORINTHIANS 4:8–9

If you think about it, God uses His power to make us into mini superheroes.

Imagine yourself trapped in a situation where there seems to be no way out. What does God do? He provides some wiggle room so you can escape by following His commands. When you feel like you've done all you can, God gives you courage not to give up. The enemy might make it hard for you, but God is always by your side, helping you to fight. You might be knocked down a few times, but you will never be destroyed, because God promises you eternal life!

God is great, and He uses His greatness to work through us. Nothing can overpower us when we put all of our faith in Him. Paul knew it when he wrote the words in 2 Corinthians 4:8–9—and, now, you know it too!

Heavenly Father, nothing, no one is greater or more powerful than You! Thank You for using Your power to help me overcome any trouble in my life. Amen.

DAY 316

You do not know about tomorrow. What is your life?
It is like fog. You see it and soon it is gone.

JAMES 4:14

For thirty-five years, a man named Arthur Stace wrote *eternity* in chalk across Sydney, Australia. His graffiti of the word *eternity*—meaning "forever"—became so popular that it was written in lights across the Sydney Harbor Bridge during the 2000 Olympics.

Stace had been a criminal before finding faith in Jesus and turning his life around. His one-man campaign was an attempt to start people thinking about where they were headed, in not only this life but the next.

In today's Bible verse, James also wants us to think about where we are headed.

Without Jesus in our lives, we walk around as if in a fog, the way Arthur Stace had before he put his faith in the Lord.

We don't know what tomorrow will bring. It might be a good day or a not-so-good one. But, whatever, tomorrow will come and go quickly. Putting our faith in Jesus *every* day means we are headed in the right direction—toward forever life in heaven with Him—never-ending tomorrows!

Eternity.

Jesus, I feel joyful knowing that I will spend eternity with You. Thank You for coming into my heart and guiding me every day. Amen.

DAY 317

So David. . .ruled over all Israel. And he ruled over Israel for forty years. . . . Then he died as an old man. . . . And his son Solomon ruled in his place. The acts of King David. . .are written in the books of Samuel, Nathan, and Gad, the men of God.

1 Chronicles 29:26–29

Today's Bible passage helps us to understand a little more about King David, the king mentioned most often in the Bible. Much is written about him from the time he was a boy until he died an old man.

As king, David ruled over Israel for forty years. When he died, Solomon became the new king–Solomon is known for his wisdom; many of his wise sayings are found in the book of Proverbs.

Much of what we know about David came from Samuel, Nathan, and Gad. Samuel is a well-known Old Testament prophet, but Nathan and Gad are not. Some Bible teachers believe that their "books" are part of the books of First and Second Samuel in the Bible.

Ask your parents to allow you to search for David's name in an online Bible. See what you can find out about this great king.

God, I want to learn more about the people in the Bible. You have told their stories so I can learn from them. Teach me, Lord. Amen.

DAY 318

When we arrived in the country of Macedonia, we had no rest. We had all kinds of trouble. There was fighting all around us. Our hearts were afraid.

2 CORINTHIANS 7:5

When you read the Bible, you discover that God's people have always faced situations where they felt afraid. For example, 2 Corinthians 7:5 tells us that Paul and his friends felt afraid after arriving in the country of Macedonia. They had gone there to preach the good news, but they were tired. There was all kinds of trouble and fighting around them, and they were scared. Whom could they turn to? God!

Often when we are afraid, God sends someone to help. And that's exactly what He did for Paul and his companions. God sent Paul's friend Titus to comfort them. Just seeing and talking with Titus made Paul feel happy (vv. 6–7).

God understands when you are afraid, and He will help you. You can count on it!

Maybe God will send you to be a friend to someone who is worried or afraid. Do you know someone, right now, who you might help comfort with a hug or some gentle words?

Father, is there someone I know who is worried or afraid? Teach me, please, how I might comfort them and bring them some happiness. Amen.

DAY 319

All these many people who have had faith in God are around us like a cloud. Let us put every thing out of our lives that keeps us from doing what we should. Let us keep running in the race that God has planned for us.

HEBREWS 12:1

The first Olympic competition, in 776 BC, was a marathon running race. Runners knew the route. It was marked out for them well in advance. As they neared completing the race, the crowds cheered them on to the finish line. The arena was full of spectators, many of them athletes who had run in the past and knew how hard it was to finish well.

Being a Christian is sort of like running a marathon, a race in which heaven is our goal. As we race through life, other Christians cheer us on. They encourage us to get past anything that gets in our way and keeps us from finishing. Our Christian friends surround us like a great "cloud" as they help us run toward Jesus.

Don't give up. Keep running! Someday, you will reach the finish line—heaven—and God Himself will be there cheering you on.

This race through life is hard, but I will stay strong and give it my best effort. If I fall, Lord, lift me up. If I become weak, carry me. We'll cross the finish line together. Amen.

DAY 320

"Do not be afraid of them or of what they say, even if thistles and thorns are with you and you sit on scorpions."

EZEKIEL 2:6

Don't be afraid—even if thistles and thorns are with you and you sit on scorpions. Ouch! If anyone else but God had said it, the prophet Ezekiel probably would have answered, "How can I *not* be afraid?" But Ezekiel trusted God, and he did what God wanted. He went to tell the Israelites to shape up and stop sinning. He went knowing that the people would want to kill him!

What if God asked you to step out of your comfort zone and do something that you were afraid to do? Would you trust God and do it?

God has a plan for your life, and sometimes it will take courage to follow His plan. New people, places, and things can be scary. But God will be with you all the way. So, don't be afraid.

And don't be afraid, either, to stand up for what you know is right and to tell others about Jesus. God will handle anything that gets in your way—even if thistles and thorns are with you and you sit on scorpions!

Dear Lord, remove my fear so that I can boldly follow Your plan for my life. And encourage me never to be afraid to tell others about Jesus. Amen.

DAY 321

Watch and keep awake! Stand true to the Lord.
Keep on acting like men and be strong.
1 CORINTHIANS 16:13

When Paul wrote his letters, he chose his words wisely. He often wrote in a way that created pictures in the minds of his readers. The Bible verse today is from Paul's letter to his church friends in Corinth.

"Watch and keep awake! Stand true to the Lord." Paul's words create an image of God's army facing its enemy. Instead of running, the army stands and fights. Its soldiers stay strong and brave.

Paul's friends were facing a difficult time for their Christian beliefs. People hated them for loving Jesus. So Paul, through his word picture, told them to be on the lookout for trouble, to stand up to trouble instead of run, and to be brave and strong.

That's how all Christians should be when trouble comes to steal their faith. We need to imagine ourselves as soldiers in God's army, prepared to face trouble with courage and strength.

How about you? Are you a soldier in God's army?

Dear God, help me to be ready when trouble comes. Bless me with courage. Strengthen my faith so that I can stand up and fight for what's right and true. Amen.

DAY 322

He gives strength to the weak. And He gives power to him who has little strength.

Isaiah 40:29

The Bible is filled with God's promises, and today's verse is one of them. God says that when we think we aren't strong enough to accomplish what He has planned for us, He will boost our strength.

Strength comes in different forms. Sometimes we need body strength to complete a task, like the nineteen-year-old girl who lifted a pickup truck that fell onto her dad, or the guy who ran fifty marathons in fifty states in fifty days! Other times we need brainpower strength to learn something new or to study hard for a test, and we need inner strength to face whatever makes us nervous or afraid.

To tap into God's strength booster, we need faith. We have to believe in God's promises and trust Him. Prayer is important too. When we face something difficult, we should pray and ask God to help us. He will. How can we be sure? Because He promised! And God cannot lie. It's in the Bible: Numbers 23:19.

Father God, it makes me feel good to know that whatever kind of strength I need, You will certainly give it to me. Thank You, Father. Amen.

DAY 323

Tell of your joy to each other by singing the Songs of David and church songs. Sing in your heart to the Lord.

EPHESIANS 5:19

Music surrounds us. It's everywhere: radios, televisions, computers, phones, smart watches, portable media players. . . We live in a world filled with sound.

Now, rewind your thoughts to a different time two thousand years ago. Electricity was limited to lightning in the night sky. There were no cell towers or anything else to carry sound from one place to another. Music was limited to simple musical instruments and the human voice.

In this quiet setting Paul wrote to his friends in Ephesus and suggested that making music together is a good way to connect with God. He told them to sing the psalms that David wrote, to sing joyfully, and to put heartfelt emotions into their singing.

Imagine how beautiful the music must have been when the people in Ephesus, and many other places in the world, broke the silence of starlit nights and sang praises to God.

Step away from the loudness of our world and create your own times of silence. Then, in the stillness, sing your own songs of praise to the Lord.

Thank You, Father, for the gift of music. Let me remember to use it often to connect with You in praise and in song. Amen.

DAY 324

The voice of the Lord is powerful. The voice of the Lord is great.

Psalm 29:4

Finish this sentence: The loudest sound I ever heard was. . . Then compare your answer with a family member's or friend's.

In Bible times, the people of Jericho might have thought the sound of trumpets was the loudest sound they ever heard—a sound loud enough to bring down the city walls! Daniel might have answered that a lion's roar was the loudest sound he ever heard—just before he was thrown into the lions' den. For the Israelites fleeing Egypt, the loudest sound was probably the thundering hooves of horses pulling chariots filled with enemy soldiers, hot on their trail. And Noah? The loudest sound he ever heard must have been the sound of gigantic waves pushing the ark through the floodwaters.

What power there is in sound!

God's voice is more powerful than any sound anyone has ever heard. It is more powerful than any sound you can imagine. The Bible says His voice is so powerful that it shakes the desert and breaks trees into pieces! Now, that's loud! Read more about it in Psalm 29:3–9.

O God, You are so powerful that if You speak, the sound of Your voice shakes the earth! How great and mighty You are! Amen.

DAY 325

God has given each of you a gift. Use it to help each other. This will show God's loving-favor.

1 PETER 4:10

Maybe you have been to a talent show at your school or church. You might even have participated in one. A talent show is usually where people show off their musical talents and dancing. Some might even include poetry. But there are many other kinds of talents not seen in talent shows.

Our talents are gifts from God, and everyone has them. They are, simply put, things that we are good at.

Today's verse tells us that God gives us these gifts so we can use them to help others.

Maybe you are really good at reading. Then use that talent to read to your younger brothers or sisters. Are you good at drawing? You might make some cards to take to people in a nursing home. Are you good at cheering people up? Then get out there and be cheerful!

Take a few minutes to think about your talent—can you think of more than one? Now, get creative and think of ways to use your talents to help others.

Father, when I share my talents with others, it's like I'm spreading Your love around! Thank You for giving me things that I'm good at. Amen.

DAY 326

"You have done well. You are a good and faithful servant. You have been faithful over a few things. I will put many things in your care."

MATTHEW 25:23

Jesus told a story about three servants.

Before their master went on a trip, he put his servants in charge of his money. He gave one man five coins. He gave another two coins. The third received one coin.

The servant who had five coins went out and traded until he made five more. The servant who had two coins did the same. He made two more. The servant who had the one coin went and hid it in a hole in the ground.

When their master returned, he praised the two servants who had doubled his money. "You have been faithful over a few things," he said. "I will put many things in your care." But the master had nothing good to say to the servant who had hidden away his coin (Matthew 25:14-30).

Are you using God's gifts—your talents—or have you hidden them away? Use your gifts to help others, and God will bless you with even more talents if you keep doing good for Him.

God, You have given me special gifts to put to use for You. Help me to use them wisely so I can do even more to serve You. Amen.

DAY 327

Punish your son when he does wrong and he will give you comfort. Yes, he will give joy to your soul.

PROVERBS 29:17

Imagine a world where no one cares about laws. There is total chaos! Cars travel every which way causing accidents. People don't think twice about stealing and doing so many other things that they know are wrong. And worse, those in charge of enforcing the laws do nothing.

Laws are in place for a purpose, and breaking them leads to consequences—in other words, punishment.

Rules are made for reasons; and just like in the real world, when kids break their parents' rules, there are consequences. Otherwise, kids grow up out of control, not knowing right from wrong.

Proverbs 29:17 is about respect. It's comforting for parents to see their sons and daughters learning to obey rules and become respectful adults. It brings joy to their souls!

Try your very best to obey your parents' rules and God's rules. If you mess up and have some privileges taken away, accept the punishment willingly. When your parents—and God—see you doing what is right, it will fill them up with joy.

Heavenly Father, I do my best to obey my parents, but I slip up sometimes and don't follow their rules. Help me to try harder, God. I want to please them and You. Amen.

DAY 328

In the same way, you who are younger, submit yourselves to your elders. All of you, clothe yourselves with humility toward one another, because, "God opposes the proud but shows favor to the humble."

1 PETER 5:5 NIV

We can all find someone older and wiser to learn from. But sometimes we become know-it-alls and decide that we know more than our elders. Our pride gets in the way of our learning.

Suppose your older brother wants to teach you how to win at a video game you both enjoy playing. You would love to win, but you don't want your brother to think that he is better than you. So, you say something like "Never mind. I know what I'm doing!" That's pride, and it's not something good.

Older kids, parents, grandparents, teachers—you can learn something from all of them.

Humility is a word that means "setting pride aside." When you admit that there is something you don't know and you are open to someone teaching you, that's humility.

Jesus is a good example of humility, and God wants you to learn from Him. Practice humility and see what God does in your life.

Father, open my heart to wisdom offered by those older than I. Set their wise words inside my heart so I might learn from them and someday pass their wisdom to someone younger than I. Amen.

DAY 329

There is nothing better for a man than to eat and drink and find joy in his work. I have seen that this also is from the hand of God.

ECCLESIASTES 2:24

Eating your favorite foods. Enjoying a cold drink on a hot day. Finishing your homework early and knowing you've done it well. These are just a few simple things that God blesses you with to bring you joy.

God's little blessings are all around and even inside you. Many are blessings you never even notice: The sun rises and sets every day, gravity holds you down on earth, you wake up, you go to sleep, your heart beats, your lungs push air in and out. You see, hear, taste, touch, and smell things! When was the last time you thought of those things as blessings?

Ecclesiastes 2:24 encourages us to remember that all good things—even the smallest ones—are gifted to us as blessings from God.

Look around. What other simple things do you see that you haven't thought of as blessings? Remember to tell God, "Thank You!"

Dear God, open my eyes to the simple things in life, the things that I forget to notice. You have done so many wonderful things in and around me. Help me to enjoy them more thankfully. I'm grateful, Lord. Amen.

DAY 330

"Come now, let us think about this together," says the Lord. "Even though your sins are bright red, they will be as white as snow. Even though they are dark red, they will be like wool."

Isaiah 1:18

Colors have meanings. For example, a traffic signal has a green light that means go, a yellow light that means caution, and a red light that means stop.

Maybe you have noticed that red is a color connected with danger. Stop signs are red. Most emergency vehicles have red flashing lights. The lights at railroad crossings are red to warn us that a train is near. The Bible has a meaning for the color red too. Red is connected with sin.

In Isaiah 1:18, God describes our sins as bright red and dark red. But He says they will be white as snow.

White is a color connected with pure and clean. When God sent Jesus to save us, He took the sin out of our hearts and turned all that red stuff to freshly washed white! No need for emergency vehicles with red flashing lights to come to our rescue. Jesus has already saved us!

I will confess my sins to You, God. I praise You for Your forgiveness. How wonderful You are to forgive even my worst sins and reward me with a clean heart. Amen.

DAY 331

But Ruth said, "Do not beg me to leave you or turn away from following you. I will go where you go. . . . Your people will be my people. And your God will be my God."

RUTH 1:16

Elimelech, his wife, Naomi, and their two sons moved to a place called Moab. While there, the sons married women named Orpah and Ruth. Sadness came when Elimelech and both sons died, leaving the women alone.

Naomi decided to return home to Israel, and Orpah and Ruth went along. But, on the way, Naomi told the girls to go back home; she was old and they needn't follow her (Ruth 1:8). Orpah went. But not Ruth! She refused. She wanted to stay with her mother-in-law and worship Naomi's God—the only God.

Why was Ruth so close to Naomi, a woman much older than she? Maybe it was because when Naomi's husband and sons died, Naomi showed great faith in God. Maybe Ruth wanted a faith like Naomi's too so she would be strong and not feel so alone.

God will strengthen your faith when you need it. Trust Him during your not-so-good times. Trust Him to keep your faith strong, and maybe others will notice, like Ruth did.

Father, I learn a lot about faith from Bible people like Naomi. Help me to have a strong faith like hers, faith that others will notice. Amen.

DAY 332

The love of money is the beginning of all kinds of sin. Some people have turned from the faith because of their love for money. They have made much pain for themselves because of this.

1 TIMOTHY 6:10

You can substitute the word *stuff* for *money* in this verse, and it will mean the same thing. Paul is telling his friend Timothy that loving money or other possessions too much allows sin to creep in.

Paul's warning to Timothy, almost two thousand years ago, is just as fresh today. Loving our stuff too much pulls us away from God. And when that happens, we are more likely to sin, and sin leads to us feeling unhappy.

Stuff isn't that important, really. Sure, there are things we need and things we want. But we can't take anything with us to heaven. We should see our stuff as blessings—gifts to us from God. When we shift the focus away from our things and toward Him, sin is less likely to sneak into our lives.

Take a look around your room. As your eyes set on each thing, take a moment to thank God for it.

Dear Lord, sometimes I pray asking You for more stuff. Teach me to be right with those prayers and to thank You for everything I have. Amen.

DAY 333

"They have healed the hurt of My people only a little, saying, 'Peace, peace,' when there is no peace."

JEREMIAH 6:14

Jeremiah had warned the Israelites that God said to shape up and stop worshiping idols. But they kept doing it. They worshiped false gods and sinned in many other ways. Trouble brewed all around them. God was angry. Still, the leaders stood up and said, "Don't worry. Everything is fine."

Jeremiah knew that everything was not fine! The leaders' words might have comforted the people just a little, but still, trouble was coming—trouble that would hurt.

It was sort of like a doctor about to put medicine on a deep cut and saying, "Don't worry. This isn't going to hurt at all." You know it's going to sting. And if someone tells you that it won't, they aren't telling the truth.

The Israelites believed the lies. But peace never comes from sin. They kept on sinning—and trouble came!

When the Holy Spirit whispers in your heart, "Stop doing what you're doing," listen. Don't obey Satan's voice when he tells you, "It's okay. Go on. Everything's going to be fine."

God, please don't allow me to fall into Satan's sinful traps. When he says, "Go on, sin," let me obey Your voice telling me to stop. Amen.

DAY 334

Dear friend, you are doing a good work by being kind to the Christians, and for sure, to the strangers.

3 JOHN 1:5

Kindness is awesome because it multiplies itself. One act of kindness leads to another and another and another. That's how kindness is supposed to work. But often it doesn't. Our kind acts go unnoticed. But does that mean we should stop being kind?

Today's Bible verse speaks to missionaries serving strangers in faraway lands. Maybe you would like to be a missionary someday. That would be great! But a missionary's work is hard.

You could live in a tent among strangers. Often, you won't have what you need, not even simple things like running water or a stove. Your job is to teach others about Jesus and, hopefully, to make them fellow Christians. But some might hate you and want to hurt you. You could be the only one showing kindness. You might wonder, sometimes, if being a missionary is worth it.

It *is* worth it. But there are many ways to serve God. Pray today, and ask Him to lead you where He wants you to go. Ask God to use you to show kindness to others.

Lord, I pray for missionaries serving in the most dangerous parts of the world. Protect them! God, how can I serve You through acts of kindness? Amen.

DAY 335

"While the earth lasts, planting time and gathering time, cold and heat, summer and winter, and day and night will not end."
GENESIS 8:22

Today's verse comes at the end of Noah's story in the Bible (Genesis 6:9–8:22). When the great flood had done its damage and the water came down, God invited the ark family to come out. God promised never again to destroy His creatures in an earth-covering flood. Even as He made His promise, new growth came from the earth.

Since then, Earth has continued to go through its natural cycles of beauty—summer, fall, winter, spring. The sun rises and sets. Day becomes night, and night becomes day. Cold days give way to hot ones, and hot days give way to cold. Gently, God leads His Earth through these cycles, year after year.

As a pledge of His faithfulness, the Creator promises to keep the world spinning on its axis, allowing His cycles and beauty of nature to continue, until the end.

Read Genesis 1, and you'll see that God created Adam and Eve to care for His Earth. You are today's Adam or Eve. It's your responsibility, as best as you can, to care for His creation.

Think about it: What can you do to help care for Earth?

Heavenly Father, thank You for the Earth!
Help me to respect and care for Your creation. Amen.

DAY 336

All things can be seen when they are in the light.
Everything that can be seen is in the light.
EPHESIANS 5:13

Have you ever experienced such total darkness that you couldn't see your hand in front of your face? Being in complete darkness can be scary but kind of cool too!

Imagine living in total darkness, though. After a short while, you would bump into things all the time, and that's not fun! It would leave you shouting, "Somebody, turn on the light!"

In Ephesians 5:13, the author, Paul, is speaking about spiritual darkness—living without Jesus in your heart. When your heart is without Him, it is like you are walking around in total darkness bumping into sin all the time. Sin keeps knocking you down until you shout, "Somebody, turn on the light!"

To get rid of spiritual darkness, people have to ask Jesus into their hearts. When they accept Jesus as their Savior, it's like warm, bright sunlight floods their hearts.

Jesus said, "I am the Light of the world. Anyone who follows Me will not walk in darkness. He will have the Light of Life" (John 8:12). Do you know someone who needs Jesus to light up their heart? Pray today for that person to accept Jesus.

Dear Jesus, I want ______ to accept You as Savior.
Please, Jesus, light up their heart. Amen.

DAY 337

"Hear, O Israel! The Lord our God is one Lord!"

DEUTERONOMY 6:4

In the Ten Commandments God puts Himself first. His first two commands are "Have no gods other than Me. Do not make for yourselves a god to look like anything that is in heaven above or on the earth below or in the waters under the earth" (Exodus 20:3–4).

You would think that the Israelites would have listened and obeyed, but they didn't. Again and again, they worshiped false gods and put more faith in their stuff than they did in God. Again and again, God's prophets told them to stop it: "Hear, O Israel! The Lord our God is one Lord!" (Deuteronomy 6:4).

Still, they didn't listen. So then, God sent Jesus, and the Holy Spirit too.

Some people think of Jesus, God, and the Holy Spirit as three separate beings. But they're not. Jesus and the Holy Spirit are part of God. God is three persons: the Father, Jesus, and the Spirit—one God, one Lord. It's hard for us to understand because we humans exist only as one person. God exists as three persons! It is just one of the amazing things about Him that make Him God!

Father God, I can't completely understand how You are three persons all at once, but I do know that You are my one-and-only God! Amen.

DAY 338

O man, He has told you what is good. What does the Lord ask of you but to do what is fair and to love kindness, and to walk without pride with your God?

MICAH 6:8

Have you read the story of King Arthur? He ruled over a kingdom called Camelot, and his knights did good deeds. In the legend, Camelot was once a happy place. But Arthur spent more time being king than he did caring about his wife, Lady Guinevere. Because of this, Lady Guinevere fell in love with the handsome Sir Lancelot, and that led to Arthur becoming jealous and losing his kingdom.

Kings and queens in stories and in real life are not perfect. Sin reigns. Kingdoms rise and fall. But there is a sin-free land ruled by a perfect King—heaven! His kingdom is forever. It will never end.

God rules both heaven and earth. Because He is the only good and true King, we should serve Him well, doing our best to be fair, kind, and loving toward each other. Always, we should honor our King with worship and praise. He is the only one worthy of such things.

O God, my King. How great You are! You lead perfectly, rule justly, and teach wisely. I am so blessed to be Your child and to live in Your kingdom forever. Amen.

DAY 339

At once the father cried out. He said with tears in his eyes, "Lord, I have faith. Help my weak faith to be stronger!"

MARK 9:24

Mark 9:14-29 tells of a father who brings his son to the disciples asking them to cast out an evil spirit. The disciples fail just before Jesus arrives. The father says to Jesus, "If You can do anything to help us, take pity on us!" Jesus answers him, "Why do you ask Me that? The one who has faith can do all things" (vv. 22-23). After saying this, Jesus heals the boy.

The words "*If* You can do anything" show that the man did not have complete faith in Jesus. So, why did Jesus still heal the boy? The answer might be in the father's words—"Lord, I have faith. Help my weak faith to be stronger!" Sometimes a little faith is enough.

Jesus says that even a little faith can accomplish great things (Matthew 17:20; Luke 17:6). When you have only a little faith, you can pray to God to strengthen your faith and make it bigger. Only then can God truly begin to work through you.

Dear Lord, there are days when my faith is strong and others when I slip into doubt. Please keep my doubt from getting bigger. Strengthen my faith, Lord! Amen.

DAY 340

Of what great worth is Your loving-kindness, O God! The children of men come and are safe in the shadow of Your wings.

PSALM 36:7

If you ever got close enough to a bird's nest with the mother bird and babies inside, you would see the baby birds slip under the mother's wings. The sight of your big eyes peering into the nest would frighten the little ones! But under their mother's wings, the babies feel safe and secure.

Today's scripture verse holds a comforting thought for kids—and grown-ups too. It paints a picture of a kind and loving God. A God whose children know that whenever they feel afraid, they can run to Him. He will cover them with protection the way a mother bird protects her babies with her wings.

God loves you! He loves you more than you can ever imagine, and He will never leave you alone and unprotected. His loving-kindness is all around you all the time.

You never have to feel afraid with God as your Father. But you are human, and all humans feel fear. So, whenever you feel frightened, remember this: God has His arms around you. He will hold you tight and keep you safe.

Thank You, Father, for Your loving protection. I know that I am always safe with You holding me in Your arms. Amen.

DAY 341

"It will not be said, 'See, here it is!' or, 'There it is!' For the holy nation of God is in you."
LUKE 17:21

For centuries, the Jewish people waited for God's kingdom to arrive. Through the words of ancient prophets, they had mental pictures of a kingdom on earth with a king they could see. The picture in their minds was wrong.

The words of the prophets were not about some new kingdom on earth with a new king but instead about the kingdom of heaven and God, our great King.

In Luke 17, the Pharisees demanded that Jesus tell them when the kingdom of God would arrive. Jesus' answer, that the kingdom of God already existed, surely confused them. Probably more puzzling to them was *where* it existed.

As Christians, we know that God's kingdom exists in our hearts. If we've discovered the kingdom, it means that God (our King) has delivered us from sin through His Son, Jesus. It's like God sits on a throne in our very own heart, ruling our souls and consciences. God promises to live within us until that day when we are free from our bodies and our souls go to be with Him in heaven. Isn't that awesome?

Dear Father, Your kingdom is within me—in my heart. I look forward to when I will live with You forever in heaven. Amen.

DAY 342

Then Saul became very angry. . . . He said, "They have given David honor for ten thousands, but for me only thousands. Now what more can he have but to be king?" And Saul was jealous and did not trust David from that day on.

1 SAMUEL 18:8–9

King Saul was a powerful king who fought his enemies and won (1 Samuel 14:47). But pride got to Saul, and he no longer followed God's commands.

At that time, David was a smart young soldier in Saul's army. He was such a successful soldier that he received higher praises than Saul. And that made the king jealous and angry. Instead of celebrating David's success, Saul became a raving madman.

Although David had proved himself loyal to the king, Saul's jealousy blinded him to the talents and accomplishments of his faithful subject. David's success on the battlefield made everyday life in Israel more secure, but Saul couldn't see or appreciate that. As a result, God removed Saul as king of Israel (1 Samuel 15:26).

Jealousy is a feeling that leads to nothing good. When others succeed, especially at something we want, God expects us to be genuinely happy for them and cheer them on.

God, jealousy slips into my heart. When others succeed, I sometimes pretend about my happiness for them. Help me to overcome jealousy and to treat others as Jesus would. Amen.

DAY 343

Do not quench the Spirit.

1 THESSALONIANS 5:19 NIV

Fire can destroy things. However, fire also gives off warmth and light. In Paul's letter to the Thessalonians, he compares the Holy Spirit to fire and warns his friends to be careful not to let the fire go out.

These are the things Paul said his friends should do: Pray, have a thankful attitude in all circumstances, and believe in God's will for their lives. In addition, they were to speak out against laziness, help those who were shy about sharing the good news, and examine the things they were being taught. They needed to hang on to what was good and stay away from evil. By doing all these things they wouldn't be quenching—putting out—the fire of the Holy Spirit.

Jesus spoke of the importance of the Holy Spirit. He said that the Spirit not only teaches us about God but brings to mind the lessons we have already learned (John 14:25–26).

We know that when water is poured on a campfire, the fire begins to go out. With proper attention, though, a fire will continue burning, giving off warmth and light to those around it.

Follow Paul's instructions to his friends. Then you will keep the Spirit burning brightly in your heart.

Lord, help me to keep the warmth and light of the Holy Spirit burning inside my heart. Amen.

DAY 344

But if I say, "I will not remember Him or speak any more in His name," then in my heart it is like a burning fire shut up in my bones. I am tired of holding it in, and I cannot do that.

JEREMIAH 20:9

The prophet Jeremiah faced a challenge. He'd been called by God to warn the people that unless they stopped sinning and asked God to forgive them, trouble would come.

Jeremiah preached with all his might, and the people only made fun of him. Frustrated, Jeremiah said, "The Word of the Lord has become a shame and a cause of laughing at me all day long" (Jeremiah 20:8). So, Jeremiah decided to stay silent.

But, no matter how hard he tried, Jeremiah couldn't stop thinking about God's warning. It was there in his heart. He couldn't stay silent! So, Jeremiah continued preaching the Word of God.

God is looking for Christians like Jeremiah who are willing to share the truth of His Word—no matter what. Don't be shy or ashamed of sharing the good news about Jesus! If people make fun of you, let God be their judge.

Jesus, help me never to stay silent where I can share the good news—that You came to save us from sin and open up our way to heaven. Amen.

DAY 345

And God said to Moses, "I AM WHO I AM."

Exodus 3:14

Look at yourself in the mirror. Then finish this sentence with words that describe how you look. "I am ______."

"I am tall."

"I am wearing a green shirt."

It's easy to describe what you see, but what about something you can't see? How would you describe God?

No one knows what God looks like because He doesn't have a physical body like humans. When He described Himself to Moses, God said simply, "I AM WHO I AM." Humans can't describe God because there is no one to compare Him to. He is who He is—God.

We can describe things about God's personality. We know that He is perfect, loving, forgiving, all-knowing, forever. . . He has always existed and He always will. God thinks of us as His children, and we know what He says because He speaks to us through the Bible.

And here is something else—we know that God wants us to be His voice on earth. He wants us to tell the whole world about Him. So, do it! Get out there right now and be the voice of the Great I AM!

Heavenly Father, what an awesome responsibility to be Your voice in the world! Help me to speak Your Word. Amen.

DAY 346

These also are wise sayings of Solomon, which were written down by the men of Hezekiah, king of Judah.

PROVERBS 25:1

King Solomon had a way with words. The Bible tells us that he spoke three thousand proverbs—wise sayings—and he wrote 1,005 songs (1 Kings 4:32)! Only one of his songs is in the Bible, the Old Testament book Song of Songs. And only about nine hundred of Solomon's proverbs exist today.

In ancient times, the Bible was not complete, the way we know it. Scribes—writers—had to write the words on scrolls, and that took time. Some of the scrolls were lost or misplaced.

At first only about seven hundred of Solomon's proverbs were preserved. Then in King Hezekiah's day, over two centuries after Solomon, someone discovered a treasure: an old scroll containing about two hundred more of Solomon's proverbs. We don't know where the other 2,100 proverbs went, but we can be thankful for what we do have.

Thanks to scribes and others, the Word of God was written down and has been passed from generation to generation. We know that the Bible will last forever. Jesus said, "Heaven and earth will pass away, but My words will not pass away" (Matthew 24:35).

Dear God, Your Word will live on forever. Nothing can take it from us. It is Your voice speaking to Your children from generation to generation. Amen.

DAY 347

I have seen that all the work done is because a man wants what his neighbor has. This also is for nothing, like trying to catch the wind.

ECCLESIASTES 4:4

Some people go through life always wanting what others have. God warned about it in His Ten Commandments: "Do not have a desire for your neighbor's house. . .or anything that belongs to your neighbor" (Exodus 20:17). The author of Ecclesiastes 4:4, wise King Solomon, said that working to be like your neighbor, or anyone else, is like trying to catch the wind.

There is nothing wrong with following someone's good example. Jesus, for instance, is our best example, and trying to be like Him is a good thing. But when we work to be like other people so we can get all the wonderful stuff they have—that's when it becomes a problem. Solomon says that our work is for nothing when we try to be like others to get what they have.

God wants everything we work at to bring us closer to Him. That means not chasing after what our neighbors have but instead reaching out to help those neighbors and others in need.

How can you work for the Lord today?

Lord, remind me that my work and all that I do should be pleasing to Your sight. Amen.

DAY 348

When He had given thanks, He broke it and said, "Take this bread and eat it. This is My body which is broken for you. Do this to remember Me."
1 CORINTHIANS 11:24

Maybe you've heard today's Bible verse spoken when communion is offered in your church. The words are Jesus' words to us, asking us to remember His death on the cross.

Remembering someone's death is usually a sad thing. But Jesus does not want us to remember His death that way. He allowed His body to be hurt and die because He loves us. If Jesus hadn't done what He did, there would be no way for us to get into heaven and live forever one day. It's such an awesome thing that it makes us feel humble inside. We might think, *Wow, I didn't deserve for Him to do that for me!* And it's true—none of us deserved Jesus' gift to us. But, He gave it to us anyway.

When we remember His death on the cross, we should be thankful, and when we remember that He rose from His grave, we should be glad! His resurrection reminds us that we will have forever life too—with Him in heaven.

Jesus, fill my mind and heart with thoughts of Your death, burial, and resurrection. I am so grateful for Your sacrifice. I don't ever want to take it for granted. Amen.

DAY 349

We know that God makes all things work together for the good of those who love Him and are chosen to be a part of His plan.

ROMANS 8:28

Maybe you've visited an art gallery or an art fair in your community. If so, you likely saw some amazing works of art: paintings, photographs, drawings—and maybe even some sculptures made from junk!

Some artists are really good at putting together pieces of junk to create something beautiful. Old pipes, a bicycle wheel, a rusty shovel, maybe a tin bucket or two. . .it might look like junk to us, but the artist has already planned how all those things can work together to make something good.

God, the great Creator, is that sort of artist. He takes the junk in our lives, the bad stuff that happens, and somehow makes it all into something good!

The Creator doesn't just throw stuff together and call it art. He always has a plan, and His plan is perfect.

God has a plan for each of us. So, when bad stuff happens, ask God to take it and make it into something good. Trust Him. He will!

Dear God, here, take all the bad stuff that has ever happened and create something good. I can't wait to see what You will do with it. Amen.

DAY 350

"If you get your life from Me and My Words live in you, ask whatever you want. It will be done for you."

JOHN 15:7

There are people who pray thinking that God will give them everything they ask for. But the Creator is smarter than that. He won't give us what we want unless it lines up with what He wants us to have.

If your parents gave you everything you wanted, that would be awesome, wouldn't it? But wait. Maybe it wouldn't be so great. You would grow up thinking that you can have whatever you want, and when you find out that you can't—well, that would take some getting used to.

As we pray and ask God for what we want, we need to understand that He knows what is best for us, and we should never demand "our way."

Read again the first part of John 15:7 that says, "If you get your life from Me and My Words live in you." This shows that God wants us to put our trust in Him.

When you pray, ask God for what you want, but then tell Him that you want Him to give you what's best. He knows how to make that happen.

Father, You know best. I want what You want for me, even if it's not what I ask for. Amen.

DAY 351

And the Lord said, "Have you any reason to be angry?"
JONAH 4:4

Jonah's adventure began when God told him to go and tell the wicked people of Nineveh that God would soon be passing judgment on them. Jonah refused to go and ran away. He ended up on a boat that he got tossed off of in the middle of a raging storm. Jonah didn't drown though; instead, God was generous and spared Jonah by sending a big fish to swallow him.

When Jonah asked for forgiveness, God delivered him out of the fish. Jonah then traveled to Nineveh and told the people that God would destroy their city. The people listened and asked God for forgiveness. He forgave and decided not to destroy them.

That made Jonah angry! It made him look foolish when God did not do as Jonah had said. "O Lord," Jonah complained, "is this not what I said You would do?" (Jonah 4:2).

Jonah had forgotten that God is in charge. God is God, and His actions are always fair. We have no right to question what He does—even when it makes us angry.

I'm guilty of questioning You, God. I wonder why You do what You do, and sometimes I get angry. Forgive me, please. Amen.

DAY 352

The missionaries told with much power how Jesus was raised from the dead. God's favor was on them all.
Acts 4:33

Missionaries perform many tasks to help people, but their most important job is telling others the story of Jesus, especially the good news that Jesus is our way to heaven.

Missionaries trust God to lead them wherever they go. They trust God to give them His power to preach the good news. They pray, asking God to open up the hearts of the people to hear about Jesus and accept Him as their Savior.

It isn't an easy job. Often, missionaries run into trouble in faraway lands. A few have even lost their lives for preaching the good news. But if you think about it, that is exactly what happened to Jesus' followers in ancient days. They were turned away, punished, and killed for loving Jesus and sharing His story. Still, that didn't stop missionaries from sharing the good news. They have kept on working for the Lord to this very day!

Pray for the missionaries today. Ask God to keep them safe and to give them His power when they preach the good news.

Father, please bring safety to all missionaries wherever they are. Give them the power and strength to do Your work. And, God, help me to work for You too. Amen.

DAY 353

Who could have power over the world except by believing that Jesus is the Son of God?

1 JOHN 5:5

Kings, queens, presidents, prime ministers, generals—all are powerful world leaders, but do they have power over the world? No! And neither do fictional characters, like book characters, superheroes, or beings from other planets! God is the only one who truly has control over every bit of the world.

We Christians do have some power over the world. Our power is different from God's, though. For us, the world is a sinful place full of temptation. Almost everywhere we go, we face things that we know are wrong. We have to choose. Do we go the right way or the wrong way?

Faith helps us make the right choices. When we welcome the Son of God into our hearts, we have faith that Jesus will help us take power over the worldly sins that tempt us. When we listen to Him and make right choices, that is how we have power over a world filled with sin.

Can you think of a time when you faced a right-or-wrong decision? If you made the right choice, then *congratulations!* You used your faith to have power over the world!

Jesus, I believe in You! Help me to overpower any sin that gets in my way. Amen.

DAY 354

"So I bought the field at Anathoth from Hanamel, the son of my father's brother. And I weighed out seventeen pieces of silver for him."

JEREMIAH 32:9

Jeremiah warned the Jews that if they didn't shape up, God would send the Babylonians to conquer them. Sure enough, the Babylonian army was now camped around Jerusalem. The Jews were trapped inside the city, away from their fields, and were low on food. Jeremiah was worst off. Jerusalem's rulers had thrown him in prison because of his warnings.

In Jeremiah's lowest moment, his cousin Hanamel showed up. Hanamel needed money for food and wanted to sell his field. The only problem was, it was in the village of Anathoth, some distance outside the walls of Jerusalem where it couldn't do Jeremiah any good. Yet, because God told him to, Jeremiah bought the field. As hopeless as things seemed, God told Jeremiah that his situation would soon get much better (Jeremiah 32:36–44). Jeremiah believed God. He trusted that it would happen—and it did!

If you feel trapped by a situation, like Jeremiah did, remember these words that God spoke to him: "I am the Lord. . . . Is anything too hard for Me?" (Jeremiah 32:27). God will help you!

When I face problems, Lord, I know that You have the answers. Show me the way. Nothing is impossible for You. Amen.

DAY 355

Wear a belt of truth around your body. Wear a piece of iron over your chest which is being right with God. Wear shoes on your feet which are the Good News of peace. Most important of all, you need a covering of faith in front of you. This is to put out the fire-arrows of the devil. The covering for your head is that you have been saved from the punishment of sin. Take the sword of the Spirit which is the Word of God.

EPHESIANS 6:14–17

Soldiers in ancient times wore armor to protect them from their enemies. In today's verses, Paul describes the kind of "armor" (behavior) Christians need to protect themselves from Satan.

Paul said that we need to believe the truth about God and be right with Him. We should be ready to share the good news about Jesus wherever our feet take us. Most important, we need faith so we don't fall into Satan's traps. We need to remember Jesus' gift of forgiveness for our sins. And, finally, arming ourselves with God's Word helps us fight Satan's lies.

How does your armor measure up? Are you ready to be a soldier in God's army?

I have put on my armor, God. When Satan gets in my way, I will be ready. Amen.

DAY 356

All at once the fingers of a man's hand were seen writing on the wall. . . . Then the king's face turned white, and his thoughts turned to fear. His legs became weak and his knees began shaking.

DANIEL 5:5–6

You've thrown a party for a thousand friends. Everyone is having a good time, when a human hand with no body appears and begins writing graffiti on the wall! Who wouldn't be afraid?

That's what happened at King Belshazzar's banquet.

The king had ordered his servants to build a giant wall around his kingdom to keep the enemy soldiers out. He'd hauled in plenty of supplies and even created a way for a nearby river to flow inside so his people would have water. King Belshazzar was so proud of what he'd done—making his kingdom perfectly safe—that he threw himself a party.

No one could read that creepy message on the wall except a man named Daniel. He read it to the king: "God has numbered the days of your rule and has brought it to an end" (v. 26). Soon, God allowed the enemy soldiers to get past the wall and invade the kingdom.

What's the message of this real story from the Bible? Great pride can get you into great trouble!

God, please don't let pride take hold of me. You are the one who allows me to do great things. Amen.

DAY 357

While Jesus spoke, men came from the house of the leader of the place of worship. They said, "Your daughter is dead. Why trouble the Teacher anymore?"

MARK 5:35

Jairus asked Jesus to heal his daughter. But while Jairus and Jesus were on the way, they received news that the girl had died. "Don't bother Jesus anymore," Jairus' friends suggested. But Jesus wasn't bothered. He told Jairus, "Do not be afraid, just believe" (v. 36).

When they got to Jairus' house, everyone was sad. "Why is there so much. . .crying? The girl is not dead. She is sleeping," Jesus said. But they laughed at Him. Jesus sent everyone away but the girl's parents. Then He took the girl by her hand and said, "Little girl, I say to you, get up!" and the girl was brought back to life (vv. 39–42)!

This is only one of the miracles Jesus did while He was on earth, and He is just as able to do great things today. What's important is that we have faith in Him. Jesus is never bothered when we pray and ask for His help.

If there's something you are praying for, don't lose hope. Keep praying. Jesus hears your prayers.

Jesus, even when it seems that You won't give me what I'm praying for, I will continue to hope and trust in You. Amen.

DAY 358

We are His work. He has made us to belong to Christ Jesus so we can work for Him. He planned that we should do this.
EPHESIANS 2:10

We are created by God to do God's work. Don't you wonder what His plan is for you?

We can know one thing about His plan for all of us. Jesus sets the example for how we should live. The more you learn about Him from the Bible, the more you can work at being patient, kind, loving, and caring, the way He is. You will learn to put what God wants before what you want, the way Jesus did.

But what about His plan for *your* life? Pray and ask God about it. Read your Bible. Often, God speaks to us through His Word (Psalm 119:105). Then have faith that God will work out His plan for your life and that His plan is good. "'For I know the plans I have for you,' says the Lord, 'plans for well-being and not for trouble, to give you a future and a hope' " (Jeremiah 29:11).

Trust God, and every day He will lead you toward His good plan—His excellent plan—for your life.

Father, what is Your plan for me? I know that it is good. Speak to me through prayer and Your Word. Amen.

DAY 359

But God, the One Who saves, showed how kind He was and how He loved us.

TITUS 3:4

The message in Titus 3:4 is simple: when Jesus' love and kindness come into our hearts, changes happen.

In Paul's letter to Titus, he wrote about how people who love Jesus should behave. They should respect authority, not say bad things about anyone, live in peace, and have a humble attitude.

Paul also reminded his friends how to act with those who don't know Jesus. Instead of being prideful because Jesus had already saved them from their sinful lives, they should remember their behavior before they met Jesus—things like jealousy, lying, hatred, and disobedience. It was only when Jesus came into their hearts that those behaviors changed.

Paul knew what he was writing about. He once hated others and approved of the mistreatment of those who believed in Jesus. Paul wasn't about peace at all. But then Jesus came (Acts 9:1–19). Suddenly Paul exchanged his bad behavior for the kind of behavior that showed Jesus was inside his heart.

God's love and kindness are powerful things that change hearts for good. How has His love changed your heart?

Jesus, I'm so thankful that You came into my heart. You make me want to be good and do good things. Amen.

DAY 360

"While I am in the world, I am the Light of the world."
JOHN 9:5

What did Jesus mean when He said, "I am the Light of the world"? To understand, you need to remember some of the Bible history you learned while reading this book.

The Old Testament is about life before Jesus. It contains stories about people misbehaving and displeasing God. But throughout the Old Testament, we see that God continued to love us. He sent messages through His prophets warning people to shape up. And even when they didn't, He hinted through the prophets about sending a special someone to save us from sin.

The New Testament is all about Jesus! When He came, it was like God's love began to shine a bright light on the world. As Jesus spread God's message to the people, God's light grew brighter. Then Jesus did the greatest thing of all—He died on the cross so our sins would be forgiven and we would go to heaven someday! That's when God's beautiful light shone the brightest.

Jesus said that while He was in the world, He was the light. But now it's our turn to keep His light burning. How do we do that? By telling others about Him and the way to heaven.

**Jesus, I will keep Your light burning brightly.
I will tell all my friends about You. Amen.**

DAY 361

This is the reason we do not give up. Our human body is wearing out. But our spirits are getting stronger every day. The little troubles we suffer now for a short time are making us ready for the great things God is going to give us forever.

2 CORINTHIANS 4:16–17

People come in all shapes and sizes. Tall. Short. Round. Thin. Young, like you! And old. Think about that young and old part for a minute.

When you look at old people, what do you see? Probably, you notice their bodies. Their skin has wrinkles. Their hair might be gray. Some walk slowly and have trouble getting around. But what you see on the outside isn't what's on the inside.

Paul said that the human body wears out but the spirit inside grows stronger. That strength comes from many years of wisdom and especially from living for Jesus.

Christians grow old looking forward to life in heaven. Many old people continue to serve God through their communities and churches. And old people are great at giving advice because they've gathered lots of wisdom.

The next time you see an old person, focus on what's on the inside rather than what's on the outside. Learn from that person how to live for God.

Father, lead me to older adults who can teach me more about You. Amen.

DAY 362

"I am Jesus. . . . I am the bright Morning Star."
REVELATION 22:16

The sun is the closest star to Earth, and without it we couldn't exist. Earth would be a big frozen, lifeless mass.

The surface of the sun is about ten thousand degrees Fahrenheit. That's hot! And all that heat warms the Earth. Once a year, Earth makes a complete trip around the sun, causing the Earth's crust to heat evenly. As the Earth rotates around the sun and tilts on its axis, seasons change.

Everything about the sun works perfectly to sustain life on Earth because God planned it that way.

In addition to providing for life, God made the sun to give us beautiful sunrises and sunsets. Most mornings, the eastern sky is ablaze in colors of orange, red, pink, and yellow—a warm-up act for that moment when the brilliant morning star peeks over the horizon.

It's no wonder that Jesus compared Himself to the sunrise. He is the light of the world! His love shines bright like the morning star. So, whenever you see a sunrise or feel the warmth of the sun on your skin, think of Him!

Jesus, Your love shines like the sun. It warms me and gives me everything I need to live. Thank You, Jesus. Amen.

DAY 363

On the day He comes, His shining-greatness will be seen in those who belong to Him. On that day, He will receive honor from all those who put their trust in Him.

2 THESSALONIANS 1:10

Throughout his life, Paul had plenty of trouble. Much of it came because he wasn't shy about sharing the good news. Still, with all that suffering, Paul never lost faith in Jesus. He firmly trusted in the Lord.

Paul talked often about getting to heaven. It was his goal. He knew that he didn't have to earn his place there. It was promised to him the moment he accepted Jesus as his Savior. He looked forward to heaven and seeing Jesus.

But it wasn't enough for Paul to be content that he had a place there. He wanted the whole world to believe and be saved!

This is the hope all Christians have—that everyone will believe and be saved. But the Bible tells us that, at some time in the future, Jesus is coming back to earth. On that day, everyone will see Him, and all who love and trust Him will honor Him. Those who have not accepted Him as Savior will be punished and sent away forever.

We don't know when Jesus is coming, so be ready. Honor Him every day.

I look forward to meeting You face-to-face, Jesus, whether here on earth or in heaven. Amen.

DAY 364

Make the best use of your time. These are sinful days.
EPHESIANS 5:16

Maybe Jesus will come back to earth in your lifetime, or maybe not. The Bible tells us that no one but God knows the date or the time of day when He will return (Matthew 24:36). And because we don't know, we need to be ready.

Every day, as you've read this book, you learned something new. You learned about God's love, beginning with Adam and Eve, continuing with the ancient Israelites, all the way to His people today. You learned about Jesus' time here on earth, the good example He set for us all, and His gift of forever life in heaven. And you've learned from people like Paul to bravely share the good news about Jesus.

You have a long life ahead, so take everything you learn and use it to serve God and others. Do your best to follow God's commands. Share the Good News so more people will accept Jesus as their Savior. Make the best use of your time by making good choices and loving the Lord with all your heart. If you do these things, then you will be ready for Jesus!

Help me to use my time wisely. Make me ready for the day You come, Lord. Amen.

DAY 365

Amen.

REVELATION 22:21 NIV

One simple word, *Amen*. It means "let it be so." *Amen* is the word we use to end our prayers to God, and it is the word He uses to end the Bible, His Word to us!

You've learned that God gave us every word of the Bible. He makes it come alive as we read. That means God makes the Bible perfectly yours. Sometimes its words will have special meaning to you or make you think. That's one way God speaks to you through His Word.

The Bible is like a textbook for Christians. It teaches God's rules and how He wants us to live. It shows what is wrong in our lives and helps us to change and make those wrongs right.

There are thousands of God's promises to us in the Bible including the most important one—His promise of forever life through Jesus.

Everything in the Bible is 100 percent true. God warns that no one should ever add to His words or take away any part that tells what will happen in the future (vv. 18–19).

And, just before the Bible ends, God reminds us of one big promise: Jesus is coming soon (v. 20).

Let it be so.

Amen!

God, thank You for the Bible and all that You've taught me so far. Remind me to keep reading Your Word. I want to learn more. Amen.

SCRIPTURE INDEX

OLD TESTAMENT

Luke

John

Acts

Romans